CAPITALIZING KNOWLEDGE

SUNY series
FRONTIERS IN EDUCATION
Philip G. Altbach, Editor

The Frontiers in Education Series draws upon a range of disciplines and approaches in the analysis of contemporary educational issues and concerns. Books in the series help to reinterpret established fields of scholarship in education by encouraging the latest synthesis and research. A special focus highlights educational policy issues from a multidisciplinary perspective. The series is published in cooperation with the School of Education, Boston College. A complete listing of books in the series can be found at the end of this volume.

CAPITALIZING KNOWLEDGE

New Intersections of Industry and Academia

EDITED BY

Henry Etzkowitz, Andrew Webster,

and Peter Healey

STATE UNIVERSITY OF NEW YORK PRESS

Published by
State University of New York Press, Albany

© 1998 State University of New York

For information, address State University of New York Press,
State University Plaza, Albany, N.Y. 12246

Production by M. R. Mulholland
Marketing by Patrick Durocher

Library of Congress Cataloging-in-Publication Data

Capitalizing knowledge : new intersections of industry and academia /
    edited by Henry Etzkowitz, Andrew Webster, and Peter Healey.
        p.   cm. — (SUNY series, frontiers in education)
    Includes bibliographical references and index.
    ISBN 0-7914-3947-X (hardcover : alk. paper). — ISBN 0-7914-3948-8
(pbk. : alk. paper)
    1. Education, Higher—Economic aspects—Cross-cultural studies.
2. Industry and education—Cross-cultural studies. 3. Research—
Economic aspects—Cross-cultural studies. 4. Higher education and
state—Cross-cultural studies. 5. Technology transfer—Cross-
cultural studies. I. Etzkowitz, Henry, 1940–   . II. Webster,
Andrew. III. Healey, Peter, 1942–   . IV. Series.
LC67.6.C37 1998
338.4′7378—dc21   98-13322
                                                                             CIP

10 9 8 7 6 5 4 3 2 1

Contents

Tables

Figures

Foreword

The "ivory tower" is no longer a viable academic structure. Cracks in the framework of academic isolation have appeared in part due to the very success of a university research enterprise that has produced a cornucopia of results, many of which have been successfully translated into use. Not surprisingly, the benefits produced have led to increased interest on the part of government and industry in closer ties to the university. Government has also made an effort to encourage the development within the academic enterprise of an interest in maintaining industrial linkages. The practice of creating ties among researchers, within and without academia, has emerged behind a facade of universities viewed as the locus of curiosity-driven research conducted by individual investigators.

The ideology of basic research was created in the late nineteenth century to protect a relatively weak academic sphere from untoward outside influences. The triumph of this ideology weakened academic connections to industry at the time. The concept of basic research culminated in the linear model of innovation, a one-way flow from fundamental to applied research to product development. The linear model is currently being supplanted by new ideas and alternative models based upon interdisciplinarity and spiral feedback links between technology and science. Perhaps ironically, this shift reflects the substantial growth and practical contributions of the academic research enterprise in both wartime and peacetime.

Academic research capacities have arisen from a variety of impetuses in different countries. Some capabilities emerged as an outgrowth of the training of students. Others were left behind as a colonial heritage. Still others were created to gain national prestige by contributing to international science. Whatever their origin, a common interest in a "third mission" for the university, in addition to teaching and research, has emerged worldwide. Along with these developments, a parallel set of issues has arisen on the other side of the traditional academic-industrial divide.

A science-based company can no longer be an island unto itself. In a highly competitive global environment it is necessary to access sources of knowledge and technology outside the firm. Companies increasingly look to universities, as well as other firms and government laboratories, as a potential source of useful knowledge and technology, especially in biotechnology and software. Cooperative initiatives are emanating from both the academic and industrial spheres, often encouraged by government, at the regional and national levels and by multinational organizations.

Just as companies seek new ways to collaborate with academic research groups, universities also want to expand their role in the economic development of their region. A variety of ways have been created, going well beyond traditional means such as graduation of students and consultation, to bridge the gap. The creation of intermediary offices, spinoff firms, science parks, and other interface mechanisms has raised a new set of issues about the role of academia in society, beyond traditional concerns about community service, on the one hand, and academic freedom, on the other. Conflict of interest, intellectual property, and limited secrecy are among the new terms of policy debate among academics, government science policy officials, and industrial laboratory directors.

The above issues, accompanying the organizational transformation of the university to carry out its new mission, have also posed a challenge to the social studies of science and technology (SSTS). SSTS is an emerging interdisciplinary field that, for the past two decades, has primarily focused on the micro-world of the laboratory. The interaction of scientists with their object of study, or what they believed to be the natural world as transmitted to them by their instrumentation, has been the focus of this social constructivist approach to understanding science. Although the laboratory is an essential part of the interaction of science with the larger world, a new set of science and society issues has arisen that is not entirely captured by this approach.

An attempt to develop new theoretical frameworks and research programs to address the broader science policy issues exemplified by the academic-industrial interface has arisen in recent years. "It all began at Acquafredda," remarked Brazilian S&T researcher Ary Plonski, referring to the international network of researchers on university-industry relations that initially came together at a NATO workshop in southernmost Italy in 1991. Several years before there was an official NATO science policy series, the London-based Science Policy Support Group (SPSG), in collaboration with the Fondazionne Rosselli of Milan and Torino, Italy, took the lead in organizing a meeting to bring together S&T researchers and practitioners, focusing upon the intersections of academia and industry. The North Atlantic Treaty Organization (NATO) Scientific Affairs directorate creatively accepted this initiative and made it its own.

The NATO scientific directorate, traditionally devoted to sponsoring interdisciplinary and specialist workshops and volumes in the "hard" sciences, is a little-known part of the widely known multinational organization devoted to furthering the mutual security, cultural interests, and scientific advance of its member states. The Scientific Affairs Directorate has played an increasingly important role in science policy studies in recent years, especially in fostering cooperation among researchers from Eastern Europe and the Former Soviet Union and their Western counterparts. The editors express their appreciation to Dr. Jubier and his predecessors at NATO for their continuing interest and support.

By the late 1980s the interface between academia and industry was increasingly identified as a factor in economic growth, a source of new products and companies, on the one hand, and of flows of knowledge to existing firms, on the other. The strengthening ties between the two institutional spheres was also seen as a force reshaping the mission of the university, both positively and negatively. A series of international research collaborations and conferences blossomed from the Acquafredda meeting (UNAM Mexico City, 1992, SUNY Purchase, New York, 1993) and the "Triple Helix" university-industry-government meetings (Amsterdam, 1996, Purchase, New York, 1998) that provided a forum and helped shape the identity of the emerging field.

This volume is the first comparative analysis of the role of academic-industry relations in national innovation systems. The first two chapters of this book are based upon the "theme paper" for the Acquafredda conference. Several of the following chapters originated as talks at the meeting while other complementary work published here was identified later. The volume attempts to synthesize and disseminate the major concepts and analyses in the field (e.g., the theses of the "second academic revolution" and "knowledge flows") to a broader audience of policy makers, academics, scientists, and industrialists, concerned with the issues of interface, and suggest some directions for future investigation.

Introduction

HENRY ETZKOWITZ, ANDREW WEBSTER, and PETER HEALEY

A new common form of academic institution is emerging in the late twentieth century. From its medieval origin as a corporation of scholars or students, the university is evolving into the contemporary entrepreneurial university. Specialized institutions such as the Princeton Institute of Advanced Study have not proven to be as effective producers of research as universities with students. Research universities, combining research with teaching, have long since displaced teaching colleges as the academic norm. Recently, a broader class of research universities has taken on economic development as an institutional mission. In the United States, technology transfer tasks had largely been confined to the "land grant" schools, a special class of universities created in the mid-nineteenth century to foster scientific agriculture. The Massachussetts Institute of Technology, for decades virtually a unique anomaly in United States higher education, originated as part of a contemporaneous movement to infuse industry with science.

An academic revolution is a change in the purpose or mission of the university. As medieval institutions, going back more than one thousand years to their establishment in Paris and Bologna, universities appear to change at a glacial pace. An academic revolution would appear to be a contradiction in terms. Originally conceived as institutions of cultural conservation, preservation, and transmission, they existed solely for that purpose for many centuries. As an institution of medieval origins for the conservation, renewal, and transmission of knowledge, the university, has retained its original characteristics even as it has expanded its purview to encompass new missions. The continuity of the university resides in its history of development: each new task has evolved out of an effort to meet a previous goal.

The first academic revolution was the transformation of universities from institutions of cultural preservation to institutions for the creation of new knowledge. Putting that knowledge into use followed soon after. The second revolution, the translation of research into products and into new enterprises,

1

started almost at the same time as the first; the former almost immediately engendering the latter. Until recently, many leading research universities eschewed an active role in the transfer of knowledge. This stance has changed due to external pressures arising from constriction in government funding for academic research accompanied by growing awareness of opportunities for the practical uses of academic knowledge.

Knowledge as Capital

The transformation of science into economic goods is not new. Certainly most technological knowledge derives from industrial practice. Indeed, these innovations have stimulated scientific progress as well, in fields such thermodynamics and information theory. There have also been significant instances of the transformation of scientific ideas into industrial use since the advent of the Industrial Revolution, classic examples being the chemical and electrical industries. What is new is the intensification of this process, including the shortening of the time span between discovery and utilization, and increased reliance of industry on knowledge originated in academic institutions. During the past two decades the capitalization of knowledge, formerly confined to a few disciplines and applied sciences and to a relatively few institutions (such as MIT and Stanford in the United States, Salford in the United Kingdom, and Campinas in Brazil), has been generalized to a much broader range of academic institutions.

This process is increasingly international, taking place not only in the United States but around the world in both developed and underdeveloped countries. It is a feature of capitalist-free market, mixed economies and socialist and post-socialist economic systems, North-South, East-West; nations and regions, each for their own reasons and, at times, at the instance of international agencies such as the World Bank and the United Nations International Development Organization (UNIDO) have focused on the the the intersection of academia and industry as a potential fulcrum of future economic development (Ogbimi 1990).

Creating science-based industries from academic research is a common theme of industrial policy, whether made explicit as in France and Mexico or left implicit as in the United States. Such policies are constructed on the basis of a new relationship between universities and industry, involving transfer of technology as well as access to trained personnel. The perception that university-based science and technology is of use to industry has led to changes in the rules governing how universities and companies interact with each other, shifting the relationship from an eleemosynary to a business basis. Similarly, the decline of traditional industries and the struggle to revive or replace them has politicized scientific and technological spheres, heretofore viewed as non-economic, self-organized, and best left unregulated. It has resulted in a change in the mission of the research university, giving it an economic development as well as an educational and training responsibility.

Leading liberal arts universities, when they became involved in practical affairs during the postwar era, oriented themselves to the national political arena. They typically eschewed any interest in the economy of their region until the recent era of uncertainty in research funding. University policies to capture the economic outcomes of campus-based research and campus involvement in efforts to aid the local economy have raised explicit discussion and caused controversy over the norms of science and the university. Of course, there was always an economic side to the university, since it received tuition payments, research grants, and gifts. But until recently, even when university endowments were invested, neither liberal arts professors nor administrators directly participated in the capitalization of knowledge.

Now, as the research university moves to assume a third function—economic development—there is concern that attention to economic issues will negatively affect the conduct of research. Transfer of knowledge to industry was theoretically freely available through the literature. But in practice industry needed relationships with academic scientists to translate this knowledge into a usable form. This is one of the driving forces behind normative change in academic science, although the relationships were initially formulated to insulate academic scientists from industry pressures. Academic scientists have a long history of working with industry, having helped establish the early industrial research laboratories in many countries.

Until quite recently most university-industry connections separated academic and commercial practices. Limits were placed on how much time an academic could devote to outside concerns. In the United States, the "one-fifth rule" allowing one day per week became commonplace. Even as ongoing relationships, consulting arrangements were usually conducted apart from academic research, although based on the academic's expertise accumulated from campus-based research. Consulting relationships typically involved brief visits to industrial sites or the conduct of discrete projects on university premises. A consequence of this separation was that it left control of commercial opportunities of academic research in the hands of industry whereas control over the direction of research and choice of research topics was left to academic scientists. Although regular payments were made to individual consultants, the large-scale transfer of funds from industry to the university was left up to the generosity of companies. Thus, the traffic between university and industry was policed so that boundaries were maintained even as exchanges took place through consultation and philanthropy.

Even the advent of federal funding appeared to support the existing social structure of academic science. Since research funds were largely controlled by committees of academic peers the postwar federal funding of science tended to support traditional academic models of autonomy. Nevertheless, the internal working of these forms was modified through scientists' interaction with granting agencies and attending to their priorities as part of the process of securing research funds. In addition to writing articles when they felt ready to present knowledge to peers, scientists had to at least project a future "product" from their research such as a cure for a disease or an economically relevant technology. This was the implicit contract between scientists and society set forth in Vannevar Bush's government report *Science: The Endless Frontier*, the charter document for the National Science Foundation. Since support for research was virtually guaranteed by the government during the early postwar era, researchers could afford to be relatively unconcerned with the practical outcomes of their research. Now the bill has become due and those earlier promises, whether they were meant to be taken literally or not, have become a contributing factor to changing the purpose of the university.

Even as issues of the balance between research and teaching emanating from the first academic revolution remain in dispute, the question of the appropriate relationship between academic research and the disposition of the economic value from that research was not settled at that time. Should the economic value of research be captured, enhanced, and marketed by the university, or are these tasks best left to other institutions to undertake? Different countries, and separate classes of universities in the same country, have taken one or the other course. As each new mission overlays older ones, there are disputes over whether the new task enriches or detracts from its predecessors. A natural experiment in the social organization of the appropriation of economic value from research, and on the relationship between research and teaching, has been underway for more than a century. Various formats have arisen in different countries either to integrate one or more of the functions of teaching, research, and economic development in single settings, as is common in the United States, or to divide them among separate settings, more typical of Europe.

A series of disputes, and their resolution, at MIT in the early twentieth century have provided U.S. universities with models for the conduct of relations with industry in succeeding years. The "one-fifth rule" allowing consultation one day per week, the decision to patent and market academic research, initially through an intermediary organization and later by the university itself, and the role of the university in regional economic development, capitalizing firms from academic research, originated at MIT. During the past two decades these formats for academic-industrial relations, heretofore relegated to a special academic sector, have spread throughout the U.S. academic system (Etzkowitz 1994).

Academic-industrial relations have become a central theme of economic renewal not only through government policy initiatives, but also from changes within universities and companies associated with the emergence of an innovation system based on lateral ties. Conflicts between universities and companies have arisen in the course of these developments from negotiators' divergent conceptions of the appropriate role of their counterpart's organization, as well as from disagreements over contract terms. Researchers, as well as practitioners, base their analyses on different assumptions about institutional mission and often talk past each other, as well.

Alternative Models of Academic-Industrial Relations:
Knowledge Flows and the Triple Helix

Two contrasting models of academic-industrial relations have been posed: "knowledge flows," based upon separation, and the "triple helix," denoting integration of institutional spheres. Explicating these models, and the assumptions on which they are based, could clarify various aspects of university-industry relations, including conflict of interest and commitment and the appropriate role of government at the academic-industrial interface. The triple helix model is based on ties among overlapping institutions, whereas the knowledge flows schema is premised upon separate academic, industrial, and governmental spheres. Real differences exist between universities as well as faculty members in devising strategies for industrial relations. To clarify controversial issues it is often helpful to sharpen them in "ideal typical" theoretical dichotomies even through reality is, of course, more complex and, as we shall see, occurs along a continuum (Weber 1922).

The definition offered here of knowledge flows is a synthesis derived from academic analyses (Feller 1986; Faulkner and Senker 1995) and statements by practitioners such as the Director of R&D at Philips (Bulthuis 1996). According to this model, universities produce knowledge, transmit it through publication, and ideally do not sell it. Linkages between the spheres and flows of knowledge across them are shaped, both organizationally and ideologically. For example, many academic departments value only publications for promotion and their members attend to the practical implications of research incidentally. Traditional academic ideology allows a narrow, yet highly effective, one-way channel from basic research to industrial innovation, the so-called linear model.

This hydraulic system of knowledge flows consists of reservoirs, dams, locks, and flowgates through which knowledge, codified and tacit, is exchanged for resources across clearly delimited boundaries. Transfer of technology, as opposed to knowledge, is conducted solely through intermediaries, such as a technology transfer office collecting invention disclosures and obtaining patents for sale to industry. However, such pecuniary efforts are viewed as counterproductive to the academic mission and cost ineffective, to boot. In this view, academia's special research mission lies at the basic end of the spectrum and governmental efforts to divert universities from this course are misguided.

The knowledge flows model specifies institutional missions narrowly: universities are assigned functions of education and research; industry, production; government, regulation. In its traditional role, the university is the producer of trained persons to send to industry according to IRDAC in the European Union and the Government, University, Industry Research Roundtable in the United States. The academic side of this perspective is a zero-sum game: if universities and their faculties become involved in development activities or firm-formation ventures, their basic research effort will inevitably decline. In the industrial view, the primary role of firms in innovation is to produce incremental improvements derived from experience with production and closely associated R&D. On the other hand, universities as a site of basic research are expected to be a source of discontinuous innovation.

The knowledge flows thesis is based on the assumption of a linear model, with a one-way flow from basic research to innovation. Alternatively, a spiral model has been suggested with a reverse flow from industry to academia, as well. Such an iterative effect, in which industrial innovation opens up new basic research questions, suggests that academic involvement in industrial innovation enhances the performance of basic research. Indeed, survey data showing that academics with industrial connections publish more than their peers lacking same indirectly supports this thesis (Blumenthal et al. 1986).

Knowledge flows are a key element of university-industry relations; some suggest it should be the only dimension! Yet as more intensive relations of increasing complexity emerge, often involving government, a new model, the triple helix, is required as an overlay upon knowledge flows (Etzkowitz and Leydesdorff 1997). In addition to linkages among institutional spheres, each sphere takes the role of the other. Thus, universities assume entrepreneurial tasks such as marketing knowledge and creating companies even as firms take on an academic dimension, sharing knowledge among each other and training employees at ever-higher skill levels.

As we suggested above, dichotomous models of academic-industrial relations seldom precisely reflect reality. Various parts of the same university can be found to operate according to different models. Indeed, members of the same department or research unit may operating according to contrasting conceptions of the proper relationship between university and industry. Such differences often result in conflict of interest and commitment controversies when viewpoints collide in the interpretation of particular cases in the same academic institution. In addition, linkage varies as one moves from one technology sector to another. The linear model may apply most clearly to the pharmaceutical sector, whereas a "chain" and "spiral" model may apply to ceramics, while neither model seems to clearly encompass the data on parallel computing.

The Role of the University in Industrial Innovation

Contemporary innovation is a precarious business. This is not simply because of transitional difficulties associated with the creation of a new innovation cycle. Rather, innovation, in the context of late modernity, is intrinsically more difficult to control, to be sure of, and to anticipate than in the past. And this condition is likely to prevail. In the fields of science and technology, the more powerful our knowledge the more difficult it is to control or decide what direction it is to take, even more to agree upon the most appropriate criteria to evaluate and regulate it.

This pressure to differentiate and specialize is met by as strong a desire to reintegrate our understanding according to new intellectual and professional boundaries. So one of the dynamics of society today is that boundaries are continually being eroded and renegotiated. New knowledge grows at such a pace that skills and the boundaries they define rapidly outdate, while there is a simultaneous tendency toward what has been called innovation overload. As a result, there is a continual pressure to audit and evaluate our knowledge base, to filter critical from non-critical technologies (Branscomb 1993), and to protect at institutional and national levels the intellectual and material capital on which future innovation depends.

As the intellectual boundaries within the knowledge base—between the sciences, for example—become more permeable, traditional professional and sectoral divisions (within industry) also begin to break down. A new division of labor has emerged, a more complex system of users and producers of knowledge and information, which has enabled the growth of new types of trans- or inter-organizational structures. Indeed, networking, cross-institutional linkage, informal and formal collaboration are all not merely possible but necessary if public and private agencies and individuals are to cope with the increasing differentiation and complexity of today's innovation systems. Companies, for example, coping with the demands of the globalization of production have sought to increase their involvement in strategic partnering at national and international levels.

This is leading to a growth in not only vertical but also, more significantly, of horizontal ties between firms. Large firms' innovative capacities will depend on access to both basic science and a key set of core technologies. Many science-based firms have sought to restructure their activities around a key generic technology, such as the U.S. corporation Monsanto, which uses biotechnology across a wide range of its research and development (R&D) areas in agricultural, chemical, and pharmaceutical innovation. In short, new organizational opportunities and demands exist for all organizations closely tied to the knowledge base.

This book explores how these processes are reshaping the specific relationships between academia, industry, and government, the principal players in the innovation system. In particular, universities and firms have become more alike in that both are involved in translating knowledge into marketable products, even though they still retain their distinctive missions for education and research on the one hand, and production and marketing on the other. Moreover, the circumstances of the innovation system make the two sectors more dependent on each other. Companies seek relevant knowledge wherever it is available: from other firms, government research laboratories, and universities. Technology transfer personnel are commonplace in larger firms and regularly attend meetings where universities, small firms, and government laboratories present their intellectual property to potential customers.

Universities have experienced a similar transformation through the development of offices to seek out and market useful knowledge developed on campus. As a result of financial pressures and incentives, universities have broadened their activities from education and research for its own sake to meeting specific research needs of industry. Although is it still a relatively small proportion of their income, universities are beginning to earn substantial sums from their technology transfer activities (Etzkowitz and Stevens, this volume).

As the third player in the innovation system, government—at regional, national and international levels—has been instrumental in encouraging universities to undertake responsibilities for economic development. Most notably, the university as a producer of knowledge on which new firms can be based and as an administrative structure to provide a home for the early stages of firm formation has become a key element in a high-tech regional economic development strategy. Working the interface of academic-industrial relations has become a watchword among institutional sectors and across national boundaries. These relations, formerly the special interests of a small coterie of academic institutions and firms, have formed the basis of a general model of how to create knowledge and wealth simultaneously in the late twentieth century.

The book's title, *Capitalizing Knowledge*, is intended to convey a process that has both economic and symbolic meaning. That is, it refers to the translation of knowledge into commercial property in the literal sense of capitalizing on one's intellectual (scientific) assets; more generally, it refers to the way in which society at large draws on, uses, and exploits its universities, government-funded research labs, and so on to build the innovative capacity of the future. These two are related of course: university spinoff firms, for example, may commercialize a technique developed during basic research in a particular area, which provides short term revenue. But the income-generating technique is also likely to feed back on and enhance further basic research, contributing to the wider knowledge base of that discipline.

Getting the right balance between these private and public functions of knowledge is often more difficult than the preceding comment suggests. Indeed, there are many who have written about a growth in conflict of interest between the public and private interests of contemporary research. Harvey Brooks (1993), for example, has argued that the level of privatization of university research that has already taken place in the last decade should not be encouraged to grow (225). Others express concern that the moves toward further commercialization of science will erode the basic science base, that the focus on patenting and exploitation of university research is misplaced and unlikely to yield net returns (Feller, ibid.), while many point to the complications a more commercial university orientation can generate for the academic experience of students (Louis and Anderson, this volume).

On the other hand, there are also many advocates of further ties between the academic and industrial sectors. These include government, as is evident in the British government's recent White Paper on science and technology (*Realising Our Potential* [HMSO 1993]) and the U.S. administration's move toward a more formal industrial policy that pushes national research laboratories toward a more extensive technology transfer role. Industrialists, too, often argue for stronger ties, summarized, perhaps, in the recent statement by the president of R&D at Hoffmann-La Roche that university departments and institutes should gear their research projects more closely to society's needs (Drews 1993). Evidence (Mansfield 1991) indicates that some sectors are notably reliant on academic research for the development of new products and processes, especially information technology and the medical instruments, drugs, and metal industries.

These very contrasting positions can only be evaluated by a close examination of the changing relationship between academia and industry. This is precisely what this book sets out to do. There are a number of key questions, which the different contributions to this volume seek to address. These include:

- What changes are taking place in the relationship between academia and industry, and how is this to be related to the wider changes in the innovation system?
- Are there limits to the capitalization of knowledge, and have these been reached?
- Are there any trends in the direction and form of academic-industrial relations, and how do these vary as you move from advanced industrial states to developing, middle-income, and post-socialist economies?
- What are the critical issues that we need to address now and in the future both about conflict or interest questions (and their ethical dimensions) and the development of a stronger research activity in the field of academic-industry relations?

Only by answering these can we begin to deconstruct the polarized positions on the relations between academia and industry sketched out above.

Stages and Forms of Knowledge Capitalization

Today, most industrialized states in the world strive to secure the most effective exploitation of their respective knowledge bases. These bases are reproduced and developed through the activities of both public and private research scientists and engineers, a battery of legally secured intellectual property rights, and a broad range of science and technology policies geared toward market-led investment in the economy. Much of this is taken for granted, the cultural and economic infrastructure on which it depends only apparent perhaps when efforts are made at constructing similar institutions in post-socialist Central European states. In other words, the capacity to initiate new forms of academic-industrial relations depends upon a wider infrastructural capacity to capitalize knowledge.

The processes that drive this capitalization are many and varied, and include: reductions in state funding for public sector science that force establishments to look elsewhere to sustain their research and training programs; a devolved responsibility—and so opportunity—to universities and the like to commercialize their activities; pressure on firms to both access the wider innovation environment and buy into it when and where appropriate; and finally, what Elzinga (1985, 1988) has called an epistemic drift toward measuring the utility of science in terms of criteria that are steered by market considerations. All these factors have brought changes to the institutional character of university and related science, which can be said to have occurred primarily—though not exclusively—over the past fifty years in western Europe and the United States.

Thus, at the level of the university the process of capitalization has occurred in three stages: first, the securing of intellectual property; secondly, the restructuring of research groups to generate a large intellectual property base; and thirdly, the establishing of corporate vehicles—such as spinoff firms—within universities to maximize the return on intellectual property. These three, broadly, follow on from each other historically, the earlier stages not being displaced by the later but developing in tandem with them as new demands and opportunities arise. The actual speed and timing of the three have varied between different countries, though the more recent tendency to monitor and match science policy changes has meant that there has been a growing convergence of both the timing and content of initiatives. So, for example, in 1985 the U.K. government invited universities to take up responsibility for patenting their intellectual property rights, a move that was a direct response to similar changes introduced in the United States in 1980.

The securing of intellectual property generated by universities began to be taken seriously in the early 1900s, although patent laws had existed for almost 200 years by then. One of the earlier examples of this was Banting and Best's discovery of insulin, the rights to which they assigned to the University of Toronto where they were faculty members. Wisconsin's Alumni Foundation was one of the more successful agencies securing rights to agro-biological research and through licensing patented work brought a growing level of income to the university to improve its science base. The U.S.-based Research Corporation, again established in the early 1900s, was another important private sector agency that licensed-in intellectual property from universities in return for royalty payments.

In the United Kingdom, the equivalent agency was the (publicly funded) National Research Development Corporation, established in 1950, subsequently subsumed within the British Technology Group, now privatized, but still serving to help identify and commercialize university invention. The role of these national agencies, while of continuing importance, has been weakened by the parallel emergence of technology transfer organizations within universities themselves which patent, license, and market intellectual property generated on campus. One of the most ambitious of these is the University of California's for-profit Technology Development Corporation, which was initiated in 1993 with a target income of $100 million through the licensing of prototype developments to industry.

The second stage of organizing research activities to create a greater volume of exploitable knowledge can be traced back to the development of group research in the university. While the individual scholar pursuing his or her research is still the predominant model in the arts and humanities, in the physical and biological sciences and to a considerable extent in the social sciences the increases in productivity that can be obtained through the division of labor has led to more organized modes of research. In the United States, organized research units date from the establishment of Agricultural Experiment Stations during the Jacksonian era, and in France and the United Kingdom, it was also agriculture but geology too (in relation to the search for minerals) which saw the development of state-funded research groups. Many other areas followed quickly in response to the economic, military, and health demands of the state through the first half of this century.

More significant changes have followed during the postwar era with the advent of research teams heavily reliant on their professor—the academic entrepreneur—who must act as fund raiser, personnel manager, publicity agent, and research director. These groups operate today as "quasi-firms" within universities, lacking only a direct profit motive to make them a business. Larger groups will be required (by contract) to provide their own corporate development plans, may operate on full economic cost accounting, secure their own patenting rights, and engender a range of technological spinoffs from their continuing basic or strategic research. The more successful they become the more likely they will find that a smaller proportion of their income comes from the core funding they receive from the university or government research budget: as such, they will be under further pressure to commercialize their research results to secure additional income.

This leads to the third stage in the capitalization process, the establishing of corporate vehicles—such as spinoff firms—to generate revenue. Spinoff firms can be of three types (Stankiewicz, this volume): contract and consulting firms, technology asset firms, and product-oriented firms. The first tend to remain relatively small, service-oriented companies, the second sell developed technologies to the market, while the third provide hard product lines (such as purified enzyme production, or specialized equipment) to larger corporations. The capacity to grow varies considerably across these different types of spinoff, related to technology sector, level of financing, relation to the wider marketplace, and organizational infrastructure they require. They tend to locate in close proximity to their parent university, typically on a neighboring science park: Stanford, for example, has spawned more than ninety high-tech firms employing more than 25,000 people and returning an annual $14 million in licensing income.

The terms on which universities capitalize their intellectual property through spinoff firms also varies. Typically, universities prefer to share in the proceeds from spinoffs via royalties rather than equity, although the latter method is increasing. Indeed, it has recently been argued that equity rather than the apparently safer (though lower value) return of royalty payments can in fact provide higher and, over the long term, more secure income for universities (Lefkoff and Gander 1993).

The three stages of capitalization can often be found to have come together in major universities that have developed large industrial liaison divisions for handling the commercialization of university intellectual property rights, through whom large joint collaborations have been established (perhaps with a pharmaceutical firm, for example) from which discrete spinoff firms are created to cash in on some specific technology or expertise which the collaboration has brought to fruition. Government research establishments replicate this process, increasingly so in the United Kingdom, where research agencies are required to market test their expertise, or where Research Council institutes have established joint firms with the private sector to market their products, such as the Medical Research Council's equity share in the firm Therexsys, initially funded by venture capital to develop new gene therapy techniques. The Medical Research Council also holds 106 licensing agreements (*Scrip* 1993).

In addition, there has been growing pressure on publicly funded research organizations, such as TNO in the Netherlands and the CNRS in France, to relate their basic and strategic research activities to the commercial market. In the United States, government has encouraged national research laboratories to establish cooperative research and development agreements (CRADAs) with industry (following legislation in 1989), through which more than 500 agreements had been contracted by 1993.

Conflicts over the Capitalization of Knowledge

Not surprisingly, these changes imply a shift in the orientation of the academic and public research culture, from being devoted exclusively to the research and training interests of professional staff toward being open to more entrepreneurial activity. The latter raises potential conflict of interest questions and normative conflict between the expectations and standards of academia and those of private enterprise. Conflict of interest may be said to exist when an individual is diverted from a group's broader goal to an individual or private goal. The issue arises most clearly when an individual within organizational responsibilities seeks to gain a personal private profit through her or his position. Thus, if the pursuit of disinterested knowledge is raised as the banner of the research university then the receipt of private profit for research pursued is *ipso facto* a conflict of interest.

In academia, of course, this issue has arisen most strongly when faculty members have organized firms based on their research or have equity in commercial developments sponsored by corporations funding their work. Some of the more notable examples of both forms of cross-sectoral interest have been in the biotechnology field, as new firms were spawned during the 1980s to commercialize the new techniques and processes developed in the area. After something of a lull here, the technologies and information needs of the Human Genome Project have led to a recent rash in academic-based firm formation, or firms whose principal executives were key players in the genetics research community.

Academics who embark on commercial activities can respond to this in at least two ways. On the one hand, it can be seen as an activity that must be kept separate from their more traditional roles and responsibilities, ensuring in particular that the research and development agendas of the two are discrete. On the other hand, such activity can be redefined as part of the legitimate role of academics and universities who define their tasks as contributing to innovation and economic growth as well as to the pursuit of knowledge. Since government science and technology policies appear to support this second view it is not surprising to find it in the ascendancy. Yet the more university scientists are involved in exploiting intellectual property the more their need to restrict the dissemination of detailed information about their work.

It is, of course, nothing new to find scientists reluctant to publish their work fully and freely because of professional competition with others; yet because of the new commercial pressures, this can be increased to a point where collaboration, dissemination (even in its more guarded mode), and proper peer review become compromised (Packer and Webster 1996). It is important therefore to determine whether the normative and ethical codes that have been traditional to academia have shadowed the institutional shifts implied by the three stages of capitalization outlined above. It would not be surprising to find that these shifts toward more commercial activities in universities have affected the relationships between faculty and students and the definition of academic work itself.

Transitions are seldom smooth as institutional spheres are transformed and boundaries among them redrawn. Survivals from the past, including feudal structures from the medieval period, have persisted and been extended to cover new relationships between faculty members and graduate students in areas such as the conduct of research. For example, in the assignment of authorship, quite often the intellectual producers are graduate students but professors automatically become co-authors in exchange for providing the infrastructure to produce the research for the article. This was an acceptable system under conditions when students were assured of the reward of the doctorate and movement into their own professorship. However, when such jobs are not as available the system starts to break down. Graduate students have organized unions at Yale and other universities, demanding better pay and working conditions during their "indenture" period. In some instances, they have gone on strike, withdrawing their teaching services, in an attempt to achieve status as a recognized group with negotiating rights.

The relations among faculty, students, and administration are subject to further strain when pecuniary as well as reputational rights are subsumed within a medieval structure. In recent years, the concept of graduate students as inventors has taken hold as academic administrators have been made aware that intellectual property as well as papers are produced in the course of research. Universities have asserted ownership rights to inventions on the grounds that students are "officers" of the university by virtue of their appointment to research assistantships with putatively the same status as faculty. Faculty prerogatives have been extended to intellectual property rights with the assumption that the professor will receive credit as inventor as well as author. The inherently one-sided power relationship based upon the right to grant or withhold a degree has thus been further reinforced through the expansion of the mission of the university. If students were to receive automatic rewards upon graduation, perhaps even this extension of the academic feudal system might be acceptable. Since this is no longer the case, the disposition of intellectual property rights has introduced a new level of conflict into the university.

The Ph.D. degree has declined in value as opportunities in the academic system have decreased. A student's best chance at a job and a future career may lie in establishing their own company on the basis of the inventions they have made in the course of their student career. Indeed, intellectual property rights issues have percolated to the undergraduate level as some universities, acting similarly to companies that by contract own the intellectual property rights to employee inventions, have claimed ownership rights to student inventions even without written policies and agreements. A former undergraduate student at the University of Florida, Peter Taborsky, was recently jailed as a result of criminal charges brought by the university, claiming ownership of an invention that the former student had patented. Taking the format of a typical business dispute over the provenance of intellectual property, the university held that the invention was made during the student's academic career and belonged to the university and the company that had sponsored the research. The former student responded from his cell that "the idea for the invention came to him after the sponsorship ended" (*Wall Street Journal* 1996).

The graduate student role has expanded from its feudal format of acolyte to incorporate teaching, research, and invention activities. Pay and status have lagged the reinvention of the role, although a few research units such as the Materials Characterization and Service Center at the University of Puerto Rico pay their students technicians' wages, in recognition of their contribution to relations with industry. In general, though, the graduate student–professor relationship has yet to be revised from its feudal format, which extends virtually absolute faculty power over the student across the multiplicity of tasks that the latter's role has accrued, including generation of intellectual property.

Nor is the status of faculty-originated intellectual property entirely clarified. Columbia University has been charged with unfairly appropriating the intellectual property rights of an adjunct faculty member in exchange for honorary faculty status. The economist Dr. Geoffrey Moore, a creator of the leading index of economic indicators, is suing the university for $23 million in damages. In another instance, a University of California researcher has sued a colleague, charging that corporate research funding, and implicitly any resulting intellectual property, was inappropriately diverted from the university to a private foundation. Despite these disputes, faculty-administration conflicts over intellectual property rights have largely been settled through a three-way split among the investigator, the sponsoring research unit, whether department or center, and the university administration.

The Entrepreneurial University

Some critics of academic-industrial relations would resolve conflicts over intellectual property by having the university retreat behind traditional boundary lines. However, the genie of capitalizable knowledge, whose potential was recognized as early as the seventeenth century, has emerged in the late twentieth century from the "ivory tower" created by the proponents of an ideology of pure research in the late nineteenth century. Moreover, the expansion of academic research has irrevocably changed the function of the university, since potentially commercializable knowledge is created as a byproduct of normal research activities even without new subventions directed toward that purpose. There is likely no return to an earlier era, especially given the university's external resource constraints and the growing contribution of technology transfer to regional economies and the university's bottom line. Instead, the university is changing its organization and ideology to accommodate its new role in economic development. Indeed, the role of professor has already been subject to considerable revision through the working out of a new balance among teaching, research, and invention, despite continuing tensions.

Changes within academia are accompanied by the organization of corporatist arrangements among academia, industry, and government, with universities having a greater say in setting the terms of relationships given their increased importance to meeting the goals of their partners. A spiral model of innovation has also emerged in which basic research spurs industrial innovation and vice versa, as an overlay upon the linear model. Economic development is increasingly based upon utilization of research resources to enhance regional innovation environments. Knowledge-producing institutions such as universities are called upon, or take the initiative themselves, and play a leading role in bringing firms and local governments together to support new initiatives. Universities, both those with long-standing and newly emerging industrial ties, are changing from a mode of separation to one of integration, in organizing their relationships with industry (Etzkowitz 1996). As this change takes place, the triple helix replaces knowledge flows as the appropriate metaphor and model for academic-industrial relations.

The entrepreneurial university, with faculty and administration directly involved in translating knowledge into intellectual property and economic development, attempts to create an industrial penumbra around the university with varying degrees of success. In the following sections of this book, we analyze these developments at three levels. Section I, "The Entrepreneurial University," interprets the changing role of the university in society, the costs and benefits as academia shifts to an entrepreneurial mode. Section II, "The Capitalization of Knowledge," evaluates the viability of different forms of linkage mechanisms that exchange knowledge and technology across the shifting boundaries between academia and industry. Section III, "International Comparisons," analyzes the growth of academic-industry relations in different national contexts and comparatively, across world regions.

I

The Entrepreneurial University

CHAPTER 1

Entrepreneurial Science:
The Second Academic Revolution

HENRY ETZKOWITZ and ANDREW WEBSTER

There is a specter haunting the academic world of externally driven influence upon the mission of universities. Change in academia has always been notoriously slow when driven from within. As a conservative institution of medieval origins the university is always fearful of change, especially of revisions of academic norms that appear to be initiated by forces outside of the academy. In the 1930s, most academics rejected government funding of research despite the ravages of the Depression, fearing that the university would be unalterably transformed and autonomy lost (Genuth 1987). However, the university was soon transformed and a new status quo created in which the autonomy of the academic enterprise became identified with government funding procedures that a new generation came to view as traditional during the postwar era (Greenberg 1967).

Today, universities are undergoing a "second revolution." Whether one is talking about the considerable funds that a pharmaceutical company might give to establish or sustain an academic center in return for exclusive property or marketing rights (such as the $85 million that Shiseido gave to Massachusetts General Hospital for a dermatological research institute, or the $75 million that Eisai gave to fund neuroscience at University College London) or the smaller but more extensive pre-competitive and contract research collaboration that industry and academia share, academic-industrial relations and the growth in the commercialization of academic science have become major items on any science policy agenda. The academic revolution of the late nineteenth and early twentieth centuries introduced a research mission into an institution hitherto devoted to the conservation and transmission of knowledge (Jencks and Riesman 1968). Building upon the first revolution, the second academic revolution is the translation of research findings into intellectual property, a marketable commodity, and economic development.

Perhaps even more significant is the fact that science policy itself has become tied to economic development policy. This is the case in industrial-

21

ized and industrializing countries (capitalist or post-socialist), at the national and regional levels, in the First, Second, and Third Worlds. Although Marx predicted in the nineteenth century that modern industry would increasingly be based on science, his prediction has come true in a way that he did not entirely foresee. Similarly, Marx's intellectual nemesis, Max Weber, who predicted that science-based industry would become increasingly centralized and bureaucratized, due to increase in scale of technology, has also been partially disconfirmed. Much science-based technology is developed and marketed by entities such as IBM, Mitsubishi, Siemens, and Phillips—multinational corporations, larger than any organization that Marx or Weber imagined. But much science-based technology also comes out of small firms, companies such as SUN (Stanford University Network) that grow out of universities or hive off from larger firms. Some of these companies, such as EG&G and DEC, formed out of the Massachusetts Institute of Technology in the early postwar era, have grown to take a position among the 500 largest firms in the United States. How to create the conditions to produce a self-sustaining chain reaction of high technology firms, a Silicon Valley, Cambridge phenomenon, or a Route 128, linking universities to firm formation through private and state venture capital has become a central issue of economic development policy, along with infrastructure and location decisions.

Modes of Linkage

Linking older firms to universities to infuse them with new science-based technologies is one form of university-industry relationship. In forming new firms, scientists and engineers have become capitalists even as science and technology becomes a more central element of production, as important as and now more limiting than labor or financial capital. The rapid growth in new and traditional forms of linkage, the strong belief that future economic growth will become dependent not simply on a new cycle of innovation but on a new structure for innovation that ties basic and applied research ever more closely together, has led to a mushrooming of national and international state policies and programs geared toward the promotion and, to a lesser extent, evaluation of academic-industrial ties. Corporations themselves are not merely witnesses to this revolution, as knowledge becomes the "axial principle" (Bell 1989) of contemporary industrial society, accessing and managing science and technology information becomes vital. It can be asked, then, whether there are just as important institutional changes taking place within the corporate context as in academia.

    At the same time, the past two decades have seen a growth of academic research and informed practitioner commentary on the pattern of collaboration between the two sectors. There has also been a plethora of descriptive and prescriptive material relating to the range of mechanisms that are or should be in place promoting links between the two sectors. Of particular value have been the occasional synoptic reviews of the issue produced by the OECD (1984) and national agencies such as the French CNRS (1989),the Australian ASTEC (1989), the late U.S. Office of Technology Assessment (OTA) (1984, 1994), as well as professional associations exemplified by the European Industrial Research Managers Association (EIRMA) (1986), cross-sector groups such as the University-Industry-Government Roundtable (1996), multinational entities, including the Research Directorate of the European Union, and international organizations such as the United Nations (UNESCO, 1994). However, this material is difficult to combine in any sensible way and is of differing degrees of analytical depth and range. In part this is because of the speed with which developments have taken place, mapping new initiatives is a demanding enough task itself.

Nevertheless, a number of features characterize the contemporary linkage between the two sectors. Those who advocate an increasing collaboration between the two believe that this is made more possible and indeed necessary because of recent institutional changes in academia and scientific research: universities and equivalent institutions are becoming increasingly autonomous and prepared to play a role—at least at the margins—that is similar to industry, spawning a wide range of local and regional linkages with the private sector as well as generating spinoff companies that may service larger corporations or develop into much more important corporate actors, as has happened in biotechnology; the science and technology infrastructure is becoming more flexible and dynamic; and finally, apart from the more traditional short-term contract research ties, it is likely that there will be a greater incidence of longer-term collaborations, especially in terms of sponsorship of fundamental, "discovery" oriented programs. Some sectors of industry (especially in the bioscience/biomedical fields) are increasingly prepared to enter into long-term strategic research alliances. More generally, the commercialization of academic science is caught up with and to some extent fostered by the restructuring of academic institutions. This last point highlights the role of a third, most important player in the collaborative context: government. Government has become more concerned with developing new organizational structures that can strengthen national knowledge and economic bases typically via new mechanisms for linking industry and academia and/or industry and industry.

Together, therefore, we see three main sectors acting in concert and independently, developing new forms of relationship between public and private organizations. Given the variation here, it is not surprising to find the OECD's (1990) review of the field commenting that, "Any observer of the current system of university-enterprise relations . . . will note that our understanding of these ties needs to be improved. The wide variety of the many relations which they can develop implies that their effects may widely differ from case to case." And, unusually, the OECD goes on to comment, "In a few circumstances, some latent drawbacks may even outweigh the potential benefits of collaboration" (8). The report does not go on, however, to suggest what these latent drawbacks might be, nor how they might be uncovered. Understandably so, for as the report itself acknowledges, there is insufficient understanding of the institutional dynamics involved in collaboration, both overt and hidden.

It is for this reason that there is a need to take stock of our understanding of the changing relationship between the two sectors both empirically and theoretically and thereby to determine appropriate strategies for future research and policy making. Four tasks require our immediate attention:

1. the review and mapping of trends in the changing relationship between academia and industry to determine the spread and extent of new developments and to situate them in their historical and social contexts;
2. the development of a deeper theoretical analysis of those institutional changes this collaboration has brought about;
3. the development of comparative methods for distinguishing between forms of collaboration as well as highlighting neglected areas of research; and finally
4. the determination of implications for both science policy, practice and research: are all the efforts at enhanced collaboration always beneficial and are the benefits necessarily the anticipated ones?

In evaluating the positive and negative aspects of collaboration it is important to distinguish between different levels of analysis. Hence the impact of any particular collaboration may be measured at the level of the university/research center and differentiated by its impact on research and administrative sectors; moreover, this impact will have both short- and long-term effects. At regional and the wider national levels there may be a varying impact of different collaborations on economic growth, employment, and value-added innovation; to what extent are we in a position to measure the value-added effect of collaboration for innovation and competitiveness within industrial sectors? What measures of benefit and disbenefit can we draw on to answer this and do we have any cross-national data that records the uptake of university research by industry?

These questions provide a framework for analyzing the capitalization of academic knowledge in this volume. They raise general themes and issues associated with the four areas outlined above that researchers and practitioners of academic-industrial relations and the university and business communities, at large, need to address.

Mapping and Review of Trends

The intimate connection of science to economic and political forces was well established as early as the seventeenth century. According to one estimate, between thirty and sixty percent of scientific innovations during that era were made to meet commerce and government needs (Merton 1938). Scientific research, developed in the academies from the sixteenth century and typically conducted in researchers' homes, was brought into the universities during the nineteenth century. From then on, academic science developed in close connection with industrial innovation.

Research emerged, initially in philology and then in other disciplines, from a concerted effort to revive classical learning in the eighteenth century. New knowledge was inevitably created and a better understanding gained through the innovative methodological techniques invented to retrieve the meaning of Greek and Roman texts. The seminar, an innovative advanced teaching method, also arose out of the development of philological research. The cooperative examination of texts though presentations by advanced students and professors, with discussion of findings among them, led to both levels of academics being jointly conceived as inquirers. The seminar supplemented lectures and enhanced the educational mission of universities even as it became a basic format for organizing research in the humanistic disciplines. The first academic revolution originated in the humanities; as it spread to the sciences, a second revolution was set in motion.

As research became a distinctive activity at some universities in Europe, the experimental sciences were also incorporated into the academy. Disciplines such as chemistry developed from craft-based apprenticeship training into a larger-scale mode of instruction based, in part, on the invention of the teaching laboratory (Gustin 1975). For example, the teaching laboratory created by Justus Liebig at the University of Giessen made possible the training of large numbers of chemists and the conduct of systematic supervised research based on standardized analytical techniques. As chemistry spread through academia, some graduates used these techniques to invent new products such as artificial dyes and founded chemical companies in cooperation with their professors. Research was cultivated in these laboratories as an offshoot of organized instruction. In the chemical, electrical, and pharmaceutical fields, close relationships between academic and industrial science were pervasive at the beginning of the era of science-based corporations and universities in the late nineteenth century. The expansion of industrial opportunities created demands for additional trained personnel and industrial problems inspired much academic research (Wise 1985).

With the rise of "pure" science, beginning in the late nineteenth century, some of these close ties were either discarded or encapsulated in special sectors of the university world such as engineering and agricultural schools. In subsequent decades, academic and industrial science grew apart, each developing its own norms and traditions. Although industrial scientists were trained in academia, it came to be expected that they went through a transitional period in their recruitment to industry in which either their expectations about science were revised to meet company needs or, if unable to return to academia, they were condemned to the strains of role incompatibility (Cotgrove and Box 1970).

During this period the primary research ties between academia and industry took place through consulting relationships in chemistry and engineering. There was a rise in interest in university-industry connections during the 1920s but this was largely disrupted by the Depression of the 1930s. In the 1930s, foundations became an important source of sponsored research—particularly in the United States, developing precursors of later government programs.

During the era of relative scarcity of university-industry interaction, a new series of formats for the relationship were being created at Massachusetts Institute of Technology. These included the faculty-formed firm, an explicit role for the university in shaping regional economic development strategy, the interdisciplinary research center, and the invention of the venture capital firm. During the postwar era, these innovations were transferred to Stanford University, where the model for the university-initiated firm had been independently invented just before the war and where a scheme for land development grew into the concept of the science park. During World War II and the postwar era, government sponsorship of research eclipsed all other sources, as state support for frontier science grew so rapidly that during the 1950s and 1960s industrial support for academia declined in relative terms.

State support for science, within all NATO and generally all Organization for Economic Cooperation and Develoment (OECD) countries, has grown over the past three decades, apart from a period during the 1970s when funding was hit by the then structural instability of most industrial economies. As with any statistical series, comparisons of spending on science across countries have to be treated with great care as they may not be measures of the same phenomenon: statistical methods vary from country to country, the boundaries of R&D are regarded differently, and the relative buying power of state funding (allied to fiscal policy) mean that the domestic and international "terms of trade" in R&D are very uneven.

With these caveats in mind, the most recent figures indicate that the Gross Expenditure on Research and Development (GERD) is on average approximately 2.3 percent of GDP for all OECD countries. The ratio of GERD to GDP has grown steadily over the past two decades reaching more than three percent in the more affluent economies. Moreover, as the OECD itself comments, "The fact the R&D expenditures increase faster than GDP both in years with sustained economic growth and during low-growth periods clearly reflects the importance given to R&D—or more generally to science and technology—both by industry and by governments."

Relative contributions to GERD by government and industry have shifted since the 1970s, such that private enterprise is now the major source of research funding. For example, in West Germany, of total GERD, sixty-five percent is financed by industry while in Japan the equivalent figure is seventy-three pecent. While this trend can be generalized across a range of countries, a number of points need to be borne in mind. First, industrial support for R&D varies considerably by sector and by technology, being most important for the research-intensive pharmaceutical industry. Moreover, within this industry expenditure on basic or "discovery" oriented research can be particularly high: the U.S./U.K. pharmaceutical SmithKline Beecham, for example, devotes thirty percent of its annual R&D budget to discovery research. In such circumstances, the institutional impetus for linkage with other centers of basic research can be very strong. Secondly, absolute and relative figures for industrial R&D say nothing about how effective this expenditure is in terms of generating innovative products or techniques. The more industry supports R&D the greater will be the demand that the organization of research be structured in such a way as to minimize uncertainty and risk. This could well rebound on the innovative process as hierarchical and overly bureaucratic managerial patterns come to dominate. Thirdly, in many industrial sectors, R&D funding is heavily concentrated within a relatively small number of lead corporations. Finally, relative amounts of GERD funded by industry have differing effects depending on the institutional context in which they apply: both Japan and Turkey have similar figures here (of about eighty percent) yet clearly—notwithstanding the obvious absolute difference—their industries structure this funding in very different ways.

Most of the industrial financing for R&D goes to sustain in-house scientific work. But there has been a marked increase in extramural funding for research, especially in academia. Again, this varies considerably by country, by sector, and even within sectors. On average, only about four percent of total academic research activity is funded by industry—with the U.S. figure approaching eight percent—while as a proportion of industrial R&D expenditure this represents, again on average, about one percent. Some countries, such as Germany, Sweden, and Norway, exhibit twice this level of funding. It is, of course, important to know how this level of funding is affected by the role of government: for example, we need to know whether this is shaped by the presence of a formal industrial or technology policy. As we argue later, the United States and United Kingdom are very different in this regard compared with Japan and France, suggesting that the context for academic-industry relations can be significantly different. Even so, it would appear to be the case that in general, industry's contribution to Public Sector Research Science (PSRS) is marginal despite the heady predictions in the press and policy literature during the 1970s. Nevertheless, Table 1.1 shows a steady increase in real terms in the amount that industry is financing in universities.

While we need, therefore, to avoid exaggerated claims about rapid growth in industrial sponsorship, it would be wrong to ignore the very important developments that are taking place in certain areas, most especially bioscience/medicine, biotechnology, new materials science (especially polymer engineering), and information systems. Moreover, it is clear that without industrial support many scientists would find it difficult to continue their work because of a severe decline in state funding. Again, as the OECD puts it, "although the flows of R&D funds from industry to universities may appear extremely modest at the macro level, it is quite clear that at the micro level, such cooperation may be extremely important for the individual contracting partners . . . in countries where public funding for university research is becoming increasingly scarce, cooperation with industry may even in the worst of cases, become a condition of survival for some university institutions" (9).

As a result, a wide range of collaborative links as well as agencies through which academic research can be commercialized have developed (see chapter 4. Apart from the more traditional short-term contract-research relationship, joint programs between a number of companies, regional technology transfer networks, and new training initiatives that link academic and indus-

TABLE 1.1
Business Enterprise Finance in Academia
(1985 prices) $m

	1980	1981	1982	1983	1984	1985	1986	1987	1988
Australia		7		9	14				
France		26	27	27	33	42	45	82	
Germany		52		147		159	176	201	170
Italy	9	25	23	5	8	20	16	16	26
Japan	64	67	78	88	117	125	137	158	
UK		51		57		77	126	119	
US	305	344	372	413	486	561	698	763	816

trial staff are all just some of the forms in which the process of commercialization of academia has occurred. We can note too the development in recent years of multi-year, multi-million dollar collaborations between a single company sponsor and an academic research center of excellence is particularly notable. These have been primarily in the biomedicine/pharmacology area and since 1985 have increased both in frequency and in the absolute as well as relative volume of corporate investment they have attracted. Table 1.2 itemizes some of the more important of these deals made over the past fifteen years.

It is not suggested that these are all of a piece—that their rationale, structure, and contractual terms are identical. Some of the international links may have wider political dimensions as companies invest in universities or other research centers overseas in order to be seen to have an R&D presence in a country where there is a large and profitable market. Moreover, the terms of the alliance can vary significantly, from an endowment through to a managed research program targeted on a very specific area of strategic research.

The more recent deals have however, an increasing similarity in that they typically involve sponsorship of a large research team—even whole departments—with little or no other corporate funding; contracts are long term with sponsors enjoying exclusive first rights over any findings. In return, academics can enjoy a relatively secure period of funding and access to expensive technology and industrial collaboration. It is important to consider whether some companies (especially in bioscience) are beginning to regard this type of collaboration as a particularly effective model for managing the exploitation of academic expertise compared with other forms of arrangement in which they may also be involved.

Many of these deals, as is clear from the Table, are made with the most prestigious of university centers. This highlights the sense in which while relative proportions of industrial funding for universities is low on average, it can be quite high for the principal academic centers in any country. Harvard estimates, for example, that within the next decade it might receive approximately twenty-five percent of its research income from industrial sources. Peters (1987) points out that in the United States the top 150 university institutions (out of a total 1739 providing undergraduate, graduate, and research programs) account for almost ninety-two percent of the U.S. academic R&D.

In mapping these trends, however, there are a number of matters that need to be given careful consideration. As Gluck has pointed out, there are three key issues that should be addressed by both researchers and funders:

• While research funding by industry at elite universities should receive our close attention we also need to understand the phenomenon of industrial

TABLE 1.2
Principal Strategic Research Alliances

Total Alliance to date	Funds ($m)	Period (Yrs)	Est.	Area
HMS/MONSANTO	23.50	12	1974	Cancer Angiogenesis
LEICS/ICI	4.20	12	1978	Genetics
MIT/EXXON	8.00	10	1980	Combustion Technology
MGH/HOECHST	70.00	12	1981	Molecular Biology
UCDAVIS/ALLIED	2.50	3	1981	Nitrogen Fixation
SCRIPPS/J&J	30.00	—	1981	Synthetic Vaccines
WASHU/MALLINK	3.80	5	1981	Hybridomas
HMS/DUPONT	6.00	5	1981	Genetics
YALE/CELANESE	1.10	5	1981	Enzymes
JHU/J&J	1.00	—	1982	Biology
ROCK/MONS	4.00	5	1982	Photosynthesis
WASHU/MONS	100.00	12	1982	Biomedical
MIT/WRGRACE	8.00	5	1982	Amino Acids
YALE/BRMYERS	3.00	5	1982	Anticancer Drugs
CSPRING/EXXON	7.50	5	1982	Molecular Genetics
ROCHES/KODAK	0.45	—	1983	DNA
MEDUNIV/CHUGAI	0.50	3	1983	Mono. Antibodies
UILLINOIS/SOHIO	2.00	5	1983	Plant Mol. Genetics
COLUMB/BRMYERS	2.30	6	1983	Gene Structure
OXFORD/MONSANTO	20.00	5	1983	Glycoproteins
GEORGE/FIDIA	62.00	—	1985	Neurosciences
HMS/TAKEDA	1.00	—	1986	Angiogenesis Factor
OXFORD/SQUIBB	32.00	7	1987	Pharmocology (CNS)
JHU/SKB	2.20	5	1988	Respiratory Disease
CAMBRIDGE/SKF	4.00	5	1988	Molecular Medicine
OXFORD/BEECHAM	8.00	10	1989	Neuropsychobiology
ULP/SQUIBB	47.00	7	1989	Mol Biol: Proteins
MGH/SHISHEIDO	85.00	10	1989	Dermatology
UCL/EISAI	75.00	15	1990	Neuroscience
HMS/HLR	10.00	5	1990	Medicinal Chemistry
MGH/BMSQUIBB	37.00	5	1990	Cardiovascular
UCSD/CIBAGEIGY	20.00	6	1990	Rheum/Osteo Arthritis
HMS/SANDOZ	100.00	10	1991	Anti-cancer Research

Notes:
HMS: Harvard Medical School
MGH: Massachusetts General Hospital
JHU: Johns Hopkins University
UCL: University College London
HMS/TAKEDA contract is $1m per annum (open-ended)
WASHU/MONS: the $100m is a cumulative figure resulting from a large injection of funds in 1990.

collaboration at a greater diversity of universities, especially among what might be called the "second tier," regional/provincial state universities in different countries: as he asks, "How different is the prevalence of various types of industrial interaction at state and regional universities than at top schools? How do the provisions of such agreements differ? Are less research-intensive universities more likely to accept conditions of support (or behavior among faculty) that pose greater risks to traditional academic norms to get needed support?" (personal correspondence).

- What is the significance and meaning of specific industrial research contracts for academics in the context of their overall research activity or portfolio, and how does this vary in different areas of scientific investigation? It might be suggested that those in the bioscience fields attached to elite universities where industrial support is high could herald the emergence of "a new applied sub discipline of biology that attempts to take advantage of the opportunities to develop basic discoveries" (Ibid).

- How has industrial cooperation in the biosciences matured over recent years? While many of the earlier deals reflected the need to access academic research not available in house, corporations have now developed considerable local expertise in such areas. Does this make them less inclined to sponsor further work or has the collaboration provided a new modus vivendi for both academia and industry that makes additional support more rather than less likely?

In addition to "inputs" of research funds into universities from industry there is also the "output" of firms formed from university research as a measure of the economic relevance of academia. The concept of the "incubator" as a physical facility located on or near a campus to house new enterprises developed from academic research has been widely accepted, from Troy, New York's Rensselaer Polytechnic Institute (RPI) to Mexico City's National Autonomous University of Mexico (UNAM). Nevertheless, it was not too long ago that the administrator of a liberal arts state university upon being asked if his school had an incubator facility referred the caller to the Poultry Science department of the state's "land grant" university. Although enterprise development has become formally organized as a separate administrative activity at some universities, it has a long pre-history as a concomitant feature of departments, research centers, and laboratories at MIT and more recently at other universities, as well. A series of studies by Edward Roberts and his students at the Sloan school over the past twenty-five years has documented the incidence and natural history of the development of firms from MIT as they make the transition from campus, to east and west Cambridge, then to Route 128 (see Table 1.3).

TABLE 1.3
Sources of New Enterprises

MIT major laboratories	107
MIT academic departments	74
Total	181

Source: Roberts (1990)

Second generation spinoff firms with an academic pedigree, mergers and bankruptcies have also been tracked. This work has received greater prominence as part of a more general theme developed in David Birch's research on the significance of small firms for creating employment growth. The emergence of the venture capital industry out of MIT's involvement in the formation of the American Research and Development Corporation and the focus upon new high-tech firms as the centerpiece of regional economic development by state and regional governments have made the issue of the role of universities and academic research in economic development a subject of more than academic interest to political and business entities.

Even universities traditionally not known for spinoff activity find that they have been the source of new firms once they develop an interest in regional economic development. When the University of Texas at Austin created an organizational capacity to monitor and encourage new company development, it found a history of firm foundation activity that could be analyzed to provide an informed basis for local policy formation. Figure 1.1 depicts an analysis of the factors involved in creating spinoff firms at one such university under previous conditions of "passive" university concern.Currently the university is playing a more active role. For example, it was found that business not technological issues were the main difficulties faced by firm founders, indicating programs that could be put into place such as ". . . business angel networks, focused entrepreneurial education, entrepreneurial courses with a hands-on emphasis, and continuing education programs focusing on the management and marketing needs of emerging companies . . ." (Smilor et al. 1990).

While the level of cash support from industry is important in stimulating qualitative changes in academia, it is only one factor. The model of research is also crucial. Universities are undergoing a change from basic to applied to industrial product, from a one-way-flow linear model, in which they have been (since World War II) traditionally involved only in the first two steps, to a multidirectional spiral model in which the linear model is incorporated along with at least two other approaches:

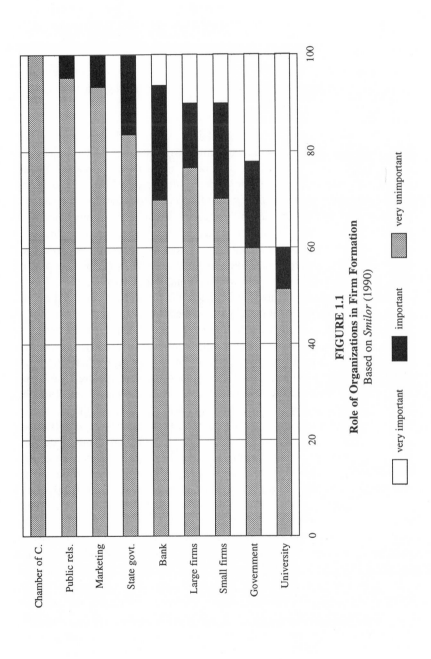

FIGURE 1.1
Role of Organizations in Firm Formation
Based on *Smilor* (1990)

☐ very important   ■ important   ▨ very unimportant

Chamber of C.
Public rels.
Marketing
State govt.
Bank
Large firms
Small firms
Government
University

0   20   40   60   80   100

- where the solution of an industrial problem leads to basic research questions, e.g., the need for improved switching devices for telephony led to basic research in solid state physics in the 1940s at Bell Labs (USA);
- where the solution to a technological problem generates basic research questions and leads to a product, e.g., the ENIAC computer project led to Von Neumann's theorizing about the nature of computing machines and the UNIVAC computer system.

The latter two approaches, the first from a theoretically oriented industrial lab, the second from an interdisciplinary military-sponsored research project at a university, are currently being incorporated into academic research models through the establishment of joint industry-university research centers and collaborative projects throughout most OECD countries, larger-scale national programs such as the U.S. NSF's Science and Engineering Centers and other state and local government supported research institutes. Moreover, this feedback cycle between basic and applied is increasingly apparent within corporate research: for example, the Dutch firm Philips have developed a model of innovation based on evidence showing that maturing technologies need to be opened up to further innovation through a return to basic research in the company, enhanced by ties to university researchers.

While the internal character of academic research appears to be broadening to incorporate approaches previously confined to industry, the internal character of much industrial research is mixing long-term fundamental R&D with short-term applied work: both are required if companies are to maintain their profitability. At different times in the innovation cycle, which varies by sector, the emphasis may be on one rather than the other of these research approaches. Rates of company basic science publications—especially those joint-authored with academics—may be indicative of such changing circumstances. For example, some leading industrial labs that were once among the leaders in the production of basic research papers have dropped off the charts. This may be a result of local, contingent factors associated with R&D strategies within specific sectors, since there is also evidence to suggest that other corporations are expanding their rate of publication. This is especially true, for example, of the major U.K., U.S., and European pharmaceutical companies: in some cases, such as SmithKline Beecham, the annual rate of publications has increased tenfold between 1979 and 1990. Even then, however, we have to consider how national factors can influence the pattern of publications, for, in Japan, pharmaceuticals publish relatively few papers compared with Japanese IT companies. Size and origin of company may also be relevant here since relatively small companies of university origin have—even when substantially large, such as Genentech—a very high rate of corporate publication.

However one is to interpret the detailed evidence about publication rates, some more general questions arise: have there been any changes in the balance between short-term and long-term research orientations within companies? What would a "balance" mean, and how are these different—potentially conflicting—orientations resolved in house? In what circumstances and to what extent might industrial (or at least some industrial) research revert to its earliest phase when it was strictly tied to the improvement of existing products, before academics were brought into industrial labs to broaden their focus? It would be worth exploring the extent to which this process, however uneven, is happening within and between industrial sectors, for clearly it may well influence the propensity to link with public sector science.

The growth of industrial patronage for academic research as described above has been encouraged by the innovation needs of industry where coverage of the technological waterfront is vital. It would also be worth considering this greater willingness to collaborate with academia as simply part of a wider need for corporations to collaborate with relevant others—corporations as well as academic research groups and centers—because of the character of the technologies and markets in which they are involved. Indeed, it might well be argued that the development of company-company links between large and small, and organized either horizontally or vertically, is of growing importance in innovative contexts dependent on new technologies. As Loveridge and Pitt (1990) have argued, "If [firms] are to sustain competitive advantage they need to distinguish technologies in which they have a distinctive competence from those that are basic, albeit necessary to competitive survival and those which confer no advantage, hence should be bought in" (9). A variety of collaborative strategies may be required to meet these varying needs, including joint ventures (where two firms establish a new corporation), cooperative research, licensing and manufacturing deals. Organizational analysts have shown how such relationships vary according to the specific sector, organizational form and strategy any one firm has.

At the same time, academic institutions are experiencing an erosion of the grants economy within which they have traditionally operated, as a more competitive exchange economy requires them too to identify their own specific competence (in teaching and research) and the way this might be enhanced through collaborative deals with others. In these twin circumstances, government pressure to encourage greater linkage between the two sectors has found only limited, and then often only ritualistic resistance. Government has been keen to generate more interaction through:

- an increasing selectivity in the choice and direction of R&D in response to both perceived needs and opportunities for technological innovation: this

has meant a growth in strategic research and an expansion of mechanisms whereby the technologies it generates can be transferred to industry;
• a tying of public sector funds to matched industrial expenditure on R&D, with the hope that commercial sponsorship of academic R&D will grow steadily: this involves both a redirection of existing funds as well as new funding.

Governments in some countries, especially in the United States and the United Kingdom, have sought to promote this growth in the commercialization of academia as a surrogate for the introduction of a formal industrial policy where national planning for science and technology and innovation more generally is regarded as politically unacceptable, contrary to the principles of the "free-market" economy. Such an "indirect industrial policy" identifies the locus of opportunity for stimulating economic development in the new technologies found at the academic-industrial collaborative interface. Whether this will be adequate to the task, particularly in terms of having a sufficiently wide national effect is open to debate. That is, can academic-industry linkage on its own promote economic development and if not what other steps, such as government-industry cooperative programs, need to be taken.

Here, the experience of those countries with a more interventionist industrial policy, such as France, Germany, Japan, and more recently Australia and Brazil (via its Industrial Technological Capability Program), needs to be properly explored and evaluated. Of course, neither approach is necessarily mutually exclusive. As traditionally laissez-faire countries such as the United States begin to experiment with government programs that subsidize companies to collaborate, traditionally interventionist countries, such as France, that supported government-industry ties have also attempted to encourage spinoffs from academia (Mustar 1997). More recently, we have seen the emergence of trilateral academic-industry-university projects in which the three institutional spheres work together, especially at the regional level, to promote knowledge-based economic development (Etzkowitz 1997).

It should be noted that as governments become more interventionist, they tend to establish research centers and schemes to evaluate these selfsame developments: otherwise monitoring is much more fragmentary.

Commercialization within Academia

Apart from the commercialization of academia in the sense of a growth in the corporate investment of and participation in research activities, there has of course been a rapid growth in the internal commercialization of academia.

Most higher education and research institutes in industrialized countries have established agencies designed to exploit their own intellectual property. Rather than being a secondary consideration, research or training courses are often judged first in terms of the commercial value they might have for their institution. Attainment of research funds from government granting agencies has long been an informal criterion for permanent status in many research-oriented departments. Although a patent or research contract from a company has not yet acquired such currency, it may not be long in coming.

Technology transfer offices have been established that are either developments out of existing administrative units, such as campus legal departments, or entirely new organizational structures, perhaps beginning in the central administration of a multi-unit campus and then gradually being decentralized to individual campuses in an effort to move transfer professionals closer to invention activity. The State University of New York and the University of California both experienced this transition, with individual units established on all but the smallest research-oriented campuses. More radical proposals have been made to attach technology transfer professionals to individual departments, centers, and research groups. Indeed, a faculty member in the Columbia University Medical School serves as a part-time technology transfer officer, representing the members of her department to the university technology office, and vice versa, of course.

While there have been reviews of these organizations and agencies, there has been relatively little systematic research on the nature of academic entrepreneurship on which they depend. Earlier studies have been valuable but limited: some have argued that entrepreneurs are more likely to be those who have a predisposition toward commercializing their research (Peters and Fusfeld [1982]). While this is clearly important, we still need to know under what circumstances such a predisposition is likely to generate genuine entrepreneurship. Seashore Louis et al. (1989), in one of the more detailed examinations published thus far on the topic, argue that individual characteristics (such as motivational predisposition) "provide weak and unsystematic predictions of the forms of entrepreneurship" that are said to relate to innovation. Much has to do with a combination of local institutional factors that provide the catalyst for successful commercial academic activity (see also Stankiewicz [1986]).

One factor is that academic science has also been transformed into a more organized mode, closer to industrial lab formats (Kemelgor 1989; Etzkowitz 1991). The model of the professor supervising a few Ph.D. students in one-on-one meetings has largely been relegated to the humanities. In larger research-intensive universities, the so-called individual investigator is the leader of a science research group comprising some or all of the categories of

B.A., M.A., Ph.D students, post docs, research associates, and technicians. In some countries the professor has become the fund raiser, personnel manager, publicity agent, and research director of a team of researchers. These groups operate as firm-like entities or "quasi-firms" within the university, lacking only a direct profit motive to make them a firm. When professors move outside of the university to form a firm, their academic experience as entrepreneurs often stands them in good stead. They negotiate with venture capitalists instead of research agency program managers, hire employees instead of recruiting students and post docs.

This is in contrast to an earlier generation of technical entrepreneurs and firm founders who were viewed as bringing only technical expertise to a new firm, lacking the managerial skills and entrepreneurial background of many contemporary academic scientists. Indeed, the holder of a professorship at a major university has even been held to be the equivalent of a C.E.O. of a medium-sized corporation, in managerial experience. Such a proposition is in need of careful testing however, not least because what might be regarded as "management" in a research lab may be very different from that in the corporate context.

State programs for academic entrepreneurship proliferate throughout industrialized and increasingly within newly industrializing countries. Typically these are characterized by a concentration of funding to develop or sustain a critical mass of scientists whose interdisciplinary skills are valued: most countries have developed or are in the process of developing their version of the "interdisciplinary research center." At the same time, one finds government giving more support to program rather than individual project research which accentuates the trend toward large teams networked across a range of academic and industrial laboratories.

In order to discriminate between these new organizational forms located within academia but tied to industry, we need some set of criteria whereby specific forms of collaboration can be evaluated and classified. The OECD (1990) offers a typology of collaboration based on three measures:

• the institutional level of cooperation
• the sphere of cooperation
• the durability of the arrangements.

Together, these three criteria should be able to classify any specific collaborative form. Thus, joint research usually involves a long-term, broad, and trans-institutional interaction across a large number of individuals, whereas contract research is more likely to imply short-term, more individually based, less integrated research activity between the industrial and academic partners.

A Second Academic Revolution?

Given then that there are important trends developing with regard to the commercialization of academic science, changes that affect institutional relationships within and between academia and industry, how far are we to regard them as in any way a radical shift in the organizational structures of the two sectors and, in particular, in the specific role that academia plays within the wider society and economy? As Peters herself notes, "Concern with economic issues, industrial competitiveness and technology transfer in the context of funding constraints is conducive to a period of organizational and intellectual experimentation within the university. It may bring about structures or an expansion that represent a significant departure from the past" (Op. cit., 178). A key question, however, is whether these new structures will become encapsulated within only part of the university, or have a more systemic, organizational impact across academia in general.

Among those who have explored this particular question there are broadly two views. The first argues that these developments are no more than an extension of earlier patterns and that the overall functional role of the two sectors and the nature of their relationship has not dramatically altered. The second position suggests that these quantitative and structural changes herald the appearance of a new type of academic institution, one that is oriented much more directly to playing a role on behalf of the state as an agency of economic development. It can be suggested that we are witnessing a second academic revolution, following the first when academic institutions took on the principal research role in the earlier part of this century.

The first revolution was closely though not exclusively related to the state's need for academic research to contribute toward the development of agricultural, medical, and military programs. Today the modern revolution ties in with the state's need to stimulate economic growth in the absence of formal industrial policies for doing so. Even where such policies exist, academic-industry relations are now given a very prominent, indeed central place in the many policy proposals that have appeared over the past decade. It could be argued, then, that we are seeing the beginnings of a new "social contract" between academia and society. This "contract" requires that large-scale government support for academic research will be sustained so long as the research plays a key role in the new economy. Traditional areas of research, especially military research in countries such as the United States, United Kingdom, and France, are increasingly being justified and legitimated not through a general appeal to "national interests" but through an appeal to the economic value this and all other research generates.

It is the capitalization of knowledge that lies at the heart of the new social contract. As the President of the National Academy of Science wrote, "For better or worse, the terms of a new social contract between the scientific community and the larger society are now being forged" (Handler 1980). And Remington (1988) has suggested we are seeing "the forging of a 'new social contract,' or a 'new negotiated treaty,' between scientists and society" (55). This is the new legitimating theme for the continued support for science by government today. Arguments once dominant about a critical or autonomous science are much less likely to be rehearsed today where, according to Remington, "[a]ccountability means carrying out the focused projects and ideals of dominant economic and bureaucratic groups who can deliver technological and organizational resources" (Ibid., 56). Science can be said to be capitalized as a cultural product when through its exploitation by scientists or others it generates income (see Etzkowitz 1990).

It is, of course, vital to know how far the adoption of this new social contract varies between individual institutions as the response to national and international policies is made. How can we draw the distinction between fundamental and cosmetic change? One way is to chart the emergence of highly innovative organizational structures within academia and subsequently between it and industry. For example, one important development has been the steady though stochastic growth of hybrid trans-institutional structures that combine academic and industrial R&D activities (Webster 1990). These reflect the shift toward what Orsenigo (1989) has called "quasi-integrated" institutions, or what Stankiewicz terms "intermediate peripheral" institutions (such as Enterprise Forum at MIT or the Electronics Group at the University of Lund, and the Fraunhofer Gesellschaften in Germany—many others could be mentioned).

Commenting on these developments, Wasser (1990) believes that the university "may well be heading towards a transformation so radical as to become a qualitatively different structure" such that "the present rapid and radical move to a university adaptive in a major fashion to economic development, to an entrepreneurial university" suggests that many institutions would no longer fit "the time-honored definition of a university" (121). Clearly, if this were to be the case, it would refer primarily to those universities that are predominantly science-based. More generally, we might say that the traditional distinctions between public and private sector R&D are—especially in bioscience, pharmaceuticals, and information technology—becoming blurred.

However, as Etzkowitz (1983; 1989) has suggested elsewhere, the shift toward an "entrepreneurial university" need not imply that its members will have to acknowledge they no longer operate in an academic culture, precisely because what constitute the norms of the academic culture have themselves been transformed over the past decade. The "traditional" pursuit of certified knowledge has been combined with and reinterpreted as compatible with commercially oriented research: "Among scientists, one of the most deeply held values is the extension of knowledge. The incorporation of this value into a compatible relationship with the capitalization of knowledge constitutes a normative change in science" (1989, 27). At the same time, this is not to imply that any such normative shift has been unproblematic, especially in the earlier part of this last decade.

From a corporate perspective, the new long-term trans-institutional relations may be regarded as functionally and commercially more effective (in terms of innovative outcome) compared with state-driven, bureaucratically complex technology transfer programs. Remington (1988) has suggested as much, and challenges the conventional wisdom when he declares: "Arrangements, such as those found in the new corporate-academic associations, could ultimately be more beneficial in ensuring long-term vitality of science than many critics fear. . . . Generative corporate science may be able to show the way out of a potential bottleneck created, on the one hand, by federal mega-objectives and, on the other, by a putative dissipation of community and scholarly ethos in academia" (65).

Correlatively, this argument would imply that new organizational forms that are engendered by academia exclusively rather than in conjunction with industry are less likely to be effective as agencies of technology transfer. Indeed, Dill (1990) has argued as much in his analysis of university-industry research collaborations, suggesting that "if the argument for simultaneous coupling as the organizational form most productive of innovation is close to the mark, there is significant reason to doubt the effectiveness of university-sponsored technology transfer centers in promoting innovation. Furthermore, given the imperfections of markets, and the apparent motivations of the collaborators, it may take many more years and millions in investment before this becomes common wisdom" (128). Against Dill, however, there is some evidence to suggest that small university spinoff firms (rather than technology transfer centers per se) can act as effective vehicles for the commercialization of science, as Matkin (1990) has shown.

A more direct role in the economy has become an accepted academic function and this is reflected in the way universities interact with industry. There has been a shift in emphasis from traditional modes of academic-industrial relations oriented to supplying academic "inputs" to existing firms either in the form of information flows or through licensing patent rights to technology in exchange for royalties. Utilizing academic knowledge to establish a new firm, usually located in the vicinity of the university, has become a more important objective (Rappert and Webster 1997). Indeed, the firm may initially be established on or near the campus in an incubator facility sponsored by the university to contribute to the local economy. Regional economic development is in tension with the traditional technology transfer objective, the sale of intellectual property rights to the highest bidder, whatever their location. Universities increasingly have to balance between two competing goals, the earning of funds to support the university in an era of constricting external support and a longer-term goal of growing the regional economic base. The conduct of academic science is also affected by a heightened interest in its economic potential.

Recognition of a congruence between basic research and invention vitiates the ideological separation of these spheres of activity. Until quite recently, most academic scientists assumed that the advancement of knowledge was synonymous with theoretical innovation. Recent examples of research in which theoretical advances have occurred in tandem with the invention of devices or innovation in methodology in transistors/semiconductors, superconductivity, and genetic engineering have called into question the assumption of a one-way flow from basic to applied research to industrial innovation (Gibbons et al. 1994). The acceptance of dualisms such as patents vs. publication and basic vs. applied research goals were the surface expressions of a theory of knowledge based on an underlying dichotomy that placed scientific advance, i.e. , development of theory, in opposition to technological advance.

In recent years, a non-linear recursive interaction between theory and practice, academia and industry, individual and group research has become an alternative academic mode. A significant number of faculty members have adopted multiple objectives, ". . . to not only run a successful company . . . and start a center here [at the university that would become] internationally recognized but to retain their traditional role as 'individual investigator,' directing a research group." An ideal-typical entrepreneurial scientist held that the ". . . interaction of constantly going back and forth from the field, to the university lab, to the industrial lab, has to happen all the time." These relationships involve different levels of commitment (financial and otherwise) by industrial sponsors, including the involvement of industrial sponsors in problem selection and research collaboration.

The academic-industrial interaction is at least potentially always reciprocal. If academic decisions become subject to industrial influence there is also the possibility that industrial enterprises admit academic influence. Such effects may be broader than a particular firm and can extend to an industrial sector or even the creation of a new industrial sector, such as biotechnology, that will impact existing ones. Firms formed by academics have been viewed in terms of their impact on the university but they are also a "carrier" of academic values and practices into industry and, depending upon the arrangements agreed upon, a channel from industry back to the university. In an era when firms run extensive high-level training programs, e.g., "Motorola University" and the Rand Institute, a spinoff of the Air Force, offers the Ph.D. degree, the boundaries among institutional spheres can best be modelled by the classic Venn diagram of separate circles becoming overlapped, with independent and interlocking segments (Packer and Webster 1996).

Simply an Evolution?

Against this thesis that the changes we are witnessing are radical, an alternative image is presented that conveys a much less dramatic, gradual evolution in the pattern of academic-industrial relations. Peters (1987), for example, recognizes that there might have been considerable "organizational innovation" over the past decade as a result of collaboration and that there is a greater tolerance for applied science, but believes that the academic system can accommodate quite a wide range of institutional changes without radically altering its basic character or function: as she says, "[t]he diversity and extent of the system allows for an elasticity in accommodating new developments and for outcomes which may not significantly change the whole" (185).

She emphasizes the need to put the recent changes into historical perspective by comparing them with similar periods in the past when industrial sponsorship grew dramatically in response to the mutual interests of both industry and academia. Moreover, the industrial investment in education and research has been thrown into relief by the relative decline in sponsorship from state sources: "Today's interest in the diversification of funding sources is part of a continuing theme masked in the 1950s and 1960s by the great influx of federal funding" (185). In some countries there has, of course, been not merely a relative but a real decline in state funding for civil research: in the United Kingdom, for example, civil R&D declined in real terms by fourteen percent between 1988 and 1992. Even in Japan, although corporate funding for research (in house and externally) has gradually increased over the past decade, state funding for academic science has only risen recently. Overall, Japanese spending on civil R&D is projected to rise above that of the United States, on a per capita basis, by the year 2000 (Gore 1996).

Historical research on the development of corporate-academic ties is then vital in order to assess whether the collaborative wheel is simply turning again, this time with different players and new technologies. It may well simply be the case that the character of new technologies offers more opportunity to commercialize academic R&D, rather than there being any radically new attempt by scientists to commercialize their research. Historical work is needed to help resolve this issue. On the academic side of the relationship, a series of disputes, and their resolution, at MIT have provided U.S. universities with models for the conduct of relations with industry. The "one-fifth rule" allowing consultation one day per week, the decision to patent and market academic research, initially through an intermediary organization and later by the university itself, and the role of the university in regional economic development, capitalizing firms from academic research, originated at MIT in the early twentieth century (Etzkowitz 1993, 1994). During the past two decades these formats for academic-industrial relations, heretofore relegated to a special academic sector, have spread throughout the U.S. academic system.

There are relatively few detailed historical studies of relevance on the industrial side of the equation, however, most focusing on the early links with the chemical industry (e.g., Weiner [1982], Pitzer [1955]). A recent study by Swann (1988) shows that there was considerable collaboration between American pharmaceutical companies and U.S. scientists during the 1930–1950 period and that there were university departments that established integrated long-term research alliances with certain corporations, such as Eli Lilly. Swann argues that after the war the level of support (for basic research) dropped dramatically and remained low for the next twenty-five years before being restored with unprecedented speed over the past decade. It might well be the pace of recent change then, rather than their actual substance, that has led to the impression of a radical shift in institutional structures. In other words, given time, a gradual structural evolution will occur to accommodate the industrial-academic collaboration of the twenty-first century.

In light of this, Peters (1987) has argued that the commercialization of academia needs to be put into its wider context, viz.:

- "the nature of the current pressures on the universities are often quite different from what is commonly imagined
- universities have been commercializing their research results and setting up companies for this purpose for a lot longer than the past five years
- while we worry about the impact of industry and the increasing commercialization of university research, we must remember that something like 85 per cent of industry interactions with academia takes place in professional schools of engineering, medicine and agriculture.
- many of the initiatives developed in response to the stated pressures are no more than experiments. It is not clear which of these will succeed." (189)

There is then, a need for great care in the way we characterize present trends in the commercialization of academia, most particularly the commercialization of academic scientific research. Much of the university is not affected at all, primarily the sciences and then only subsets of the scientific arena. It is true, however, that very significant, but localized, shifts are taking place in the organizational structures tying the two sectors together. Moreover, there are also changes in the normative expectations and demands of the academic role, as well as perhaps similar shifts in corporate culture. Whether these are to be regarded as revolutionary or evolutionary depends on the degree to which these changes are bounded or encapsulated within the university, having a limited impact on parts of the university rather than the institution as a whole.

Academia in Business and Business in Academia

The shift in the university system to the model of the university having a role in economic development has several consequences. Not only is it a new academic function, it also transforms the professorial role even at the level of the universe of discourse that faculty utter. For example, faculty who have become seriously involved in technology transfer have learned how much to say to someone from industry. They describe their technology at a certain level of generality but do not become too specific because they are aware that potential intellectual property rights could be given away (Etzkowitz 1996). Formerly, academics would have been willing to be more open or perhaps to disclose their knowledge to a company as a consultant for a small fee. Now their interaction with industry is carefully calculated based upon the expectation that their university wishes to patent and market that knowledge and/or that the faculty member themselves might wish to form a company based upon that commercializable knowledge. Academic-industrial relations have thus shifted to more value-added economic activities, with the consulting role declining in import except as the faculty member becomes a consultant to his or her own firm.

As faculty become more knowledgeable about business, they are able to take the role of someone in industry and relate to them from a business stance, protecting the intellectual property in which they and their university have a financial interest. Indeed, the relationship of the faculty member to the university has also been revised to take account of this change in orientation to knowledge as potential intellectual property. Heretofore, the few academics who were interested in pursuing commercial gain from their research were able to capitalize their discoveries themselves without their university claiming ownership. Under current conditions, universities typically claim ownership rights and professors must share potential financial gain with their university. Nevertheless, their commercial position is far superior to the employee of an industrial firm that typically claims one hundred percent of the intellectual property rights of their employees. Faculty members' traditional independent academic status is reflected in the substantial share they retain of the intellectual property rights to their discoveries.

The intellectual transformation of the research role of the professor that ensues from the capitalization of knowledge is that instead of thinking only in basic research terms they also think in terms of applied research funding and commercializable results. Rather than auguring a shift from a basic to applied research orientation, this broadened focus typically occurs through adding on another activity as faculty adopt a "layered" rather than a "substitution" strategy of research resource seeking and problem selection. Faculty keep their basic research program going but they also add on an applied project and interrogate each research line for implications for the other. Ironically, financial stringency causes an expansion of the academic research system as the scale and scope of research groups expand. On the other hand, some previously successful academic researchers who are unable to make the transition to multiple roles and orientations are forced out of the system and revert to purely teaching and administrative roles. The specter of externally induced change in academia is indeed palpable and real but it occurs as an overlay upon an internal dynamic of institutional development that has taken the university through two revolutions within the past century, even as it retains a recognizable resemblance to its medieval forbear.

CHAPTER 2

Toward a Theoretical Analysis of
Academic-Industry Collaboration

ANDREW WEBSTER and HENRY ETZKOWITZ

Debate about the form of collaboration between industry and academia rarely asks what it is that is the subject of collaboration. Notions of "technology transfer"—typically the focus of collaborative schemes—beg the question of what the technology actually is that is being transferred, and crucially that successful "transfer" typically involves "transformation" of the technological. Sociologists and economists have also shown that technology has both a tacit and codified dimension, each being "transferred" within and between organizations in distinct ways. Policies for collaboration may or may not recognize this; those that do. acknowledge the elasticity of the technological boundary within which the collaborative agreement can work. It would appear, for example, that Japanese and U.S. companies have recognized this tacit dimension of science and technology in the iterative approach to collaboration that they have taken with MIT.

At the same time, however, even in these more open strategic areas of collaborative R&D (the classic pre-competitive club arrangement) there is always debate and negotiation between academic and industrial partners about what should and should not be included in the research program. This reflects different judgments about appropriate research paths, significant findings, the balance between "basic" and "applied" research, the best interests of the parties concerned, and so on.

If this is recognized, it is clearly possible that the same technological arena—a specific product or techniques being developed by competitor companies—may need or lead to different science and technology inputs (STI) (Faulkner and Senker 1995) and so different forms of collaboration. Identifying scientific and technological needs, therefore, is a crucial requirement in determining appropriate linkage, as it is in determining R&D strategies and links within companies.

The Trajectory of Collaboration

Specifying the likely trajectory of a collaborative relationship may in practice be exceptionally difficult. The very nature of the STI that corporate scientists adopt from public sector science is not always easily articulated as in-house and extramural programs of research feed back on each other. Hence it may be difficult to chart and evaluate its specific impact in both the short and long terms. This in part explains why some companies, having withdrawn from a collaboration they regard as unproductive, suddenly find other companies moving into their place and emerging with commercial products relatively quickly.

In short, therefore, while the contractual terms of any collaboration will specify the scientific and technological focus of the research, in practice what this focus is deemed to mean and how "productive" it is shifts as the iterative innovation process unfolds. At times this may cause difficulties, as in some pre-competitive programs where academic scientists have pursued their inquiries in directions corporate partners felt inappropriate.

It is clear, then, that much more work needs to be done on the classification of STIs and in particular how corporations monitor and absorb the knowledge bases their collaborative links involve. Corporations are much more prepared today to take on this task for themselves through internal auditing of the technological terrain they cover. This is in part explained by the need to access a wide range of external sources of information but to filter those most relevant to firm product and process development. An appraisal of internal scientific and technological stock, competencies, capacities, and requirements is of central importance (see, e.g., Kameoka 1996).

The analytical problem of categorizing and classifying STIs has been relatively neglected compared with the attention that has been devoted toward the classification of forms of linkage between the two sectors. In a similar vein, "academic entrepreneurship" is often used rather glibly to refer to a range of activities. The traditional perception of the entrepreneur would be someone who undertakes fundraising activities to support research (Vollmer 1962). Again traditionally, the organizer and fund seeker for a research group does not affect the channels through which research results are distributed except to increase the flow through them, for example through more papers presented at conferences, additional submissions to journals, and so on. Perhaps too, the entrepreneur shapes the production of academic research by introducing a division of labor into the academic research unit over and above the traditional division of labor among researchers at different sites.

What is particularly interesting about more recent forms of academic entrepreneurialism is the role the academic plays as the organizer of startup companies based on academic research, sometimes though not always in partnership with a large private-sector company. There is an element of continuity with the prior traditional role here inasmuch as organizing a research group requires skills and power similar to those of a research manager in a firm: the research team is like a quasi-firm with the principal investigator directing the research overall and taking responsibility for personnel management, strategic direction, and fundraising.

But the key factor for the new academic entrepreneur is the need to take decisions about R&D that are informed by the profit motive. What is the effect of the introduction of the profit motive on shaping the research direction in academia? Krimsky (1991) has postulated from his data on collaborative ties (such as professors' memberships on scientific advisory boards and roles in forming firms) that such an effect exists but has not been properly documented. If such a relationship was found to exist, proponents and opponents of collaboration would interpret it quite differently: the former as a useful redirection of effort and the latter as a loss of academic autonomy. We shall return to this question of research agenda setting later.

Just as we need to unpack the concepts of STI and academic entrepreneurialism, so too must we explore the structure and function of academia in order to throw into relief significant changes brought about through its commercialization. Whereas, for example, academia has traditionally been an educational institution dependent upon philanthropic and/or governmental support, it is increasingly likely that it will become a partially self-generating institution through capitalizing the knowledge it produces. As noted earlier, in addition to its teaching and research roles, academia is gradually assuming an economic development function within regional and national contexts. This process of change is similar in form to that which occurred during the late nineteenth century, when research was added to the teaching function in Europe and the United States. Moreover, recent conflict of interest charges raised over these new economic activities and their detracting from research are reminiscent of earlier accusations made against time devoted to research that was said to conflict with the teaching duties of staff. Such conflict of interest disputes are not only symptomatic of a clash of values but reflect an underlying structural change.

This change has occurred more or less rapidly within different countries as the level of state support for public-sector research science has declined and/or been retargeted in new ways. At the ideological level there has been a shift away from the right of universities to decide their own goals toward the requirement that their principal role is to serve the economic needs of the country. Paradoxically, the more the state has sought to intervene in the management of university or other public sector establishment, the more it has done so in order to pressurize institutions to take their own initiatives to meet the economic goals it prescribes. Traditional structures are limited in what opportunities they offer for innovative, financially productive programs that can help sustain an institution. Thus, within academia, new institutional forms are developed to meet this need. In turn, academia as a whole is experiencing a shift in its functional position within society to play a more important role in a knowledge-based, postindustrial economy. It might even be suggested that universities could replace the military in the core institutional triad identified by C. Wright Mills, a shift from the "military-industrial" to the "academic-industrial" complex.

As noted earlier, these shifts are in addition associated with a broad reorientation of state policy away from nationally determined industrial policies targeted on one or more sector. As the OECD (1989), in a review of industrial policy throughout member states, noted, "it is generally not the role of the State to try, by means of selective programs, to take over from firms the task of identifying growth opportunities and deciding which resources should be devoted to seizing such opportunities: the application of this principle is even tending to become more widespread as regards government supervision of state-owned firms" (13). Corporations themselves must decide on their own long-term priorities and select those technological innovations that suit their interests best; for its part, the state will try to ensure that there are as few impediments to technological diffusion as possible. Since "one strategic stage in the commercial exploitation of scientific progress" (Ibid.) is located upstream in the ties between industry and academia, it is here that "efforts are now being made to strengthen the links between the two sectors" (Ibid.). Structural economic difficulties of regions are not to be tackled through macro-planning but through creating an environment more generally conducive to technology transfer, that is, to act in a catalytic rather than directive manner. The increasing importance of academic-industrial links as one crucial ingredient in such a policy is obvious.

Implications for Research

There are certain methodological implications that follow from the discussion thus far. Two need emphasizing most strongly. First, that analyses and commentaries of academic-industry collaboration need to develop yardsticks that can classify and measure STIs, academic entrepreneurialism, and the structure and function of the academic establishment under review. Secondly, there is need to locate collaboration in its wider socio-economic and political context, particularly with regard to state policy towards industry.

At the same time, it is vital that research focus on the structure of collaboration itself as an inter-organizational form, a structure that raises a number of general issues independently of the fact that it combines industry and academia. That is to say, there is some value to be gained in treating the linkage between the two sectors as a combination that is worth exploring through the sort of questions that are typically associated with organization theory.

In terms of transinstitutional structures, considerable work has been done on cooperative links between industrial organizations within the broad terms of this theoretical tradition. For example, Borys and Jemison (1989) have provided an analysis of inter-corporate alliance that raises a number of points that are applicable to any collaborative structure. They argue that analysis needs to:

- determine the relationships of authority and trust between the participating organizations;
- determine which parts of the organizations are to link together;
- determine whether and if so how stability mechanisms operate in order to sustain the institutional relationship over time;
- determine how the process of value creation is measured and achieved within the collaborative structure.

There has unfortunately been little or no attempt by sociologists or science policy analysts to explore these dimensions of trans-institutional structures. These points may even apply to internal organizational restructuring as a result of commercialization of academia inasmuch as it requires the repositioning of what were once peripheral activities into a more central role.

Borys and Jemison raise the central question of the overall purpose of any inter-organizational linkage, since it is this which gives both direction and legitimacy to the venture. However, there is a fine balance to be reached between the need for breadth over against specificity of purpose: "Although a broad purpose may provide sufficient 'glue' for the [collaboration] in the face of disagreements over narrow interests, a broad purpose may not provide enough detail to adjudicate among these interests. Conversely, although a narrow and focussed purpose allows partners to be clearer about what they expect from each other, it may leave many important fringe issues unaddressed" (238).

Moreover, it is important to determine how new forms of collaboration delineate the boundaries between the two sectors, especially where joint ventures are established; each party needs to decide how much resourcing can be controlled by the collaboration and how much authority remains within the partners' respective organizations. This highlights the question of what Borys and Jemison call the "boundary permeability" of collaborative forms of organization, that is, "what elements—resources, authority, obligations—are allowed" into the new collaborative structure. Furthermore, how do these elements change over the life of any one type of collaboration? It is these sorts of issues that need to be considered by both analysts and practitioners concerned with academic-industry relations. However, Borys and Jemison's work focuses on institutional practice that can provide for maximum cooperation and exchange between the two sectors. In addition, we need to explore the power relationships informing collaborative structures, the possible patterns of dominance within and between the two collaborating parties (see Benson [1978]). This broad body of organizational theory should be drawn on more fully in both theory and practice since it says much about the problematic nature of multiparty interorganizational integration.

A final area that has been subject to much needed debate in the early 1990s is the broad relationship between public and private sectors and how we are to see where their boundaries lie, or if we are better advised to see these boundaries as being more plastic, as public-private alignments associated with the commercialization of the science base create new, but changing, structures (Rip 1996). Rather than seeing these boundaries as being defined in *a priori* terms, often the assumption that underlies "conflict-of-interest" commentaries, we can see them as negotiated and often competing constituencies of interest (Webster and Rappert 1996).

The five areas discussed above—STIs, academic entrepreneurship, structure and function of academia, the nature of interorganizational structures, and the determination of contested boundaries between public and private—ought to provide the theoretical and methodological focus for both researchers and practitioners of academic-industry collaboration. Each needs to inform the analysis of any specific form of collaboration, for together they cover both behavioral and structural processes at work therein. Often, however, one finds more descriptive commentaries on the latest vehicle for technology transfer, typically depicted as a "win-win" situation; there is unfortunately little room in such discourse for a more reflexive analysis.

Developing analyses of collaboration in this way, according to some pre-defined foci, helps to distinguish between and evaluate the impact of novel (as well as traditional) collaborative forms. Moreover, whatever the specifics of the collaborative model, we want to suggest that new organizational forms might be more properly characterized as examples of a non-linear "technology flow," rather than the older forms of "technology transfer" associated with the traditional consulting and contract research arrangements. That is to say, new organizational forms break down traditional boundaries between the two sectors in which the construction of research programs displays an iterative, feedback, or spiral process.

New Institutional Forms

Three patterns seem to be worth focusing on when looking at the emergence of new institutional forms of collaboration. These are the increasing attractiveness of long-term strategic alliances, which rarely, if ever, involve state support; the development of new institutions (e.g., university spinoff firms) or agencies (e.g., ILOs) for technology transfer, sometimes with, at other times without the assistance of government; and finally, the appearance of a quasi-academic culture within corporate establishments themselves, in part caused by these shifts in academic-industrial relations. Each of these developments may involve, in both academia and industry, the parallel development of mechanisms internal to each sector that are designed to encourage or facilitate easier relations between the two, as well as organizational changes that seek to redraw (in order to break down) the boundaries between the two.

The growth in long-term academic-industrial strategic alliances (see chapter 1) has been primarily in the bioscience/biomedicine and pharmacology fields. These alliances reflect a growing corporate strategy to fund centers of academic expertise. Such coalitions normally are based on a coincidence of interests or mutual affinity between the scientific concerns of the company and the university. They are typically wide ranging and, compared with corporate in-house R&D, unfocused, often involving the funding of a whole new (embryonic) field of research or an entire academic department. They are established with the aim of drawing on the discovery skills and expertise of academics in the new area, undeveloped within the company, much as the first of these collaborations—the Hoechst/Massachusetts General Hospital (molecular biology) deal—exemplifies. In many cases it is cheaper and quicker to achieve the company's goals by funding academics, whose ideas feed the firm's in-house product development concepts. This kind of funding is high risk but can yield beneficial results. Coalitions in this bioscience area typically incorporate a clinical dimension within them even when the sponsored department has no tradition of clinical research; this clearly is of immense importance in the development of new drugs.

This type of collaboration is now extending beyond the bioscience area. For example, in France, the University of Grenoble has developed a similar type of structure involving the computer engineering department and a major French electronics company. This particular link has also led to the establishment of a joint university/company R&D subsidiary as the most efficient way of commercializing the work. In Italy, there have traditionally been very small-scale collaborative research contracts (on average worth only $4000 per annum per project); while these have been regarded as reasonably successful, there is a growing belief that much larger long-term collaborative links across all industrial sectors will be needed in order to stimulate widespread industry-university cooperation (Malerba et al. 1991). In the United Kingdom, similar (non-bioscience) links have been established with various engineering companies (such as Air Products) by Imperial College. Of particular interest was the establishment in Europe of what were called "European Discovery Capability Units," (EDCU) by the U.S. pharmaceutical Upjohn. Whereas in most long-term joint ventures there is a broad basic/strategic focus, in the case of these EDCUs basic and applied R&D programs were established across a number of universities which drew on the expertise of local biology and chemistry departments. Their aim was to produce a new chemical compound ready for phase 1 clinical trials within five years: "after five years, the EDCUs are projected to be producing 1–2 candidates a year, nearly half of Upjohn's total from domestic discovery work" (Vivo 1989). Here the academic research is clearly seen as an integral part of the corporate program; as Upjohn have commented, "The EDCUs represent our discovery labs in Europe" (Ibid.).

While the ECDUs made some progress in delivering results that could be pursued as candidate compounds, there have been difficulties in orchestrating a network of researchers across a range of different universities. (The original intention was, in fact, to secure these research competencies from single sources.) Moreover, the degree of management required was seen to pose something of an intrusion to university departments. The scheme now is being wound down because of these managerial difficulties. A similar venture can be found in the United States, in the shape of university-industry research centers (UIRC). Although the majority of these centers operate with university control over financial management and administrative operations, participating companies have quite strong control over the flow of information, both inside and outside of the centers. Controls on information go beyond controls to non-participating companies and include significant controls on academics and their communications with faculty, restrictions on disclosures to firms participating in the UIRC if they were not involved in the particular project, and in some instances delaying and deleting information for publications whether or not it was considered to be a discretionary matter for the participating firms.

The large, long-term single company coalition with university science departments has recently been advocated by Garnsey and Wright (1990) following their study of technological innovation and its relationship to organizational structure. They argue that the development of such strategic alliances allows mobile "innovation teams" to cross the institutional boundaries of industry and academia, providing a much more flexible and effective innovative environment for the large corporation. Indeed, the attractiveness of this type of coalition to industry no doubt reflects the growing need for new, flexible organizational structures within which innovation can occur. That is, it is possible to link the growth of these alliances to the shift in the character of manufacturing industry from a large-scale, less research-intensive mass production "Fordist" structure to a "post-Fordist" one. The latter denotes a situation in which modern corporations orchestrate their productive activities in a more flexible, decentralized way, reliant on new technologies while contracting out specialized functions to others—such as "discovery labs" in academia. Flexibility is required in order to remain competitive in a global economy where there are no safe havens, even for long-established large companies.

Whittington (1990) has shown how industrial R&D has been disaggregated from the large central laboratory structure to smaller in-house units or external subcontractor labs. Research workers have been exposed to the pressure of the market "by transferring them to decentralized profit-centers, with research contracts allocated on a competitive basis" (183). There may also be a relationship between this process and the apparent shift from "mechanical" to "organic" R&D management within large corporations (Hull 1988). In industrial sectors as a whole, Powell (1987) has argued that the increased pressure toward greater flexibility has meant that more firms are entering into joint agreements with each other. Where joint agreements are insufficient mergers become a more attractive solution, as has been seen in the past five years in the pharmaceutical industry (e.g., SmithKline Beecham; Bristol-Myers Squibb; and the largest pharmaceutical in the world, Glaxo Wellcome).

Another rather different form of long-term collaboration with academia that has been developed over the past decade involving bioscience, pharmaceutical, engineering, electronics, and chemical industry firms is what might be called the "co-locational" arrangement (see Constable and Webster 1990). Here, a company establishes a strategic research laboratory on a campus in property owned by the university rented out to the unit. A tenancy agreement relating to rent, refurbishments, maintenance costs, etc. forms the basis of the contract between the two parties. The unit is strongly product oriented even though it conducts some basic research. Those working in the unit are full-time employees of the company though they are likely to be academics head-hunted from the appropriate field. The unit is typically physically secure.

Collaboration here occurs on an informal, perhaps consultancy basis, through the development of informal links with neighboring scientists working within the cognate department. Sometimes the departmental head may be required by the terms of the contract to meet fairly regularly with the industrial group scientists to discuss areas that may be of common interest. Where these exchanges lead to research collaboration specific contractual terms may be drawn up for specific projects which will give the university some share in any eventual profits they generate.

Co-locational collaboration is then developed by two parties at arm's length from each other; the industrial unit is a self-sufficient enterprise. If problems were to develop with the university, it would still continue to function as a research arm of the parent company. Why should a company want to create such a unit when it would appear to limit unnecessarily the scope of collaboration that could be obtained from resident academics? This is clearly a reflection of corporate policy towards extramural research: these co-locationals seek to maximize the possibility for collaborating with academia while taking very little risk on matters such as intellectual property rights, control over employees, targeting research to meet the applied needs of the company, and, where pharmaceuticals are involved, having access to clinical material from patients associated with teaching hospitals that would have been much more difficult to effect outside of this type of collaboration. The co-locational provides an academic environment without loss of full company control, whereas the price paid for the hybrid joint venture is a ceding of some power in return for a potentially greater research output over a longer period of time. It is clearly possible that co-locationals could be restructured as hybrids should the company and academic institution agree to do so; this would require, however, a rather different use of resources geared towards transinstitutional integration. Much more work needs to be done here to document the value added benefit of a co-locational compared to a "hybrid" arrangement from both industrial and academic points of view

In contrast to these two differing forms of single company/university liaison, there have been an increasing number of schemes developed in many countries designed to encourage multi-party (company-company-academia) cooperation, typically in the so-called "precompetitive" stage of research. Again, normally these have been initiated via government action, though there are cases where corporations have jointly—often through industry associations—set up collaborative programs independently of the state (e.g., in the United Kingdom, the Polymer Synthesis Laboratory at Cambridge University, sponsored by ICI, Unilever, 3M, and the Davy Corporation). The propensity to link and the character of linkage varies, however, between sectors and across different countries. For example, sectorally, data for the United Kingdom show that there is much more large company collaboration in the IT than there is in the biotechnology sector.

New Developments within Academia

Apart from these novel collaborative links, which reflect changes in corporate strategy toward academia, we have seen over the past decade the emergence of academic/government-inspired initiatives geared toward the exploitation of public-sector research. Most notably, these include science parks, interdisciplinary research centers (IRCs), and startup companies from within academia. Each of these, while a significant development, has emerged within a local context of considerable variety—from, say, the university-inspired technology parks of the Netherlands to those more heavily dependent on local and national state support, as in the United Kingdom or Canada. Moreover, the role played by each can also vary depending on local context.

Science parks have played differing roles, but there are three that have been most important:

- as a university development strategy to raise funds by selling or leasing underutilized land, as was the case initially, for example, at Stanford and Cambridge;
- as a strategy to create a technical environment for an engineering school, a source of jobs for graduates and consulting opportunities for faculty (e.g., Rensselear Polytechnic Institute; Heriot Watt [Edinburgh];
- as a regional economic development strategy to attract industrial and governmental labs (e.g., Research Triangle [USA]; University-enterprise Foundations [Spain]).

Science parks in general have had a fairly limited success as agencies for the exploitation of academic knowledge; indeed, links with academia can sometimes be fairly peripheral, especially in the case of the first type outlined above. Some analysts have even argued that science parks can act as a barrier to technology transfer and links between firms and academia because of their high-tech image which can intimidate firms, especially SMEs. More generally, the analysis suggests that the parks can encourage social and geographical polarization (see Massey et al. 1992). In part, in response to their equivocal success, many science parks within OECD countries have recently sought to incorporate a more centralized management structure in the way they are run in order to promote closer intellectual and not just physical proximity to the neighboring academic and industrial base in the region. This has been a key objective for parks in less-developed areas of southern Europe, for example (see Cricelli et al. 1996).

While science parks have been said to allow what Stankiewicz (1986) has called an "intellectual osmosis" between industry and academia to occur, though at arm's length from the actual academic site and in many ways without disturbing the departmental, disciplinary character of that site, the more recent development of IRCs during the latter part of the 1980s has involved a deliberate attempt to join industry and academia at a more fundamental but interdisciplinary level of research. As Hoch (1990) notes, "the effort has moved further upstream to focus on strategic basic science . . . which is foreseen to underlie the next generation of new generic technology in areas like high temperature superconductivity and biotechnology" (39). In some ways, IRCs are an expansion of earlier models of this type of research effort, such as the Rockefeller Foundation's early and mid-twentieth century efforts at the construction of new scientific fields through merging the elements of existing ones, or the efforts of the U.S. National Science Foundation's University-Industry Cooperative Research Centers in the 1970s. It is too early to say whether these new organizational structures—being developed in most OECD and other countries—will do the job they are supposed to do, though many involved feel that they are inadequately resourced or, where so, take resources from other more traditional academic centers. But recent research by Hicks et al. (1995) has shown empirically the rise in interdisciplinarity as a feature of the current research enterprise.

At a more philosophical level, Stankiewicz emphasizes the importance of disciplinary research for the maintenance of a healthy science base: "The integrity of disciplinary departments is essential to the health of science. It is largely through the departments that the scientific community of a discipline socializes its members, exercises control over the quality of their work and collectively governs the direction of their scientific efforts" (56). If this is true, IRCs are likely to have to create new forms of quality control and intellectual loyalty for those participating in interdisciplinary work. This will be made doubly difficult by the need to do a similar sort of job to encourage the participating industrial members to collaborate as well. All those questions raised earlier by Borys and Jemison's analysis of inter-organizational linkage will apply here where we have not only trans-institutional but also trans-disciplinary ties being made. The organizational issues connected with the encouragement of interdisciplinary research and training are important matters for science policy analysts to debate.

One of the most important agencies that can act as an interface between industry and academia is the start-up company where individual academics or their institutions as a whole form a separate company to exploit and commercialize in-house R&D. By translating research into products and even taking the next step of participating in the formation of firms to bring products to market, universities are entering into a domain traditionally reserved for business. Moreover, the capital for such firms is increasingly likely to come from the academic establishment, itself prepared to act as a venture capitalist investor. Universities may regard themselves as particularly well suited to this role since, unlike fully commercial venture capitalists, they do not need to satisfy stockholders' immediate needs for dividends and can therefore invest for the long term. Such developments (such as Oxford University's Oxford Molecular, or UCL Ventures Ltd [London]) are yet another indication of the way in which academia is beginning to create its own industrial sector. A key issue here is how these new firms and their parent universities manage and exploit the intellectual property rights derived from their research (see Webster and Packer 1996). This spinoff activity is happening not only within higher education establishments but also within government and research council institutes and laboratories as the state has gradually removed the bureaucratic and legal constraints on its own institutions.

All three developments—science parks, IRCs, and start-up companies—have become increasingly important agencies for the commercialization of science. This is reflected in the growth of administrative structures, often associated with the old (and some might claim ad hoc procedures of the) industrial liaison office, to oversee and promote their effective—and profitable—functioning. In this sense, we can see how extra-departmental structures have moved from their more peripheral status of a decade ago to being of central importance in the long-term planning of universities and other establishments along with other more traditional concerns. Rather than being mere brokers for industry-academic collaboration, these structures themselves take on the responsibility for meeting the requirements of industrial clients—e.g., through university extension services to new businesses in a region—as well as commercializing their own intellectual property (Samuelson 1987). Of course, the greater the commercial pressure on the PSR base the more likely will areas of knowledge be regarded as commercially exploitable and so subject to protection. However, expectations here can often be unfulfilled as commercialization of new research confronts many obstacles (Packer 1995). And, as has been noted elsewhere, "From whom one is protecting one's knowledge is not always clear, especially for those working within the PSR science base who are increasingly likely to find that fellow members of PSR are simultaneously sponsors, collaborators and competitors" (Webster 1988, 26).

Academia in the Corporation?

The third trend we may be witnessing that is linked to the new forms of transinstitutional relations between the two sectors is the development within companies of aspects of the academic culture itself. There has been little or no detailed research conducted on this question by the science studies/science policy research community yet it could well play a vital role in facilitating any further expansion of long-term collaborative links. Is it only those companies that have a strong basic-research orientation that are likely to adopt "academic" features in the way they manage and evaluate research programs. Do these companies collaborate more or less with academia? How might more liaison affect other companies such that their own in-house research takes on the collegiality of the campus too? Some indication of what is happening in this regard might be suggested by the rapid increase in sole and joint publication with academics (Hicks et al. 1996), a preparedness for a long-term view in some sectors, the growth in applications from corporate staff for government research grants, and a willingness to handle research in a more organic, less mechanistic manner. Some corporations dub their own central research laboratories—often with 750-plus staff—"campuses" and even run them in a departmental rather than line-management way (e.g., Merck, one of the world's larger pharmaceutical companies). To the extent, as mentioned above, that this research effort is disaggregated into profit centers there may thereby be a less conducive environment for academic culture to emerge. On the other hand, most departments in academia are themselves being designated profit/cost centers that must not simply balance their books but seek to generate profitable income.

More generally, some corporations not only participate in structures to share knowledge but also in ones geared toward training; to the extent that they train students, they are taking on an academic role. In the past, there were considerable difficulties experienced in this regard by companies. In the United States, for example, Frederick Terman's proposal in the late 1960s to form an industrially related university based on the research laboratories of northern New Jersey did not come to fruition at the time. Instead, the companies decided to establish closer relations with the universities in the region (Rutgers and Princeton). More recently, however, a number of corporations in a range of areas—management, engineering, computing, textiles, health care, and banking—have successfully established higher education institutions that award their own degrees, that have been accredited by State Educational Boards, and that, in many cases, are open as nonprofit institutions to all applicants, not just company personnel. In Europe, there have been similar initiatives taken by companies, especially in terms of the development of in-house or collaborative training programs for staff. In the United Kingdom, the first "corporate college" to be given approval to award its own qualifications was the one run from British Telecom's (BT) training department: this was the first time a nationally recognized course was run entirely in house. Since then, many other corporations have taken advantage of a much looser validation regime in the United Kingdom, which has provided new opportunities for in-company credit-rated academic programs.

We need to know more of these developments in training on an international basis and why they are occurring. Corporations often go down this track having found academic institutions unable to meet their needs quickly or precisely enough. These needs are, however, less likely to be tied to the research requirements of companies research staff will still be drawn via the eminent postgraduate schools and research centers.

Institutional Issues

Analysis of the emergence of new forms of collaboration is important, especially where it can respond to the deeper theoretical and methodological issues discussed earlier. At the same time, there are generic institutional questions that cut across specific forms of linkage that need addressing. Three, which have been very unevenly covered in the literature, are the ways in which commercialization:

- tends to steer scientists toward setting research agendas that are not merely applied but also overly accommodating to the commercial interests of their sponsors;
- generates forms of normative conflict;
- creates acute and/or chronic periods of institutional instability and volatility.

A significant concern with long-term and large-scale industrial funding of academic basic/strategic research is that the agenda of the work being undertaken will be influenced by the company in such a way that university departments simply become little more than outposts of the companies' research activities. Aware of these problems, corporations and academics involved go to great lengths to stress the intellectually driven nature of the projects being funded, projects that would have been pursued anyway.

Corporations are not (unless one is referring to endowments) simply an alternative source of funding through which scientists can continue to follow their disciplinary noses. Obviously, research will—as in the UIRC example mentioned earlier—be expected to contribute in the strategic term to the companies' portfolio of products or technologies.

But while companies will only support research that complements their long-term development plans, this research is—where it is not directly contract research focused on a very specific applied problem—normally within areas where the science or at least its technological application is still relatively immature, such that the sense in which agendas could be set is less obvious. The objective behind collaboration is often to fund long-term work in as broad a way as possible and to avoid interfering with the scientists in the labs; it is often said that this would kill the goose that lays the (genetically engineered!) golden egg. Researchers do, of course, subject project proposals to industrial sponsors in the way that is most likely to maximize their chances of obtaining finance. Some have suggested that this process is little different from that associated with submitting grant applications to public-sector agencies.

It is important, therefore, to develop techniques that can properly determine the genuine sense in which agenda setting may be going on. This problem is made more difficult because the linkage between the two sectors develops over a period of time and in an iterative way such that academics involved may hardly notice or may be unable to articulate the point at which they might feel their independence is being compromised. To help answer this problem we might consider asking some of the following questions;

- Is there any substantive difference between the papers that are published by a research group before and after the arrival of large-scale commercial sponsorship? The problem here is discriminating between what might be regarded as a "natural" development within the field and that which is commercially informed. Without some sort of control group elsewhere it would be difficult to come to any firm conclusions about this.
- What terms are being set when collaborations come up for renewal? This is in principle more promising, since corporate interests in directing the research program are most likely to be expressed at this point in time. However, in practice there may be difficulty in getting access to the confidential documents that spell out the terms of the contract. But this strategy still seems worth pursuing.
- What managerial autonomy does the research team involved in collaboration have in deciding their own programs and in allocating resources to facilitate them? Clearly, agenda setting would depend on a sponsor's capacity to control and direct academic research; hence the need to understand the sort of organizational issues that have been raised by Borys and Jemison, as discussed earlier.
- What is the relationship between any spinoff (or start-up) companies and the research base in academia that they depend on for new STIs; does the company tail wag the research dog?
- Finally, what is the cultural and organizational link between the in-house corporate R&D and the academic center's own research; how much interchange of personnel, findings, technologies, and materials occurs?

It will be detailed answers to these sorts of questions that will help resolve this question of agenda setting. There is evidence, for example, in relation to academic publications, that commercial interests do shape the sort of speculations that are made in the concluding sections to papers. Academics involved in patenting have revealed that they sometimes "doctor" their conclusions to ensure they do not compromise any future patent application they might make related to the area under discussion (Webster and Packer 1996). It may, of course, be the case that even if academics recognize that a skewing of research agendas does occur, those involved may believe that the fruit of the collaboration even on these terms is in fact scientifically and technologically better than it would have been had there been limited or no interaction between the two parties. Moreover, if the distinctive feature of any "second academic revolution" lies in academia's playing a new economic role in society, the more programs (from basic through to applied) that deliver exploitable technologies the better. Academics may welcome this as a measure of the success of their work, but the question then becomes which parts of the program become applied and according to what broad assumptions about market interest and social welfare?

Institutional questions also arise in connection with possible conflict of interest and normative conflict between the different rules of the game as operating in academia and industry. These two forms of conflict reflect differing boundary issues; to identify a potential conflict of interest is to declare that boundaries should be preserved intact and not crossed, reflecting the belief in separate institutional spheres, whereas debate over a conflict of norms or values presupposes a debate over the exclusivity of boundaries per se, such that people may disagree over whether a particular action constitutes conflict.

Conflict of interest as an organizational issue may be said to exist when an individual is diverted from a group's broader goal to an individual or private goal. The issue arises most clearly when an individual with organizational responsibilities seeks to gain a personal private profit through his or her position. Thus, if the pursuit of disinterested knowledge is raised as the banner of the research university, then the receipt of private profit for research pursued is *ipso facto* a conflict of interest.

There are also the related issues of loyalties and obligations. Both arise from involvement in an alternative organization to the one in which an individual is primarily employed. On the one hand, such involvement is held to lead to adherence to the goals of the other organization making one beholden to an external interest, while on the other hand, the time commitment to the other organization makes it less likely that an individual will fulfill more than the formal requirements of his or her job. In academia, these issues have arisen strongly when faculty members have taken the lead in organizing firms based on their research and typically most intensely during the first instances of firm formation in a university or department.

During the initial stages of firm formation, academic involvement is most time consuming and the work of the firm is likely to be most closely related to the individual's academic research. Two alternative modes of reducing conflict over firm formation have evolved: one of separation, the other of integration. Proponents of the first strategy propose to reduce conflicts of interest and obligation by making a clear distinction between their academic research and the work of their firm, with different research programs pursued by different persons and with professors' involvement limited to leave periods and consulting time. Advocates of integration argue that attempts to "build a wall between the firm and the university" are artificial and counterproductive. These scientists attempt to untie the "gordian knot" of conflicts of interest and obligation by creating a seamless web between their academic research group and their commercial enterprise. The work of the lab and firm become one and the same with information flowing back and forth and students moving from one site to the other. On the financial level, conflicts are resolved through a sharing of the rewards between the academic entrepreneur and the university. On the ideological plane, conflicts are transcended by making the purpose of the firm, commercialization of research, into one of the goals of the university. Hence, conflict resolution should in principle become less problematic precisely because the basis for conflict is being itself displaced. While there has been much more research done on this topic than on agenda setting, there is still a need to consider carefully the following issues:

- Insofar as institutions have felt the need to develop mechanisms for dealing with conflict of interest questions, there is clearly a sense in which there is a perception that normative conflict can—and does—occur. But how far is this changing, if at all? If there is less of a perceived need for developing such mechanisms, how are we to interpret this?
- When no institutional mechanisms are available to discuss and adjudicate issues concerning academic-industry relations or conflict of interest charges, what happens? At times disputes have escalated from specific issues into matters of broad principle and institutional purpose, such as the 1980 controversy at Harvard over the formation of a biotechnology firm, the 1989 Boulder (Colorado) controversy over the formation of a start-up company to manage the entire intellectual property of the university and systematically to seek out commercialization opportunities by having representatives of the firm sit in on research group meetings, or the 1993 dispute between the Sandoz company and the National Institutes of Health (NIH) over the level of access to NIH research the firm wanted through its tie-in with the Scripps Institute. Are these disputes less likely to occur as commercialization becomes more the norm, and where they do arise, do academic establishments resolve them by explicitly revising their institutional goals, most importantly, that economic development is to be regarded as one of several academic missions?

- What conflict of interest issues arise between the arts and sciences (the two cultures within academia), the unfunded and funded sectors, with industrial connections more relevant to and likely to be accepted by the sciences, especially under conditions of financial stringency?
- What impact have scientists who oppose further commercialization had on the development of new forms of collaboration? Some oppose all connections, believing that they will ultimately interfere with the full government funding of science through peer review mechanisms. In some ways, it might be argued that peer review depends on the stability of a core set of scientists within discrete disciplines maintaining the overall quality control of their respective fields. How far does commercialization generate a new transinstitutional core set joining academic and corporate members? Typically, collaborative agreements seek to sustain the peer review process through the appointment of a science advisory board; is this as effective a peer review process as is needed?
- What conflict has arisen between administrators and faculty? Some scientists who have generated intellectual property wish to control its disposition, including its commercialization, and view administrative efforts to exploit it as an unwarranted interference, even regarding it as a breach of academic autonomy and freedom.
- Finally, what relevance have conflict of interest codes developed in the legal profession for academics involved in collaboration?

Normative conflict can generate not only periods of tension and interpersonal dispute, it can also trigger more fundamental institutional instability. This is also more generally true of commercialization itself. Conflicts over academic-industrial relations have been managed by establishing committees to deal with unresolved issues, representing both proponents and opponents. The objective is to reach a consensus so that differences will not erupt into open conflict. Typically, linkages are introduced in a regulated fashion. Thus, a patent policy that heretofore allowed only non-exclusive licenses might be changed to allow exclusive licenses under certain circumstances. In the course of committee discussion less knowledgeable academics learn that small companies cannot usually afford to take the risk of an unrestricted license, allowing others to follow up easily and copy them. They need the protection of an exclusive license in order to take the risk of bringing a product to market. Academics, usually more sympathetic to small firms than large, see the logic of this analysis and modify their total opposition to exclusivity in the licensing of intellectual property.

More generally, it is crucial that collaborative agreements are stable in their structure and function. One of the threats to this stability is that senior company personnel change frequently and with them ways of funding extra-mural research. Companies will inevitably change according to what they perceive as the correct responses to changes in the fiscal environment, but will adopt different strategies. This means that strategies for funding academic work will vary from company to company and indeed from (senior) person to person. In the pharmaceutical sector, where there has been a spate of acquisition and merger recently, collaborative links have experienced some fragility. A number of questions arise here:

- How have administrators handled different corporate philosophies toward collaboration?
- What are the different consequences for the university in negotiating with domestic, multinational, and foreign corporations for research support, collaboration, and exchange?
- Do administrators articulate the sort of inter-organizational concerns regarding such matters as collaborative boundaries, breadth of purpose, and the "permeability" of new collaborative structures discussed earlier?
- How have recent changes in central and eastern European societies affected the traditional institutional mechanisms for technology transfer from academia to industry? In socialist economies the transfer of technology was expected to take place from research institutes to production organizations through governmental coordination. The inability of bureaucratic central planning organizations to arrange such transfers effectively left an elaborate structure of basic and applied research institutes largely disconnected from the economy. Research institutes are currently being encouraged to make their own arrangements with firms, even with firms in capitalist countries, to transfer technology. As research institutes take on an entrepreneurial role in selling their discoveries and supporting their future research from such sales, they represent the introduction of a laissez faire element into centrally planned economies. In doing this, the institutes have met and are experiencing considerable institutional difficulties.

There is, then, a range of questions that needs addressing associated with these three institutional issues of agenda setting, normative conflict, and institutional stability, issues that have come to the fore in Europe (especially in the post-socialist countries [see Balázs 1995]) and the United States but that are now also of vital concern elsewhere, such as in Australia, Japan, and Brazil.

We are now at a point where we can draw together, briefly, a number of general methodological and policy implications from our discussion of the theoretical and substantive dimensions of academic-industry collaboration.

Key Methodological and Policy Implications

In summarizing the principal themes that are worth the attention of researchers and policy makers, we want to argue that the issues we highlight are theoretically derived from our understanding of the structural shifts that we believe are taking place in academia and, to a lesser extent, in research-intensive industry. This examination of collaborative changes is not just important from an academic point of view, since it clearly has implications for industrialists, scientists themselves, and policy makers; given the increasing investment (social and material) in collaboration, it is vital that we understand it. The analysis here helps to clarify what is happening and to evaluate proposals for innovative linkage; academic research needs to be embedded in that policy-making process.

We suggest in chapter 1 that it is possible that we are witnessing today a new, "second" academic revolution whereby the institutional role and character of academia is changing as it adopts a more central economic role in society, both in conjunction with industry and on its own behalf through exploiting its knowledge base. It was suggested too that this role has been encouraged by government policy, which has deliberately sought to avoid any specific industrial policies for economic development, preferring instead to encourage a general environment of growth. A number of commentaries, as noted, make similar claims, stressing in particular the appearance of a new "social contract" between academia and the wider society. Others, however, are less convinced of this process, suggesting that it is only piecemeal and where occurring does so in an evolutionary rather than revolutionary way. One could of course argue that both evolutionary and revolutionary changes occur at the same time, and that we should abandon the notion that it is either one or the other. The question then becomes how does revolutionary change impact on evolutionary processes?

We want to argue that the only way in which any sort of answer to this question can be provided is by addressing a number of theoretical concerns that should provide the main conceptual ground on which we build our analysis of any fundamental changes taking place. Three key analytical tasks lie ahead:

- the need to develop more adequate conceptions of the three principal dimensions of collaborative relations, viz., science and technology inputs, entrepreneurialism, and the structure and function of academia;
- the need to develop a much more sophisticated understanding of the inter-organizational factors involved in collaboration; in this regard, it would be valuable to explore the sense in which the specific case of academic-indus-

try linkage is just one (albeit important) example of the increasing appearance of inter-organizational relationships developing among institutions that deal actively and strategically with knowledge;

- the need to develop models—such as the example of a "hybrid coalition"—that are built from various assumptions that can be made about the sort of transinstitutional interests any particular ideal-type of collaboration may be designed to serve; such models can then be used as heuristic devices against which real collaborations can be measured and evaluated. These models need to draw on our understanding of academic and industrial institutions as distinct knowledge bases with different but now more overlapping requirements as the boundaries between the two—or more accurately, specific parts of the two—become blurred.

It was suggested further that these three issues could be usefully developed through further empirical analyses by social scientists of some notable substantive developments such as the rapid growth of long-term alliances, the emergence of new institutional structures for technology transfer, and the potential for the development of a quasi-academic culture within corporate R&D establishments. No doubt others can and should be raised for discussion.

From a policy-oriented perspective there are a number of questions that arise:

- If academic institutions are required to take on a more direct economic role, which is both internally and externally driven, what long-term implications will this second academic revolution have? The first "revolution" led to a gradual expansion of the knowledge base through the development of a new research role (Jencks and Reisman 1968); the second will provide for a more rapid and widespread exploitation of that knowledge base. There will be both costs and benefits associated with this process in both the short and long term whose effect will be felt at individual, institutional, and national levels. What is collaboration for some may ultimately end up as "exploitation" for others.
- How much do these changes vary between different countries, and what data are available to show whether clear trends in any one direction—e.g., toward any one preferred model of collaboration—are taking place?
- Will stronger links between research-intensive industry and research-intensive academia be likely to accentuate the trend toward a two-tier system where large corporations and large science-based academic centers dominate over small and medium-sized firms (SMEs) and the teaching-oriented, less well-endowed educational establishments?
- Within academic institutions, will tension be created between those departments with strong industrial links and others that have relatively few? Will

some sort of formula for redistributing wealth become necessary? Traditional academic management through conventional committee structures may be inadequate to the task. Indeed, we have seen the appearance of new forms of decision making in universities, reflecting the need for different mechanisms for managing the interface between academia and industry.

- What changes are taking place with regard to the character of industrial R&D within different sectors that relate to discernible trends in academic-industry collaboration? If companies encourage an innovative, academic-type research culture in-house, how would this affect their relationship with academia in the longer term?

- How far will any significant changes in academic-industry relations bring about changes in both the experience and occupational status of academics and industrialists involved?

- How much do senior academics who establish start-up companies in which they enjoy equity while overseeing large research teams part-funded by industry develop rather different occupational and status positions compared with the conventional academic? Apart from the marketability of their academic expertise, they enjoy new forms of ownership (via their equity rights) and—where they have managerial responsibility—control. In doing so, academics have access to novel forms of prestige and power as they straddle corporate and academic institutions. University authorities increasingly recognize this development by negotiating new individual contracts of employment for some entrepreneurial staff. This introduces new forms of recognition and reward into academia that are more highly differentiated than at present; it is uncertain the impact this might have on existing forms of collegial integration.

- What, if any, tensions are generated between academia and industry when academic companies become competitive with other private firms? Are competitive pressures reduced through joint partnerships or vertical integration? What organizational changes take place as university companies grow in size?

- What quantitative and qualitative measures and techniques are available for evaluating the contribution of different forms of collaboration to the development of the science base, the development of specific knowledge bases, technology transfer, and economic growth? Where structural difficulties of a region or country are to be tackled not through macro-planning but creating the right sort of general environment for growth, how effective have industry-academic relationships been in the past, and can we extrapolate from this previous track record to the new situation confronting us today?

- Finally, while the focus of this debate has been on the changing relationships between academic-industrial research and the wider developmental role universities are being asked to play, how do any changes affect the teaching function of academia?

Apart from the administrative, social, and political problems in managing new institutional structures and occupational statuses, there is a need to develop techniques that can monitor the collaborative links as they develop. Typically, the initial contractual relationships between industry and academia are subject to revision as the R&D process and its management evolve. Again, here, the question arises as to how much autonomy the joint venture is allowed in determining its developmental trajectory; much depends on the position the collaboration has within the parent institution—for example, external, peripheral, or fully integrated in the institution's structures.

Clearly, there are changing patterns in terms of how and where research and development activities are undertaken. How we understand these dynamics depends in part on the time frame we adopt: the longer the term the more it is possible to regard academia as making a general contribution to a wider "publicly" accessible reservoir of knowledge; the shorter the term the greater the likelihood of identifying closer and more targeted relations between universities and the private sector. Yet it also depends on our understanding of the role of research within the innovation system and the changing significance it is accorded by industry.

Thus, even as the leading technology corporations of a previous era—IBM, AT&T, GM—downsize, or even abandon, the basic research sections of their corporate laboratories, a new generation of companies that had previously only attended to near-market R&D have found that incremental improvements in a core technology are insufficient to secure their future competitive status. Countries such as Japan that pursued a similar strategy, relying upon others for discontinuous innovation, have also increased their investment in basic research. As academic investigators focus on grant renewals on 2–5-year cycles, it is especially significant that a company such as Microsoft is attracting to its new laboratory the leading academic and industrial researchers in fields such as decision theory and Bayesian nets, which they project will be relevant to creating a new generation of products.

Certainly, Microsoft's strategy differs from the old IBM of the 1960s, which supported its laboratories from mainframe profits as a "national treasure" with little or no connection between the laboratories and product development. Indeed, there is a long list of computer innovations from parallel processing to RISC computing that IBM took the research, but not the innovation, lead in developing. The new generation of corporate researchers are pursuing a strategy of directed basic research, picking areas of potential relevance to future product development. For example, Intel, "The world's largest chip maker is embarking on a modest program of long-term original research. According to a story in the Wall Street Journal, Intel has until now relied on miniaturizing older designs. To go further they feel they must look for whole new approaches to computing. Could this be the first timid step in a return to the great corporate research laboratories of the past?" (Park 1996). The renewal of industrial research also involves development of capacities in both new and old research-oriented companies with a dual function: the generation of significant research results internally that qualifies the firm to collaborate with other firms, universities, and government laboratories, allowing the incorporation of useful knowledge from external sources.

CHAPTER 3

The Changing Context of Science
and University-Industry Relations

KAREN SEASHORE LOUIS and
MELISSA S. ANDERSON

Introduction

The university is often viewed as an ivory tower—"a secluded place that affords the means of treating practical issues with an impractical, often escapist attitude; esp: a place of learning" (*Webster's Ninth New Collegiate Dictionary*). In an ivory tower, the community of scholars can develop a value system and norms of behavior that are consistent with the personal dispositions of its members. There is no real need to be concerned about competing values systems on the outside, at least in democratic environments in which the autonomy of the university is valued.

Self-regulation of values and behavior lies at the center of the norms of research universities. Historically, this arrangement has not been particularly controversial except in periods of social upheaval—and for good reason. Until recently, few people went to universities or on to any form of higher education at all. Pre–World War II universities produced very little of value to the larger society, other than educated clergy and lawyers, and "well-rounded" national leaders. Until this century, most significant scientific advances occurred outside of universities. Finally, while universities reflected changing social conditions, they were largely buffered from them, because they were not expected to be very responsive. This is hardly true today, as any academic will attest.

This chapter examines some of the changes in values that are affected by the increasingly close relationships between the larger society and the research university, focusing primarily, but not exclusively, on ties between industry and universities. Of particular consideration here is how faculty members' increasing involvement with groups outside the university leads to more opportunities for those groups to influence and even control faculty research. Decision making, once vested in the researcher, is now dispersed among funding agencies, regulatory agencies, university-level review committees, and even the general public. Ideals of faculty autonomy and academic freedom compete with complex constraints derived from increasingly complex university-environment interaction.

The Normative Structure of Self-Regulation

Cultural expectations related to academic research behavior, as defined by the classic work of Robert Merton (1942), are based on four key norms. First is norm of *universalism* or the separation of scientific statements from the personal characteristics of the scientist. This norm ensures that the quality of academic work will be evaluated on the basis of the work itself, not the scientist's prestige or lack thereof. The second is *communality*, the sharing of research results and approaches with all other researchers. Communality ensures that research will be open to all challenges, subject to verification by replication, and widely disseminated. The third norm, *disinterestedness*, requires research to be detached from personal motives, pursued only for the sake of truth and intellectual progress. Finally, *organized skepticism* demands the critical and public examination of scientific work so necessary to ensure sound theoretical structures and correct deductions.

　　Standards, however, do not always reflect the reality of scientists' behavior, which is sometimes competitive, secretive, and focused on power and politics (Goldman 1987; List 1985;. Ben-Yehuda 1986; Mitroff 1974; Chalk 1985, Sechrest 1987; Riordan and Marlin 1987). Mitroff's (1974) work has demonstrated that, in some contexts, work and relationships are shaped by normative systems that not only do not conform to the Mertonian norms but are point-for-point contrary to them. Mulkay (1979, 1980) has argued that normative structures are ideologies or "evaluative repertoires" (Mulkay 1976, 643), that is, "relatively standardized verbal formulations which are used by participants to describe the actions of scientists, to assess or evaluate such actions and to prescribe acceptable or permissible kinds of social action" (Mulkay 1976, 643–644). As such, they serve as socially constructed means for interpreting behaviors.

　　Chubin (1985), though, suggests that "Merton's norms have come to represent the official ideology of scientists, but only a crude indicator of their practices" (79). While compliance with the academic ethic is not universal, the norms continue to serve as descriptions of desirable, appropriate behavior in the academy (Rosenzweig 1985). Our research on normative orientations in the sciences, engineering, and the social sciences reveals extremely high levels of subscription to the Mertonian norms among faculty: followup analyses to our investigation of students' normative orientations (Anderson and Louis

1994) show that for each of the four Mertonian norms, more than ninety-nine percent of faculty subscribe to the norm to some extent or to a great extent.

The sociology of science during the 1960s and 1970s argued that these norms are supported by a number of social structures including peer review, replication and verification, academic freedom and tenure, scholarly autonomy, and an intensive socialization process that involves a lengthy apprenticeship "at the bench" with an esteemed faculty member.

The Changing Context for Science[1]

Changes in the social context of academic work have influenced the effectiveness of some of these supportive structures. Such changes relate to the imperatives of scientific research as well as involvement of industry and other external actors.

Large-scale research. Academic research increasingly requires big laboratories and facilities and, once established, big projects require a continuing flow of funds to maintain the staff and work. Obtaining funding to maintain a research facility can, in some instances, become an end in itself, displacing more purely scientific motivations. This trend is frequently viewed negatively. Schultz (1980) maintains that increases in scale are associated with reductions in scientific creativity (irrespective of the production of publications, which may remain high; see Cohen 1981; Louis, Blumenthal, Gluck and Stoto 1989). Larger projects may also increase the likelihood of intrusion by funding agencies, who have a greater vested interest in the results.

Changing assessments of performance. The dimensions of the research enterprise may also affect the basis for evaluating individual performance. In many fields, the size and number of research grants has come to be a "quick and dirty" indicator of the scientist's disciplinary prestige (Liebert 1977; Hackett 1990). Universities' policies have reinforced this trend (Pfeffer and Salancik 1974; Pfeffer and Moore 1980). The impact of large-scale science on the incentive system for younger scholars has also been questioned, as National Science Foundation budgets remain rather stable but the number of funded investigators decreases. This contributes to what Merton (1968) called the "Matthew effect"—to whom that hath, shall be given. The growth in large-scale research and collaboration is also viewed as good preparation for cooperative work in industry (Etzkowitz 1984), thus possibly contributing to the outflow of talent from academe.

Involvement outside the ivory tower. In the past, academics' work was characterized by their lack of concern for personal gain, in accordance with the norm of disinterestedness. As Etzkowitz (1984) has pointed out, since World

War II, more people have come to assume that scientists can maintain the ideal of basic research without sacrificing opportunities for financial reward (Etzkowitz 1984). Currently, consulting is the norm for most academics (Boyer and Lewis 1985; Marsh and Dillon 1980; Louis et al. 1989).

Commercial potential of academic research. The academic reward system theoretically gives greater prestige to research that extends the boundaries of the field, and writers often make distinctions between what properly belongs within the basic sciences and what belongs outside. In recent years, however, "hot" basic research has confounded this distinction by demonstrating potential commercial consequences almost immediately. This happened first in computer and information science but has occurred more recently in biochemistry, with biotechnological advances, and in physics, with new hopes for superconductivity research.

Growth of industrial research. As Schmandt (1984) points out, new industries in fields such as computers and biotechnology "use scientific research directly as a production force. To do so, they must engage heavily in research and development" (Schmandt 1984, 25). In the past fifteen years there has been an increase in the number of fields in which the research laboratories of private companies provide a context more favorable to long-term, innovative basic research than university laboratories (Brooks 1988). It is estimated that more than fifty percent of the U.S. national budget for basic research is allocated to scientists in non-university settings (Brooks 1988). As Blumenthal et al. (1986a) indicate, large corporations tend to view their own in-house research scientists as an adequate source of basic research results for their own development purposes and fund university research largely for philanthropic or network-building reasons. Although many university-based scientists still claim a great chasm in values between industry researchers and university researchers (Grobstein 1985), there is little evidence to suggest that there are significant differences between sectors with respect to basic science (Blumenthal et al. 1986a).

Increasing regulation by national governments. Recent historical analysis shows that the regulatory role of government has increased steadily over the past 100 years and that the government has more recently intruded into the regulation of research in the United States. This trend is also occurring in European countries. Brooks (1988) points out that shortly after World War II, science policy in the United States became based on an informal "social contract" between universities and the federal government, involving "a promise of social benefits in exchange for an unusual degree of self-governance and financial support free of strings" (Brooks 1988, 50). Schmandt's (1984) analysis of government regulation implies that this social contract may have inadvertently increased the acceptability of government regulation of new technologies.

While this regulatory thrust began in industry, it has rapidly extended into university work, in part because the public and legislators had become accustomed to seeing academic science as (1) a part of the economic base and (2) a partner to a two-sided bargain with society. Under these conditions, including the growth of industrial basic research, the special autonomy of academic science has become less clear.

We turn now to a more detailed examination of the effects of one of these trends on the locus of control of academic research: the expansion of relationships between universities and industry.

Further Exploration of the Effects of University-Industry Relations

In recent years, faculty involvement with private business and industry has substantially increased (Rosenzweig 1985), although the proportion of funding is still low and varies substantially across institutions and disciplines (Ashford 1983; Fink 1985).[2] The federal government has also encouraged university-industry linkages (Weese 1985). Nevertheless, because industry controls financial and technical resources desired by university faculty members, it has the same potential for influence and control as federal funding agencies. In addition, because the relationships between faculty and industry are not always as visible and regulated as those between government and universities, the potential for inappropriate influence over the content or use of scientific results appears greater. The issues raised by such interaction relate to the fundamental mission of public higher education, implicit and explicit terms of academic employment, and the distinctive intellectual motivation of research in the university setting (Bok 1981).

Entrepreneurship: A Definition

In the mid-1980s, a research team that included the first author of this article conducted a survey-based study of life scientists' relationships with industry. We review here some of the key findings from one of the project's publications, an analysis of the entrepreneurial behavior of life scientists (Louis, Blumenthal, Gluck and Stoto 1989).

The study identified five different forms of entrepreneurship in which academic scientists engage. The first was obtaining large, externally funded research projects, and the other four related to industry: getting research money from industry; consulting; commercializing research results through patenting, licensing, or developing trade secrets; and actually starting or investing in firms whose products are based on their research. Although these five different types of entrepreneurship were positively related to one another, the associations were very modest. We concluded—and this is rather important for studying the impact of university-industry relationships on faculty— that *these different types of behavior were, in fact, rather distinct.* In other words, a faculty member who does a lot of consulting is only slightly more likely than a randomly selected peer to be involved in commercializing his or her research.

The Informal Connections

Faculty consulting is probably the most common and least visible form of university-industry relationship, since universities frequently do not know when it occurs (Rosenzweig 1985; see also Blevins and Ewer 1988). A University of North Carolina survey reported that among those faculty who were active in externally funded research, more than seventy percent were engaged in personal consultancies (Bird and Allen 1989), although Louis, et al.'s (1989) data suggest that life science faculty who have a great deal of external funding earn less from consulting than those whose research projects are smaller.

Direct faculty involvement through ownership is also often invisible, at least when it operates on a small scale, since it occurs outside of university auspices. The University of North Carolina survey indicated that thirteen percent of research-active faculty are already involved in commercialization of their research, while thirty-two percent anticipate that they may become involved (Bird and Allen 1989). Louis et al.'s (1989) data indicated that faculty who are major publishers and are engaged in larger-scale research are also the most likely to be investing in firms whose products are based on their research.

The Formal Connection: Incentives

The variety and increasing prevalence of more formal arrangements—grants, contracts, science parks, cooperative training ventures, etc.—that involve faculty in university-industry relationships, particularly in scientific and applied fields, raises a number of issues central to the conduct of academic research. Caldart characterizes the situation thus:

> In a very real sense . . . universities are now experiencing a shift from corporate contribution to corporate investment . . . all of these recent contacts . . . can be distinguished from philanthropic contributions, in that they are designed to pro-

vide direct financial gain to parties outside the university. . . . Second, all delve, at least in part, into areas of "basic" research traditionally confined to non-commercial academic settings. And, third, all [of the cases investigated in this paper] involve large sums of money. (Caldart 1983, 25)

From the point of view of individual scientists, there is much to gain in contacts with industry. Louis et al. (1989) for example, indicated that more than fifty percent of life scientists agree to a great extent or to some extent with the statements that research support from industry "provides resources for research that could not be obtained elsewhere" and "involves less red tape than federal funding" (114–115). The "market" for obtaining industry support may be more open (e.g., less tied to the past productivity of the applicant), which makes this source more attractive to younger scholars or those with weak track records (Liebert 1977). In addition, university researchers may gain access to industrial facilities, which are usually much better equipped (Barber 1985). Finally, research assistantships rather than grants increasingly provide support for graduate students (Hackett 1990); for example, thirty-two percent of all biotechnology firms support graduate students (Blumenthal et al. 1986a). Finally, universities hope to benefit from patents and licenses that develop from industry-funded research (Brown 1985). Thus, it is not surprising that universities are frequently the initiators of cooperative ventures with industry, rather than vice versa (Olswang and Lee 1984).

From the standpoint of industry, access to researchers at the cutting edge of knowledge provides valuable advantages for commercial development. This access is viewed as the most important benefit of university research sponsorship by firms engaged in biotechnology (Blumenthal et al. 1986a). The same biotechnology study shows that industrially funded university research has a higher payoff in terms of patent applications per research dollar than industry-conducted R&D. Smith (1984) argues that university-industry collaboration:

> minimize(s) the inefficiencies and shorten(s) the period associated with the early portion of the learning process. . . . As an employer of university-trained people and as a user of university-generated knowledge, industry, too, is concerned about the value system of the university and knows that a bona fide relationship is essential. . . . (24)

The Formal Connection: Disincentives

There are disadvantages of university-industry relationships as well, however. Nora and Olivas (1988) showed that most university researchers (in Texas) believed that their institutions should not become more involved in corporate-funded research, and the Blumenthal et al. (1986b) survey also revealed that many life science faculty are concerned about increasing dependence on industry funding. We focus here on two broad concerns. On the university side, Rosenzweig (1985) points to the challenge of maintaining the distinctive role of academic research in the face of the changing external context. On industry's side, ensuring that interaction with academe will continue to be profitable is viewed as a problem. The most salient issue here is ownership of the ideas or products of sponsored or cooperative research (Varrin and Kukich 1985; Fowler 1982–83), an issue that relates both to profit and to the scientific communication process.

Academic research exists in a normative context that defines the institutional role of the research task and the professional role of the academic researcher. The implicit motive for research, as well as the basis for rewards in academic work, is the pursuit of new knowledge. Institutional autonomy for the university and academic freedom for the professor are predicated on the assumption that the independent demands of knowledge creation, tempered by a concern for the public good, determine the direction of academic work (Caldart 1983, 29).

Maintaining an appropriate balance between basic research and commercial objectives is an area of tension (Smith 1984), as is the related question of research direction. To the extent that external institutions seek to direct academic research based on their own interests, faculty members become subject to controls inconsistent with their professional roles and the purpose of their work (Blevins and Ewer 1988).

Agenda setting by external groups may lead to ethical problems or academic misconduct. Two recent cases illustrate such effects. At the University of California, researchers found that a leukemia patient was not as ill as expected, given the history of his disease. Wanting to know why, they kept some of his spleen cells in culture and isolated from them an anti-cancer substance. As Arthur Caplan (1993) explains, the researchers developed a "very lucrative arrangement" with a private firm to manufacture this anti-cancer substance from a set of cells cloned from the patient's tissues. They, however, did not tell the patient what they were doing. In fact, they called the patient back from time to time for what they termed "further treatment," which was actually further work on his spleen cells in order to control the cell line for the manufacturing process (Caplan 1993).

Arrangements between academic researchers and external organizations may be particularly complicated when investigators have equity in companies that make products based on the investigators' own research. David Knighton at the University of Minnesota developed a product that appears to help wounds heal. He held equity in a company that developed the product, now called Procuren, for commercialization. The ethical complications in this case involve questions about whether Knighton either deceptively or prematurely reported favorable research results because of his equity holding (Caplan 1993). Also, it is interesting to note that when Knighton's research project went through extensive review by University of Minnesota medical school peers each time it was funded, no one objected to the fact that the research agenda was being affected by external groups, namely, the commercializing organization. To the contrary, the peer review panel found each time that there was no conflict of interest. Clearly, in this case, the internal and external standards for conflict of interest were in contradiction, for when this case received media attention and closer administrative investigation, Knighton left the university.

Ashford argues that at each critical decision point in the development of a research project, industrial funding can influence the incentives that cause a researcher to choose one direction over another. Blumenthal et al. (1986b) support this concern, showing that biology and biochemistry faculty who receive research funds from industry are four times more likely than others to report that their choice of research topics was influenced by the likelihood of commercial implications of the results.

Differences in industrial and academic orientations are often viewed as reflective of basic cultural differences between the two sectors:

> Existing barriers to a greater degree of cooperation and collaboration between universities and the corporate world are identified as "cultural differences." To a large extent, these differences relate to the process of work itself. There is the academics' self-paced nature of working, the discretion of faculty members over the organization and management of their research, the rules and understandings concerning freedom of communication and publication. Contrasted to these aspects of the academic environment are the orientation toward profit and commercialization, the need to meet deadlines, proprietary rights, and the maintenance of a competitive edge in the marketplace, all of which are seen to be characteristic of the corporate environment. (Buchbinder and Newsome 1985, 45)

Differences in values, breadth of focus, nature of rewards, standards of success, and lifestyles may explain some of the difficulties of interaction between academics and industrialists (Bird and Allen 1989). For example, industry grants to universities tend to be much shorter term than federal grants (Blumenthal et al. 1987), suggesting a focus on narrow research questions. The matter of time frame reflects not only cultural differences but also different perspectives on the purpose of research. Blevins and Ewer (1988) caution:

> The one difference that threatens a lasting relationship between industry and higher education is industry's propensity to work toward short term profit maximization while the university maintains a philosophy of long term considerations. All other differences between the two institutions pale in comparison. It is of dire necessity that universities not lose their long term perspectives. (654)

Another value difference introduced by industrial funding concerns openness of communication. Academic research culture is based on this value, while industrial profit motives require some secrecy to protect competitive advantage. One-quarter of faculty with industrial research support in biotechnology report that they are restricted from circulating research results by the terms of their funding, a rate that is five times higher than for those without funding (Blumenthal et al. 1986b). In response, most research universities (seventy-four percent) have developed guidelines that indicate how long such restrictions may apply (Louis, Anderson, and Swazey 1988).

Counterforces from the University

Other concerns on the university side are conflict of commitment and conflict of interest (Giamatti 1982). Most faculty members have teaching and other responsibilities beyond their research. To the extent that work with industrial organizations impinges on these other duties and compromises the value of the non-research services that the university provides, universities may charge their faculty members with conflict of commitment (Burke 1985; Blevins and Ewer 1988). Consulting appears to be the primary source of difficulties: high levels of research funding from industry do not appear to have a negative effect on research productivity, but exclusive or extensive consulting is associated with lower publication rates (Blumenthal et al. 1987).[3] Ninety-five percent of all research universities regulate faculty consulting (Louis, Anderson, and Swazey 1988). However, only a few universities monitor conflict of interest in any systematic way.

Perhaps of greater concern is the possible conflict of interest in the industrially funded professors' teaching and mentoring roles: doctoral students whose education is supported by industry funds report lower publication rates, more delays in publication, and constraints in discussing their work (Gluck, Blumenthal, and Stoto 1987; see also Varrin and Kukich 1985). Doctoral students learn about the norms and assumptions that underlie academic work from their professors and learn about their practical application from watching scientists go about their daily tasks. However, if students encounter many faculty who are struggling with issues of secrecy, particularism, or personal interest in their research, doctoral students will be less likely to see the traditional norms as valuable.

The potential for conflict of interest likewise leads universities to seek to regulate faculty behavior. A survey of academic deans at research universities revealed that eighty-eight percent of these institutions have written policies concerning consulting, fifty-two percent have policies regarding faculty involvement in firms whose products are based on their own research, and forty-five percent have policies relating to other sources of conflict of interest or commitment (Louis, Anderson, and Swazey 1988).

Thus, from the university's perspective, the major problems with university-industry interaction stem from the distinctive character of academic research and the responsibilities of academic researchers as members of the university community.

Responses from Industry

From industry's perspective, the greatest concern centers on its reasons for entering into collaboration with a university in the first place. In the competitive industrial climate, exclusive control of technology or information is critical. Intellectual property resulting from academic research can be protected through statutory grants (patents, trademarks, copyrights, etc.) or through trade secrets (Buttel and Belsky 1987). Increases in university-industry arrangements have focused attention on the implications of both of these approaches (Fowler 1982–83):

> Trade secrets stemming from academic research pose the greater challenge. Companies in many fields eagerly invest large sums in the services of university researchers, asking for guarantees of secrecy in return. . . . At scientific meetings, disputes over secrecy are erupting, and in some organizations, actions are being considered which could censure or expel members who use their business obligations as shields to avoid participation in the usual sharing and discussion of new advances. (Bok 1982, 37)

To say the least, this problem has not been resolved. Secrecy contradicts the academic norms of openness. It restricts communication with colleagues, some of whom may also be competitors if they are linked with competing industrial interests. It greatly complicates the participation of graduate students in the research enterprise.

Patenting of research results with subsequent licensing arrangements is an alternative way to protect industry's interests. The temporary monopoly afforded by a patent provides an incentive to innovate (Samuelson 1987). The incidence of patent awards to university scientists or universities has been growing; many universities now contain patent offices or have stimulated independent foundations to deal with patents and royalties (Blumenthal et al.

1986b). In addition, many industries report that they have made patent application based on research that has occurred in universities (Blumenthal et al. 1986a).

Patents are not without complications, however. Sponsoring corporations may have the option to review papers to check for patentable material, thus delaying publication (Coberly 1985). Most universities expect to hold patents based on research conducted under their auspices, but industrial sponsors may expect exclusive licenses to the products of research.

> Business wants fair value in return for its investment and therefore wants . . . to use the research results without having to pay a second time. . . . Moreover, many business people . . . have difficulty reconciling the role of a university as a public agent with its desire to take proprietary positions. (Bremer 1985, 52)

It is not always easy, however, to assign ownership of intellectual property, particularly when it has been built up over years through the contributions of many people. A single corporation can seldom take full credit for having funded a particular research innovation (Bremer 1985; Lepkowski 1984). Finally, procedures involved in securing a patent are not completely free from the problems associated with trade secrets.

Fragmenting the Collegium

By their very nature, applied fields are more closely linked to their environments. As Ashford (1983) points out, past ties with commercial organizations have made academics in engineering, medicine, and chemistry "kindly disposed towards industrial goals" (17; see also Smith 1984). Faculty in applied fields are far more likely than faculty in non-applied fields to be involved in research centers funded either by government or by private corporations. Areas such as engineering not only have ready outlets for the results of their research, but in fact have developed in large part in response to problems posed by external constituents:

> At some institutions, in departments of engineering, physics, and biophysics, more than half the faculty are involved in some significant way in industry. And they do so not for financial gain, but because in these fields the cutting edge—or some element of the cutting edge—is, in fact, in industry. If they want to be at the cutting edge and if they want their students to be there, then they naturally work with industrial research groups. (Dialogue: Disclosure of conflicts of interest 1985, 38)

Blumenthal et al. (1987) support this assertion, reporting that more than forty-three percent of chemists and engineers receive some research support from industry, as compared with twenty-three percent in life science fields (where the tradition of applied research is less developed). Nora and Olivas (1988), in a study of research faculty in Texas, show that those in applied fields (engineering and business) are more likely to earn additional income from consulting and to support additional institutional relationships between the university and private sector organizations, and less likely to believe that the institution should retain patent rights to faculty research.

But the classification of a field as applied or non-applied is not an immutable one; it depends on the (unanticipated) results of science itself. "Pure research" fields that are establishing new linkages with outside groups confront critical issues in the management of cooperative ventures, with which faculty members may be ill-equipped to deal. The most obvious case here is microbiology with its explosion of commercially valuable research: now, a field that formerly was marked by "extreme openness" has become "the most secretive of all biological sciences today" (Chubin 1985, 77).[4]

University Responses

The above discussion clearly raises issues related to institutional responsibilities. Issues of research ethics are, at one level, based on individual and disciplinary norms. The social trend outlined above creates pressures that reduce the effectiveness of university autonomy in regulating science. It is our observation, however, that universities (and disciplines) are not really sure how to respond, and may not be well positioned to do so.

For example, more prestigious universities are less likely to use formal procedures for handling allegations of research improprieties, and less likely to incorporate formal instruction on ethical and value-related issues into course work (Louis, Swazey, and Anderson 1988). The administrators we interviewed in these universities tended to indicate that they rely heavily on the administrative vigilance of their middle-level administrators. However, department chairs from more prestigious universities are less likely formally to sanction violation of the norms of science (Braxton 1989). In addition, more prestigious universities produce a disproportionate share of ethical-violation cases (Louis, Swazey, and Anderson 1988). Although the incidence of problems is undoubtedly due to the fact that the most prestigious institutions employ the largest number of active investigators, we cannot ignore the questions of whether the status quo is operating to maintain an unholy silence about problems related to the norms of science. Not surprisingly, as situations related to the above become public knowledge, there is increasing public pressure to regulate the universities from outside.

Summary

Values are at the center of the universities' enterprise. External pressures are challenging older value systems and, while these pressures have been recognized, universities, faculties, and professional associations have not responded rapidly, increasing the probability that traditional self-regulation will disappear and that public values will regulate the university.

Strategic Interdependencies

Universities are not self-sufficient, but need to acquire resources from their environments to survive. A central problem for modern universities is the management of relations with critical actors in their environments (Shenhav 1986; Ruscio 1984). Pfeffer and Salancik's (1978) discussion of interdependency applies well to universities:

> The typical solution to problems of interdependence and uncertainty involves increasing coordination, which means increasing the mutual control over each others' activities, or, in other words, increasing the behavioral interdependence of the social actors. (43)

Industry's primary interest in universities has traditionally focused on their supply of an educated workforce. This fact explains industry's support of higher education through such mechanisms as philanthropic donations, internships for students, and participation in disciplinary advisory boards. Increasingly in recent years, industry's funding of graduate study has supplemented more traditional forms of support. Moreover, the increase in commercial value of university research has broadened industry's interest in faculty work, potentially increasing both university-industry interaction and interdependence. On industry's side, one mechanism by which organizations seek to moderate their dependence is by obtaining ownership of research results. On the university's side, strategic mechanisms for tempering industry's influence include maintaining diversity in external funding sources and approaching university-industry linkages with enough caution that overall industry support remains a relatively small proportion of funding for academic research.

One problem in regulating this interdependency—a goal that both universities and industry have in common—is the problem of faculty autonomy. Organizations with relatively permeable boundaries are more likely to have increases in critical interactions with external groups without proportional increases in control by those groups (Pfeffer and Salancik 1978). Since universities interact with environmental elements at levels and in departments virtually throughout, there are many possibilities for "letting in" sources of influence. Boundary permeability works both ways, however. To the extent that university faculty are only "partially included" (Pfeffer and Salancik 1978, 29–32) in the institution (i.e., their behavior is not fully regulated), they do not represent their university in the same way that, for instance, a corporate executive represents the corporation. Through independent arrangements with external groups, faculty manage semi-autonomous research enterprises. The external organizations, therefore, are often not able to influence academic research through well-defined bureaucratic mechanisms beyond those researchers with whom they have established links, nor do universities have full control over the faculty.

The second aspect of university organization that diminishes the potential for external control is the loosely coupled nature of the academic enterprise (Weick 1976). To the extent that research in one department has essentially no relation to research in some other department, internal loose coupling confines external influence to specific subgroups within the university. This means that universities tend to fall back on facets of faculty self-regulation such as peer review, reporting of inappropriate behavior, and socialization because the alternatives are very cumbersome (Sechrest 1987). Universities neither closely monitor the work of academic researchers (so as to prevent internal erosion of the academic ethic) nor offer significant opposition at the institutional level to external agents who would control faculty behavior (Steneck 1984).

These standard responses, in keeping with academic tradition, release the university from the responsibility of responding to each challenge. As Rosenzweig puts it, "But I'm not sure how many universities want to make the effort to find out how individual faculty members are behaving. And on the whole I think they are right. If you go about the business of learning the way people behave you are under obligation to do something about it" (quoted in Lepkowski 1984, 11). This approach may frustrate attempts by would-be influentials to change either faculty behavior or institutional response.

The "hands off" approach may reduce universities' discretion in dealing with agencies or organizations that have legitimate interests in ensuring compliance with specific regulations. Universities' reluctance to do more than they do at present or to adopt different kinds of procedures may, for example, encourage funding agencies or corporations to initiate other kinds of controls in their contractual arrangements.

Institutional Issues

While the resource-dependency perspective discussed above illuminates many aspects of the changing context of academic work, there are some aspects that can be better explained with reference to institutional theories (Scott 1987). The environment for the modern university is a source of normative assumptions about and constraints on its activities.[5] Support from the environment is necessary for organizational survival, and organizations achieve legitimacy either by genuine adaptation or by establishing structures that both conform to external expectations and shield core technologies from external scrutiny (Meyer and Rowan 1977).

Universities operate in highly institutionalized environments; that is, there are widely-held assumptions about what constitutes appropriate activity for a university. The cost of change under these circumstances is often high— support flows to a university, in part, because it maintains consonance with established expectations about its mission and appropriate activities. A university may, for example, find it less "costly" in the currency of legitimacy to continue to portray itself to the state legislature as the educator of the young (with all the normative assumptions that role involves), even as its research activity leads it into the world of lucrative patents and commercial-like enterprises.

Thus it appears that most universities adopt strategies of symbolic responses in order to cope with increasingly heterogeneous environments. For example, only a handful of research universities have adopted policies that demand that faculty discuss potential conflicts of interest prior to entering into a research or consulting relationship with an outside agency, although most have a policy that covers such conflict of interest situations (Louis, Anderson, and Swazey 1988). As more and more actors enter the research context, normative pressures can become incompatible or even mutually contradictory, but the appearance of response may be more important than actual change, particularly if one constituency can be satisfied by a symbolic response without activating opposition from another source.

The university may also seek to maintain its legitimacy in the eyes of critical external constituencies by controlling the definition of work that is appropriate for it to do. It can do so either by demonstrating the essential compatibility of current research directions with traditional university activity or by attempting to expand generally held conceptions about what constitutes appropriate research at a university. Insofar as university administrators have issued major public statements about the changing institutional pressures on university faculty and the need for university response, most have been of the first type. Nevertheless, what has been more notable is the lack of major institutional statements regarding the changing nature of academic research. If we compare universities to corporations, for example, we would expect more public announcements of the way in which the institution expects to respond to its changing environment (Hearn 1988). We are, therefore, drawn to the conclusion that the university, as an institution, is somewhat reluctant to confront these issues directly but prefers to use more indirect mechanisms.

One indirect mechanism is the development of external buffer institutions (Fink 1985). One kind is the research park, which is officially outside of normal university operations but provides an environment in which university-stimulated commercialization can take place. Another kind of buffer institution that has been established by many universities is the research foundation, which takes the profit-making activities associated with applied research out of the heart of the university, while retaining the potential financial benefits. While controversial, these buffering institutions have been much less criticized than other university strategies to invest in and profit from faculty research.

A final type of buffering agency that is becoming increasingly important is the national scientific board. In this case, an independent agency acts as a mediator between federal government and university (and, indirectly, the general public) to ensure that an appropriate balance is maintained between autonomy and accountability. Because of the high prestige of associations such as the National Institutes of Medicine or the National Academy of Sciences, this mediating role helps to create consensus while maintaining the legitimacy of the scholarly enterprise. It is also, notably, within the tradition of permitting scholars to govern their own conduct, since such boards are comprised largely of eminent academics.

Implications for Research

The arena for additional research contributions to the general topic covered in this paper is virtually limitless, since research attention to the organizational implications of university-industry relations in the recent past has been relatively minimal. Most of the literature we have reviewed is not methodologically rigorous; the great majority of the empirically solid studies are narrow in focus, covering a single discipline or a small number of cases. In this section we will outline some additional arenas for research that derive from the framework that we have used for organizing the review.

First, there is a need for research that examines in greater depth the way in which both the changing nature of science and various institutional actors actually affect the work of scientists and engineers engaged in university-industry relations, with particular reference to normative structures, conflict of interest, and conflict of commitment, as well as other emerging indicators of behavior. One group of useful studies might focus on the individual scientist as the bearer of standards of behavior.

Our review indicates that the area of differences in behavior and attitudes among disciplines is significant, and this area of research holds much promise for illuminating both the nature of changing scientific norms and the emerging conflicts and controversies that may arise as universities begin to take on the expected role as mediators between scientists and institutional pressures from groups outside the university, which include both industry and the federal government. Extending our understanding of how disciplines differ, not only in their normative structure but also in their relationships to different industrial sectors and types of firms, would extend the higher education field's often too casual acceptance of the importance of the disciplinary community as a determinant of behavior.

The same can be said for our understanding of international issues. While a few of the articles noted here mention problems related to international cooperation in science and university-industry relations, there have been no comprehensive, comparative studies.

Finally, our understanding of how universities are responding to the increasing external pressures is limited to a handful of surveys, which fail to delve deeply into the processes of institutional control, and case studies of individual cases of misconduct, potential conflict of interest, etc. Research in this area could profitably begin with a more comprehensive review of university policies in both more and less controversial areas (animal care review boards and conflict of interest, for example), examining specific institutional responses to the pressure to increase compliance. Surveys of faculty and students to examine issues related to monitoring and compliance regarding policies would also be important.

Conclusion

Our review of current directions in academic research leads us to conclude that (1) significant changes in the faculty-institution relationship are occurring; (2) increasingly complex arrangements with external groups make control of faculty behavior more problematic; (3) as research relationships come to have the character of governmental or corporate contracts, the special norms of autonomy and self-regulation which have distinguished academic work in the past tend to have less certain status.

One implication is that the academic appointment in years to come is likely to differ substantially from the traditional scholarly role—even if the individual is not directly involved in a university-industry relationship (Hackett 1988). In light of the projected need for replacements for a large proportion of the current professoriate, due to a large retirement-age cohort, changes in the academic environment raise questions about the attractiveness of academic careers (Brooks 1988). One of the primary compensations for traditionally low wages in academia has been autonomy in research and teaching. Should this autonomy be compromised by increased controls on faculty behavior, universities may be forced to find other ways to attract young scholars.

No matter what changes emerge in the nature of academic work, it is clear that university research will be increasingly related to elements in the environment. How it manages such relationships will add a fascinating chapter to the history of university life.

II

The Capitalization of Knowledge

CHAPTER 4

Strategic Research Alliances:
Testing the Collaborative Limits?

ANDREW WEBSTER

Introduction

Within the ecology of academic-industry relations, the link between the pharmaceutical industry and the wider public-sector science base is particularly strong. In fact, evidence shows that collaborative and contract research income from firms in this sector to the universities is higher than from any other (see, e.g., Thomas 1992). Not surprisingly, a number of studies have indicated the relative importance of accessing academic science for the pharmaceuticals compared with other industries. Mansfield (1991), for example has compared the relative importance of academic research for seven industries; products from the drugs industry are at least twice as dependent on academic research input as any other sector (the next in fact being instruments). Faulkner (1992), too, has shown that this dependency is reflected in the range and scale of information required by drugs firms from academia, again compared with other sectors studied (ceramics and parallel processing). Moreover, the growing costs of drug development and the need to access but also filter as wide a science base as possible has created a massive growth in absolute terms of internal research budgets and, proportionally, a similar growth in external funding of R&D in both other firms and universities and similar public research centers (Webster and Swain 1991). There is, however, the longer-term question of how company-sponsored R&D will evolve over time. For drugs firms, there are a number of options they might pursue more vigorously that would mean a reduction in in-house R&D without this being made up in academia. For example, firms might consider shifting production toward lower-cost generic drugs or, as is already happening, positioning themselves as integrated healthcare corporations with a much wider range of "products" than drugs per se.

Nevertheless, at present the conventional indicators used to measure R&D activity are particularly high for this sector. Patenting, for example, particularly important for the pharmaceutical sector, has grown dramatically within the industry—doubling every ten years (Drews 1993; Archibugi 1992). A similar growth rate has occurred in the number of patents filed by universities, which have often—though not always—emerged from work sponsored by private corporations (Webster and Packer 1996). In addition, the overall spending of corporations on R&D is typically highest in absolute terms within the pharmaceutical and chemical-related firms, as is evident among the top U.K. R&D spenders (see Table 4.1). The pressure on firms to spend so much on in-house and extramural research has led many to review their strategies toward linkage with academia. While there has long been a conventional range of collaborative relationships—such as endowments, contract research, and studentships—more firms appear to be exploring new forms of linkage which improve access to the science base while improving the ways in which knowledge and technologies produced therein are acquired. Upjohn, for example, recently established, though not without some difficulties, "discovery capability units" (DCU) in western Europe: these bring together research scientists from a number of universities into teams whose objective is to find one new chemical entity (NCE) every five years for clinical trial. These have already generated some patents and candidate drugs. In many ways, these DCUs are an academic extension of the company laboratory and not surprisingly have raised questions about where the boundary lies between "discovery" and "development" work (see Longman 1989).

Upjohn's strategy is, however, atypical of large firms' response toward the increasingly competitive research environment. More typically, we have seen the emergence of long-term strategic research alliances (SRAs). The growth in

TABLE 4.1
Principal R&D Spenders (£m):
U.K. Top Ten Firms in Declining Order

GLAXO-WELLCOME	1200
SKB	638
UNILEVER	543
ZENECA	518
SHELL	437
GE	406
BT	265
ROLLS ROYCE	218
ICI	184
BP	123

Figures reported June 1995
Source: Company Reporting Ltd (1996)

number, scale, and duration of these SRAs has been a particularly notable feature of the A-IR (Academic-Industrial Relations) ecology (Constable and Webster 1991). These multimillion dollar, multi-year collaborations involve a university (or equivalent) research team's being funded to conduct basic research (with potential for early strategic spinoff) in partnership with the sponsoring firm. In the earlier period of SRA formation (1970s–early '80s) the rationale was to link with work that was not available in house. More recent SRAs complement in-house capacity. Table 4.2 lists some of the more significant SRAs. In general they have been established in the new life sciences areas, especially biotechnology. A number have been renewed, though on more modest terms and with an agreed completion date, as the field they cover has matured and/or developed in house. These collaborations reflect the importance of basic research to the industry. But as the costs of drug development increase, as patents expire on leading drugs (Marsh 1990), and as government seeks to reduce its ethical drugs bill (OTA 1993), so the pressure on corporations to target their basic research grows, as does the structural pressure for merger. The search for the next blockbuster based on new scientific discovery grows at precisely the time when the long-term returns on investment look increasingly uncertain; as Drews (1993) notes, if a five percent growth target is not reached over the next few years "the industry will have invested more than it can earn" (40).

Clearly these costs (which include those required to meet regulatory standards) act as barriers to new firm entrants into the sector (Sapienza 1989) or

TABLE 4.2
Notable SRAs in U.S.A. and U.K. (Life Sciences)

			$	Period (yrs)
1974	HMS	Monsanto	23	12
1981	MGH	Hoechst	70	12–>19*
1981	Scripps	J & J	120	16
1982	Wash U	Monsanto	100	12
1983	Oxford	Monsanto	20	10–>15*
1987	Oxford	Squibb	32	7–>10*
1988	Camb	SKB	5	5–>10*
1989	MGH	Shiseido	85	10
1991	UCJ	Eisai	75	15
1991	HMS	Sandoz	100	10
1997	Scripps	Sandoz	300	16

*Note: period of collaboration extended to new total years, in each case with modified contract. Between 1974–97, SRA total U.S.A./U.K. = 31 Centers.

lead to the incorporation of those that do grow—such as Hoffman-La Roche's acquisition of Genentech—into the larger companies. Moreover this also means that the western European and U.S. firms that dominate globally will be unlikely to experience the same sort of threat from Japan that the electronics and semiconductor industries experienced. Nevertheless, the growing costs and oligopolistic competition within the industry will mean that its "absorptive capacity" must become increasingly efficient, and that therefore its monitoring of and collaboration with academic science become more effective. Evidence shows, however, that the capacity to acquire external knowledge is a function of in-house research competence: one has to know how and where to look (Rosenberg 1990). Some evidence shows that large firms in the sector are not all equally adept at this, and it has been suggested that those that are successful appear to be so because of their modelling their scientific research along academic department lines (Gambardella 1992), though there have been some that are similarly structured which have failed. Perhaps it is this too which has led to the growing adoption of the SRA form of collaboration; for those firms that adopt a more academic model of R&D in house it is a form of extension of a set of practices with which they are not unfamiliar; for those that find the departmental structure more problematic, the SRA provides an external version. In the latter case, there will of course remain the problem of providing the right sort of organizational framework through which the work of the SRA is incorporated in house by the company.

Strategic Research Alliances (SRAs)

In order to locate SRAs in the ecology of academic-industrial collaboration we need to define their specific structure and function. Table 4.3 outlines the

TABLE 4.3
SRA Indicators

1. Single company sponsorship of an academic research group.
2. Five years or more duration (typically with five years' notice to terminate the contract).
3. Sponsor (firm) provides new research laboratories and buildings at the host site.
4. Contracts cover capital and current costs.
5. SRAs focus on basic and strategic research.
6. Research projects, research processes, and their management involve joint agreement between and participation of corporate and academic staff.
7. Formal contracts cover intellectual property rights.

features that can be used to identify SRAs. All collaborations are at least five years in duration, some double and even triple that. Their length and resource requirements mean that they can involve a not inconsiderable research investment for a company. Even when this may be relatively small compared with a firm's total R&D budget, for some university research teams the establishment of an SRA becomes their principal source of funds. There is in fact a range of funding between a low of around fifteen percent to a high of more than 90 percent in both capital and current expenditure that SRAs have provided. Some of those listed in Table 4.2 include both high and low reliance on corporate funding for their staff's continued research activity. In real terms the level of funding has increased over the past decade, though the actual frequency of the collaborations in statistical terms is stochastic. Orsenigo (1989), one of the few to comment in some detail on SRAs, has remarked that the strong relationship between the company and university and the exclusivity of the contract "make this type of interaction resemble in many respects a relationship of quasi-integration" (80). This list of indicators separates SRAs from endowments, contract research, pre-competitive consortia involving a number of firms supporting research in academia, and other traditional links while indicating the organizational (and not merely capital) investment they require. Indeed, it is the latter that has suggested that SRAs could be said to embody the *limits* of the collaborative relations between the two sectors. This might be said to be true in three ways: SRAs might be regarded as setting the *institutional* limits of collaboration inasmuch as the inter-organizational demands they place on academic and corporate staff (with shared authority structures, research facilities, technician support, agenda-setting being practised on a daily basis) are likely to strain the most enlightened and consensually oriented managers.

Secondly, they might provide the *ethical* limits for collaboration inasmuch as the possibilities for conflict of interest between academic and corporate roles are high but less transparent than in, say, contract research, where the need to keep corporate sponsors happy is paramount (Wade 1984; NIH 1992). The reason for the greater opacity of SRAs is that typically they involve financial support to undertake broad, strategic research from which the company can take new ideas for development purposes, not targeted contract research which companies can specify in advance and which academics are under pressure to "deliver." The need to balance collaborative partnership with commercial gain is most problematic in SRAs where, over time, the scale of the investment calls out for some sort of "return." Who is to deliver this, how, and when, are questions to which the breadth of contracts rarely provides clear answers (again unlike the situation obtaining with contract research). This puts pressure on staff—felt by everyone from senior researchers to postgraduate students attached to SRAs—to engage in research whose ownership and long-term payoff may be uncertain. Managing this situation ethically requires considerable skill (Weil 1991).

Finally, SRAs may appear to pose the *political* limits to academic-industrial collaboration: more than any other links, these deals have been marked by political controversy where, especially in the United States, recent examples—such as the Sandoz-Scripps contract—are seen to provide a scientific Trojan horse for overseas pharmaceutical companies keen to access the U.S. science base (Schrage 1992). Consequently, not only have such deals been seen to lack legitimacy, they have also been challenged because they have sought to access research beyond the immediate institutional context of the SRA, pulling in the results of federally funded work which passes through the host establishment (Anderson 1993). This issue is complicated, however, by the fact that some countries actively recruit overseas corporations to help build local knowledge bases, as has happened, for example, in the Canadian approach made to Merck (Spurgeon 1992) and more recently to Amgen (Gershon 1993).

Despite these institutional, ethical, and political issues that must be addressed by those that establish SRAs, their continued appearance in the collaborative ecology indicates their attractiveness to larger firms. They are, then, worth exploring more fully, and this chapter reports on research that has examined them in detail, and that in addition locates and evaluates SRAs in the wider innovation context of the pharmaceutical industry. There were, in short, three main objectives of the research:

- to determine their essential features in order that they could be separated from other forms of linkage;
- to determine why they have been and continue to be established, and once set up whether and how they are evaluated by those involved;
- to determine whether there is any variation *within* the population of SRAs and if so, to consider whether some are in a stronger position that others to realize their objectives.

Modelling SRAs

The first of these tasks drew on work of organizational sociologists (e.g., Borys and Jemison 1989) who have examined the structural demands of inter-organizational relations. In the SRA context, we can see two organizations from very different sectors with discrete interests seeking to combine in a new type of social and economic relation, what we can call here a "hybrid coalition," that is, an organizational arrangement that combines in a novel yet coherent way the separate characters and objectives of academia and industry. Any such hybrid structure would need to balance the interests of both parties so that they were seen to be served judiciously and legitimately, while also being structured in such a way that it could sustain itself in a stable manner over a reasonable length of time.

On the basis of these general assumptions the model of the hybrid coalition was constructed (see Table 4.4), which acts as an idealized model against which it is possible to compare real SRAs. The purpose of the model is to draw attention to the range of structural demands of properly functioning SRAs, as well as mark the organizational limits of hybridization, or, in Orsenigo's phrase, "quasi-integration." The model can be used too as a checklist for comparing the features of hybrids against other forms of linkage, and indeed, though this is not reported here, this was also undertaken in the research (see Constable and Webster 1991). All these features of an "idealized" SRA would clearly test the managerial skills of both university and firm involved, and require adjustments of practice surrounding the SRA itself (e.g., specific agreements made over industrial employees on university sites and

TABLE 4.4
The Hybrid Coalition

- The HC is established through a long-term contract with an academic institution, adequately resourced and secured by a single-company sponsor.
- Intellectual property rights or the exclusive rights to license them go to the industrial sponsor in the first place.
- Corporate sponsorship should be adequate to maintain a critical mass of researchers in the new field.
- Basic and/or strategic research projects should be identified by academics in a program of research identified by the sponsor in liaison with the principal investigators.
- Corporate staff should pursue joint and integrated research with academics on both university and industrial sites.
- Results from the HC should go via the principal investigator to the senior research managers of the company in the first instance.
- Research should be managed on the HC site by the academic director, who has regular meetings with company personnel to discuss the content and significance of research.
- Research should be subject to peer review via publication and corporate research staff evaluation.
- Success of the HC should be measured in terms acceptable to both parties—patents, papers, know-how, products—without any one criterion being overly dominant.
- Constraints on information flow should be minimized.

their rates of pay compared with those of other [academic] SRA-based colleagues). It is evident then that effective absorptive capacity to pick up on new research depends as much on carrying appropriate *organizational capacities* in house as it does adequate *scientific knowledge*.

Why Establish SRAs

Four U.K.-based SRAs were examined closely over eighteen months. The senior and more junior academic and corporate staff involved were all interviewed several times during this period. Parallel visits were made to U.S. sites that had been established by the same corporations, and at each SRA site the senior industrial liaison officers for the university were also interviewed. Interviews were based on semi-structured questionnaires, were taped, transcribed, and returned to respondents for comment; most interviews lasted between one and two hours. The SRAs were chosen as they all, to a greater or lesser degree, carried those features of emergent hybridicity that the model of the hybrid coalition predicted. To what extent could such a transinstitutional relationship be built and sustained? The basic background information on the four SRAs surveyed is carried in Table 4.5. In terms of measuring the *success of SRAs*, it is important to distinguish between wider strategic goals which SRA creation is designed to achieve, such as an improvement in drug prices for firms investing in British research activity (whereby foreign companies use SRAs to secure a high return on pricing in the United Kingdom), and SRA-specific objectives with which the immediate participants were most concerned. To the extent that the wider goals were achieved—and respondents reported that the U.K. government did look favorably on their drug prices— the SRA seemed good value, whatever it was to achieve on the scientific front. But at the SRA level, there were both organizational and output measures of success that respondents used in judging the value of their collaboration.

TABLE 4.5
Strategic Research Alliances Surveyed

	SRA 1	SRA 2	SRA 3	SRA 4
Established	1983	1988	1987	1989
Period (yrs)	10	10	7	10
Projected funding (£m)	11	5	20	8
% funds research group	90	20	55	30
SRA-funded staff numbers	45	17	20	16
- of whom academic	34	13	20	8

From the outset, however, it is important to note that these did not seem to have much *stability* as measures over time as the situation within the SRA changed. This suggests that we should be wary of those few reports that have sought to measure the success of links between firms and academia through quantifying evaluative descriptions of success, assuming that such descriptions are replicable over time, constant, and relatively context free. While the better examples of this approach raise interesting questions about methodological issues (see Cukor 1992), we should expect to find that—as was the case here—participants in collaboration *redefine* "success" as the situation that confronts them in the SRA changes. For example, some members of one of the SRAs surveyed applied to external grant agencies to test the wider academic value of their industrially sponsored research; however, the subsequent rejection by grant agencies was not perceived as failure but a recognition of the quality work being conducted which was already well endowed by a corporation.

Similarly, the contextualization of "success" was evident from the way in which SRA members—both corporate and academic—redefined the value of their work to the company when it appeared in jeopardy because of internal changes in the firm's R&D strategy. Quantitative surveys that presume stable meaning and so accurate counting of achieved successes miss the varied, changing, and sometimes even inconsistent criteria used by members to define achievement. Quite often, successful research was seen to be as much a reflection of successful social relations as it was "good science"; indeed, the boundaries between the two are not watertight. Similar results have been found of measures of success used in U.S. federal labs in describing their relations to industry (Roessner and Bean 1991).

Wider objectives—and probably just as important measures of "success"—of the establishment of SRAs were identified, for industry and academia respectively (see Tables 4.6 and 4.7). There were various reasons why companies established SRAs: these were scientific, economic, and managerial. The three are related, of course. For example, access to a new market will depend on moving from an improved innovation approach to one that relies on basic research (Schimank 1988).

Economic factors had a global dimension to them inasmuch as overseas SRAs opened up new markets to secure favorable drug prices as well as to respond to the perceived challenge of Japanese pharmaceuticals now establishing SRAs in Europe and the United States for precisely the same reasons. Note that SRAs were not seen as important sources of new recruits to companies; since SRAs imply a sense of merger between academia and industry in terms of R&D expertise there was little point in trying to recruit or headhunt people in the normal sense of the term. Thus "recruitment" came via the

TABLE 4.6
Reasons for SRA—Company Perspective

Science factors	Access to new generic technology/techniques	100%
	General window on research	94%
	Links with med schools give access to tissue	45%
Economic factors	Move into new markets with high drug prices	60%
	Cheaper than in-house research	40%
	Response to declining market for existing drugs	30%
Management factors	Less cumbersome than consortia-type links	60%
	Monitor Japanese firms developing SRAs	25%
	Channel for recruitment	15%

TABLE 4.7
Reasons for SRA—University Perspective

Scientific factors	Access to technologies and compounds not normally have	100%
	Be more speculative	65%
	Avoid professional constraints	15%
Economic factors	Compensate for govt cuts in R&D	80%
	Overcome reliance on soft money	60%
Professional factors	Applied medical payoff to society	90%

contract itself (e.g., companies paying academic salaries) rather than via a formal transfer of personnel. Primacy was given to accessing new generic technologies and more specific techniques: in this sense companies selected SRA sites according to perceived in-house gaps and potential for early commercial spinoff. From the academic perspective, SRAs were again seen to have scientific and economic value (see Table 4.7). Most interestingly, and in a sense counterintuitively, they were said to allow more speculative work than public grant agencies would support. Moreover, some academics used them to short-circuit professional licensing constraints normally applied when seeking grant support through public agencies. Greatest weight was placed by respondents on the way in which SRAs gave them the opportunity to undertake more applied, drug-oriented work, which they legitimated through an appeal to the public-good value of their research.

Variation Within Sample of SRAs

Although the four SRAs surveyed in detail shared the broad indicators listed earlier (in Table 4.3), there was some significant variation in the ways in which they *more or less* conformed to the "hybrid coalition" indicators outlined above (Table 4.4). One of the most important differences was the way in which the research teams at the different sites pursued their respective scientific agendas: that all involved the negotiation between and participation of academic and industrial members is true, but some were more geared by *broad program* concerns, while others were guided by more *targeted projects.* The investigation showed how this difference was in turn linked to the level of interaction between academics and industrial employees both at the SRA site and between it and scientists in the company. The more specific question of how and what *specific agendas* were set as a result is discussed elsewhere, though a brief comment on this is made in the conclusion (see Webster 1994).

It became clear that there is a direct relationship between high levels of regular interaction and the capacity (organizationally) to sustain what is perceived to be a useful broad program of research. It was apparent that this interaction was necessary to prevent the buildup of pressure from the sponsoring company to move the research toward more targeted research once the SRA had begun generating valued output. SRA1, for example, was a form of collaboration in which *both* academic and corporate members sought to maintain a broad program of work rather than look for particular projects funded on a one-by-one basis by the company. Thus, SRA1 staff never submitted individual project proposals to the sponsor. In SRA4, in almost complete contrast, there was a much stronger contractual obligation of staff to work on project areas selected by the company, into which academics were invited to make specific proposals.

Figures 4.1a and 4.1b suggest in simplified form the broad relation between research type and pattern of interaction. In the more program-oriented SRAs there was a high degree of interaction with company staff on site but much less (or virtually none, as in SRA1) with bench scientists in the firm itself. The inverse was true of the more project-oriented SRAs. As is clear from Figure 4.1b, however, SRA4 was something of an anomaly here, since, though it was the most strongly driven in terms of company-selected projects

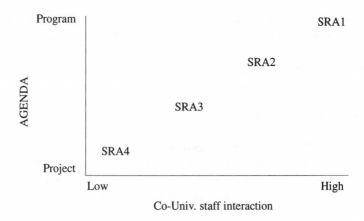

FIGURE 4.1a
Agenda-Type and Company-Academic Interation on SRA Site

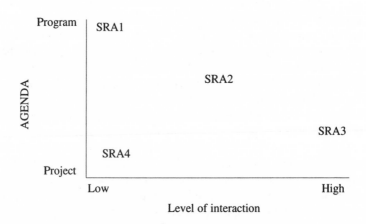

FIGURE 4.1b
Agenda-Type and Level of Interaction between
SRA Staff and In-House Company Staff

there was virtually no contact with bench scientists at the firm's in-house labs, but neither was there any possibility of interaction with firm staff locally since there were none on the SRA site itself. One of the respondents described the relationship with the company as "hands off but closely monitored." SRA4 is, then, the least like a hybrid coalition. It was not surprising, however, to learn that the host university found this contract relatively easy to manage, since there was little organizational or cultural complexity to it. SRAs that conform more clearly to the transinstitutional complexities of the hybrid coalition are much more difficult to manage. However, if levels of interaction are correlated with absorptive capacity, then, despite these difficulties of management, SRA1 might be said to carry the most potential scientific value for the company.

To achieve this is, at the same time, organizationally demanding in a number of ways. Where broad research programs are in place ring-fencing and securing intellectual property is more difficult than with targeted project work. Relating to wider communities (both academic and corporate) when one's research costs are predominantly met by a single firm can also be problematic since academics elsewhere may regard you as overprivileged (and the respondents in the survey did mention the phenomenon of "fiscal envy" of SRA staff by those not included), while other firms cannot be courted without damaging the sponsor's interests. In addition, the need to promote flexibility of research interest while doing so with some overall control that makes sense to the sponsor's long-term interests is a delicate balancing act. It might call—and indeed in one of the SRAs surveyed this was created—for a localized managerial structure bringing academic and local company staff together, as well as a standardizing of research protocols and procedures so that managers can compare the results of very different research avenues being pursued within the broad program. Again, none of this is easy to achieve. And we have already seen how evaluation of "success" is more likely to be a matter of negotiation and change in SRAs that most closely approximate the HC model.

Clearly, whatever the specific character of the SRA, a key question is, what happens as the area of work it covers is considered to be "maturing," or coming to its "natural" end? It is clear from the research results that there is a pressure on the SRA to make its work more directed, by either generating spinoff techniques or products or linking more closely with the applied needs of the company. Resisting this depends on the type of SRA and the internal capacity it has to manage its program locally as an approximation to a hybrid; without this capacity, it is likely that the SRA group will fall foul of the sponsor's internal R&D priorities and either be given notice of termination (with a five-year lead time), or collapse into a more modestly funded endowment grant that bears little or no resemblance to an SRA. If it has been project-oriented, but with little interaction between SRA staff and company-site staff (as in SRA4), the likelihood is that the list of project areas the company is prepared to fund may decline over time, and, again, necessitate contractual renegotiation leading to more modest funding and notice to terminate.

It would appear, therefore, that the most sensible route to take here, which combines the interests of both parties without placing unrealistic demands on their members, would be a mix of program and project funding in a two-tier system of support for the SRA by a firm. This was in fact what was emerging in SRA2 over the period of the review. This has a number of advantages:

- It sustains the academic research team's longer-term research focus through the broad program while allowing the sponsor to promote, either from within its own in-house research or via the SRA program, specific projects that would have their own timescale and milestones;
- So-called "fiscal-envy" is reduced by the combination of the block plus project grant since there is the opportunity for project funds, which are more modest and time-constrained, to be farmed around a whole research team on a rolling program basis;
- Required levels of integration—both personal and managerial—between firm and academic staff on the SRA site are somewhat reduced, and can be channelled as appropriate through the specific projects, rather than needing to be expressed through a broad program of research;
- Background and foreground rights over intellectual property, and the management of confidentiality may be easier to secure in the two-track research context suggested here, since the boundaries of proprietary research might be more easily identified;
- Allowing the continuation of long-term broad research as one track will if necessary enable the academic team to convince future funding agencies—whether public or private—that their work is worthy of support and not overly tied to the interest of the soon-to-be-departing SRA sponsor.

Conclusion

This chapter has reported on a survey of strategic research alliances between pharmaceutical firms and universities, which have become an important feature of the collaborative relationships between academia and industry. It was argued earlier in the chapter that SRAs can be regarded as setting the limits of collaboration on a number of counts, institutional, political, and ethical. In many ways, the last two are reflections of the first set of institutional issues posed by SRAs, which this chapter has concentrated on. What might be regarded as a more ethically related issue—the skewing of research agendas in SRA settings by sponsoring firms—has been reported on elsewhere (Webster 1994). Here we can note that the way research agendas are shaped by corporate sponsorship varies as you move from one type of SRA to another. Moreover, the capacity of research scientists in universities to resist agenda shaping by firms was found to vary too, as some were in a better position than others to defend their "institutional space." Most importantly, however, research agendas have to be seen as constructed in an iterative and interactive way, each party involved able, to a greater or lesser degree, to construct what is to be regarded as an agenda that "delivers the goods."

Clearly, from the discussion of the managerial and cultural demands of SRAs they are difficult organizations to sustain, and to that extent reveal the idealized and rather demanding model of the hybrid coalition. This is precisely the purpose behind such an ideal-type model: it throws light on the contingencies and constraints that make meeting its demands and so its realization problematic. Some SRAs, such as SRA1 reported on here, do aspire to and for a time achieve the hybrid coalition pattern, but maintaining it is demanding. Hybrid SRAs are also difficult to sustain and renew when sponsors pull out. In this, SRAs are, by analogy with the biological model, truly "hybrid" in that they do not "breed true," suggesting that subsequent generations of SRAs have to be created afresh. This contrasts with the reproduction of more traditional links (e.g., in the United Kingdom, the Teaching Company Scheme), where institutional building blocks are less complex even if the overall building they create makes a less impressive contribution to the wider science base. Where building blocks can be set in place effectively, as, I suggest, is more likely of two-tier SRA research programs, they tend to prevail over much longer periods of time. The success of SRA2 has in fact led in 1997 to the arrival from the sponsoring firm of much more substantial funding for a major building and new research labs. Yet the argument above suggests that it will be very important for the particular parties involved *not* to extend the level of collaboration to a point where the proportion of lab research sponsored and controlled by the firm becomes so large that the two-tier pattern, which allows for lab autonomy to a degree, breaks down in real terms.

In short, it is suggested that a two-track system of SRA is likely to be the best practice for the drug industry (and any other sector seeking to access the scientific waterfront and improve absorptive capacity). This seems to be structurally less problematic and perhaps, because of its more clearly defined internal boundaries between project and program research, more transparent about intellectual property rights and possible conflict of interest. It is also clear that SRAs are much more likely to be found in the pharmaceutical sector than elsewhere. It is clearly true that there are other industries that are as "knowledge-intensive" as the drug industry, such as information technology. Yet the nature of the technology in the latter case, its hard- and software developments, have a much faster turnaround time between inventive step and commercialization and typically involve a wider range of producer-supplier links among firms, not only vertically but even horizontally across firms that have to collaborate to compete. Links with universities are important at an informal level, but formalized long-term deals of an SRA type may be inappropriate to the structure of the market and the pattern of innovation it requires (Rappert and Webster 1996). There are much more important linkages to be made with neighboring firms.

The discussion of SRAs points to the need for much research on how linkage between the pharmaceutical sector and academia is changing. If the formation of SRAs is to continue—as is predicted here—and is to become part of corporate strategy from the center—as is now happening—those corporations and universities with most experience of them need to review this experience, and to identify the demands that they have (against the HC idealized model) and judge whether they have the capacity to meet them. Unfortunately, a number of SRAs have ended or been allowed to peter out in a way that has demoralized their members precisely because of a failure of the participating parties to recognize their structural and cultural needs. The economic and scientific wastage that results from this can be very high.

Science and Technology Knowledge Flows between Industrial and Academic Research: A Comparative Study

JACQUELINE SENKER, WENDY FAULKNER,
and LÉA VELHO

Introduction

This chapter reports on a study that examined companies' interaction with and use of university and government laboratories in three fields of advanced technology—the new biotechnology, advanced engineering ceramics, and parallel computing. The primary aim of this study was to analyze any cross-technology diversity in industry-academia research linkage, in the belief that public policy for such linkage would be more effective if it were grounded in an appreciation of industry's *specific* knowledge needs and *targeted* accordingly.[1] Additional significance for the purpose of this collection lies in the rather novel research design and methodology adopted. Most crucially, this research approach involves a detailed examination of the scientific and technological knowledge companies obtain from university and government laboratories—laboratories that we refer to generically as academic research.[2] We believe that this focus on knowledge flows between academia and industry is necessary if we are to understand why companies interact with academia when they do and in the ways they do.

In contrast to our concern with knowledge flows, most research on the subject of industry-academia research linkage has tended to focus on narrowly institutional aspects: either it has provided an "audit" of the range of formal mechanisms or types of linkage (e.g., CVCP 1981; NSB 1983), or it has investigated specific mechanisms, usually in order to identify particular problems associated with them (e.g., Webster and Constable 1990). Such work has been of considerable value in its own terms. In particular, it has done much to illuminate institutional features of the interaction, including differences in "culture," which may act as barriers. It has also revealed that there is considerable *diversity* in industry linkage with university and government laboratories—diversity both in the extent of that linkage and in the nature of the interactions (e.g., Segal Quince Wickstead 1988). However, few studies have sought to analyze in any detailed or systematic way the reasons for this diversity, or to identify the *limits* to industry-academia research linkage in any one instance. Such research has in the main been descriptive rather than analytical. It does not tell us *why* industry should want to interact with academia institutions, nor does it reveal much about what academia *contributes* to innovation in the process.

These questions have been more central to the innovation literature, with its focus on the industrial viewpoint. The early innovation studies tended to investigate company links with academia institutions as one of many sources contributing inputs to new product ideas and problem solving in the course of research, design, and development (RD&D)[3] leading to innovation. This work has revealed that around two-thirds of these inputs (averaged across sectors) are derived internally, i.e., from in-house RD&D activity and from the expertise held by individual RD&D staff; most of the remainder comes from other companies, often users or suppliers, while the contribution of academia institutions ranges between five and twenty percent of the total (see Rothwell 1977, Pavitt 1984, for a review).

The value of this approach is that the *scale* of the academia contribution is gauged in context—i.e., in relation to the totality of inputs from all sources, internal and external. However, with the exception of the study by Gibbons and Johnston (1974, see below), this work has done little to explore the *content* of the knowledge obtained from university and government laboratories. More recent innovation studies have tended to focus rather on the organizational and management aspects. Nonetheless, work in the emergent discipline of evolutionary economics provides a useful conceptual framework with its interest in the firm's *knowledge base*. Metcalfe and Gibbons (1988), for example, note that a firm's ability to move into new areas of innovative activity is strongly constrained by its existing capability, its "paradigmatic" (i.e., highly selective) view of technological options, and its gatekeeper activities.

Some insights into the content of what academia contributes to industrial innovation have emerged from the literature on the science-technology relation within the "science studies" tradition (e.g., in Barnes and Edge 1982). Three themes in this literature are worth noting. First, from citation studies of patents (e.g., Narin and Noma 1985) and the "technology" literature (Lieberman 1987), we know that industrial researchers in some fields make quite heavy use of the current scientific literature, especially at times when new knowledge is emerging. Second, Derek de Solla Price (1984) noted that science and technology are "linked inseparably" by *instrumentalities*—encompassing the instruments and associated techniques and skills used to conduct experiments and tests—and that instrumentalities are a vital focus of interaction at times of major change in a field.[4] Finally, recent work drawing on the science studies tradition has highlighted that the assumed *transfer* of science and technology from public to private sector generally involves a significant *transformation* of both knowledge and artifacts (e.g., Edge 1992, Peláez 1990).

Each of these literatures has strengths we were keen to integrate into the research design for our study and limitations we wished to avoid. In essence, our research design combines investigation of the *linkage activity*, or mechanisms by which industry interacts with academia (which is common to most studies of industry-academia research linkage), with investigation of the associated science and technology *knowledge flows* from academia to industrial RD&D organizations, which is the novel element (but draws on the innovation and science-technology literatures).

The chapter is in three substantive parts. Section 1 outlines our research design and methodology, and the benefits we believe it holds in this field. Section 2 summarizes the main findings on when, how, and why companies interact with university and government laboratories. Section 3 discusses the similarities and differences that emerged between the three fields; and section 4 summarizes our policy conclusions.

1. Research Design and Methodology

Simply put, our study sought to answer three central questions in each of the three technologies investigated: (i) to what extent do companies interact with university and government laboratories? (ii) how do they interact with academia? and (iii) and why, or what do they get out of interacting with academia? The design we developed in order to do this incorporates five elements.

First, as noted above, *we examine the linkage activity by which industry interacts with academia, and the knowledge flows associated with that interaction*. In this way, our approach attempts to dig deeper than the immediate institutional interface between industry and academia, by extending the focus to the knowledge requirements of the innovating organization, within a conceptual framework that recognizes both the potential economic significance of knowledge emanating from university and government laboratories, and the organizational barriers that make it difficult for firms to perceive and utilize such inputs from academia.

Second, *we investigate industry-academia research linkage from the perspective of the innovating organization*. There is a strong policy rationale for this, given that the burgeoning interest in industry-academia research relations is generally justified in terms of the potential contribution of academic and government research to industrial innovation. But in our view the industry perspective is also important because the most significant limiting factor in industry-academia research linkage is whether firms have need of knowledge and assistance from outside the firm (Fowler 1984).

Third, *knowledge flows from academia are analyzed in terms of* all *the scientific and technological knowledge inputs companies utilise in the course of new product development.* The study of knowledge flows associated with public-private research linkage is rather undeveloped.[5] The first and arguably still the most serious work in this tradition was that conducted by Michael Gibbons and Ron Johnston in 1974. Building on this study, our approach seeks to characterize and classify the range of scientific and technological inputs to innovative RD&D by *type*; to identify the *sources* from which they are obtained and the *channels* through which those emanating from academia enter the firm; and to establish their *impact* on the companies' innovative activities.[6] In this way, the knowledge contribution of academia is assessed in the context of the totality of knowledge inputs from *all* sources—i.e., individual RD&D staff and RD&D activities internally, and other companies and academia externally. The relative significance to innovation of inputs from academia is assessed by a comparison with those obtained from other sources, and the particular contribution of academia to companies' innovative activities is established by analysis of the type and impact of knowledge obtained from academia and other sources. Information on *how* companies access knowledge from academia is generated by reference to the channels used, i.e., the methods used to acquire such knowledge.

Fourth, *data generated (on both knowledge flows and linkage activity) are analyzed comparatively—between different companies in one technology, and between different technologies.* This is intended to expose and explain some of the diversity in the nature and extent of industry-academia research linkage.

Finally, *analysis is grounded in a thorough understanding of the technological field under investigation—at the level of both the sector and the individual company.* This provides the necessary context for understanding why companies embark on linkage with academia in each technology and what is the import of the academic contribution to innovative RD&D in each case.

The three fields chosen for investigation were the new biotechnology, advanced engineering ceramics, and parallel computing. All three technologies are widely seen as new and very promising. They are all the subject of serious industrial RD&D, which has resulted in several specialist products (especially in parallel computing) but has yet to yield the much heralded stream of innovations. The decision to focus on relatively new but promising technologies was made, in part, because such technologies are an important focus of public policy, but also because we might expect firms' efforts to develop their knowledge base by accessing external sources of knowledge to be more transparent in such technologies than in existing areas of competence.

The desire to investigate the subject in some detail, and at the same time to generate comparative data, necessitated an interview-based methodology. The interview schedule addressed the company's organization and strategy for the technology; its academia linkage activity; and the knowledge inputs to innovation. Our investigation of linkage activity aimed to generate reasonable indication of the range and number of academic linkages in the study firms, and of the objectives and benefits or outcomes (expected and actual) of this linkage. Information on the knowledge inputs to innovation was obtained by asking interviewees to complete charts based on the categories of type, source, impact, and channel developed by us.[7] Apart from the use of these charts, the interviews were semi-structured with minimal use of prompts for open-ended questions.

Each interview lasted at least two hours and was either taped and transcribed or written up immediately afterwards. Ideally, we spoke to the Research or Technical Director plus two more junior RD&D staff—usually project managers—in each company, but this was not always possible.[8] Overall, we talked to twelve researchers in biotechnology (four firms), twenty-three in advanced engineering ceramics (twelve firms), and twenty-five in parallel computing (fifteen firms). All of the firms are U.K.-based except for eight of the parallel computing firms, which are based in the United States. The choice of study firms was made by approaching all those identified as being actively engaged in RD&D in the respective fields; only one or two refused to cooperate. In biotechnology we focused on the large established pharmaceutical companies which had embarked on related RD&D during the 1980s. This provided a contrast with the parallel computing firms interviewed, which are mostly small independent startups. The ceramics companies were quite heterogeneous—encompassing users and suppliers, who were mostly large established firms, and processors, who were mostly small or medium sized.

The success of the study in providing some explanation for diversity in industry-academia research linkage and in pointing to some important policy implications (see Section 3 below), represents a powerful vindication of the methodology employed. We would highlight three particular strengths. First, the approach outlined here provides an important element of triangulation, since the central research questions are addressed from a number of different angles, concerning industry-academia research linkage activity on the one hand and the knowledge flows from academia to industry on the other. This has proved positive: in most instances the two types of data either concur or provide complementary insights. Second, the attention paid to the technolog-ical and commercial context, coupled with the collection of data on overall knowledge inputs to innovation, provides the necessary basis for understand-ing both the contribution of academia to innovation and the diversity in indus-try-academia research linkage.

Third and perhaps most profoundly, our categorization of scientific and technological knowledge inputs, embracing as it does artifacts and skills as well as knowledge and information (see 2.3 below), provides a reasonably complete and rounded picture of the character of knowledge used in innova-tion (and thus of the academic contribution). As a result, our approach privi-leges a number of aspects of industry interaction with university and govern-ment laboratories that tend to be neglected by other approaches: the role of informal linkage; flows of tacit knowledge; and the wider contribution of academia to industrial innovation through the literature and training. The *combined* importance of these features highlights the limitations of studies of academia-industrial linkage which focus exclusively either on audits of for-mal linkage activity or on bibliometric indicators of collaborations and knowledge flows between industry and academia.

2. Main Findings

Below is a summary of the results of the three technology studies, focusing in turn on the three central questions: when, how, and why companies interact with university and government laboratories.

2.1. To What Extent Do Companies Interact with Academia?

Evidence on how much companies interact with academia in each technology comes chiefly from (i) an audit of the *extent of linkage activities*, both formal and informal, and (ii) data comparing the *relative significance of different sources* in terms of their contribution to knowledge used in innovative RD&D.

Comparative data on the extent and range of formal (i.e., contractual) linkage activity is presented in Table 5.1. It is apparent that the pharmaceuti-cal firms in biotechnology are the most active in this regard and the parallel computing firms least so. Cutting across technologies, the larger-scale forms of academia linkage generally involve only the larger companies. By contrast,

TABLE 5.1
Range and number of formal linkages with academic research

Type of Linkage	Biotechnology	Engineering Ceramics	Parallel Computing
		Technology	
Bilateral Links			
consultants	4	5	9
studentships	5	2	—
post-doctoral fellowships	1	—	—
affiliate or graduate recruitment programs	—	—	6
use of instrumentation	—	9*	—
customer links	—	—	10*
licensing	—	—	2
RD&D contracts	6	4*	4
campus laboratories	2	1	—
Government Supported Links			
studentships	4	7	2
collaborative RD&D	2	1	5#
interfirm RD&D	3	17#	—
number of firms	4	12	15

* These include some semi-formal "barter" arrangments
\# only some of these projects involved academia

informal linkage plays a major role in all firms. Although it is difficult to generate meaningful quantitative data on such interaction, our interviews revealed that the incidence of informal linkage activity dramatically exceeds that of formal linkage activity. Moreover, far more knowledge flows through informal personal interaction than through formalized linkage.

The scale of academia's *knowledge* contribution to innovative RD&D is gauged by comparing the relative significance or use of different sources of knowledge inputs to company RD&D. It is notable that in all three technologies internal sources are more important than external sources, although a sizeable minority of respondents in both biotechnology and ceramics reported that external sources were more important than internal ones. In line with this general finding, but contrary to earlier evidence (see Rothwell 1977), researchers in all three technologies reported that new product ideas are also derived primarily from internal sources. However, our interviewees repeatedly stressed the link between knowledge generated internally and that obtained from external sources. Thus, for example, ideas for new product development tend to "coalesce," often stimulated by inputs from outside the firm; internal ideas are often checked with external sources; and considerable in-house development work is needed in order to transform external ideas into a marketable product. While the predominance of internal sources is universally acknowledged, so too is the need to know what's going on outside through search activity.

There was more divergence on the relative significance of different *external* sources, which is in line with the divergence on the extent of formal linkage activity. Biotechnology is the only field in which the contribution of academia was judged to be greater than or equal to that of other companies. In engineering ceramics the responses were fairly evenly split between academia and other companies. The contribution from other companies is explained by the vital importance to innovation of information on the specifications and performance of individual ceramic materials and components, which is exchanged across a dense network linking users, suppliers, and processors. In parallel computing, the most important external source of knowledge inputs to RD&D was either other companies—software firms, hardware suppliers, users, and (in the United States especially) competitors—or other companies and academia equally.

2.2. How Do Companies Interact with Academic Research?

Details on how companies interact with academic research are provided by investigation of (i) the *nature of the different linkage* activities, and (ii) the *channels* though which company researchers obtain scientific and technological knowledge from academia.

2.2.1. Nature of linkage activity. The formal linkage mechanisms listed in Table 5.1 may be grouped in terms of cost. The main low-cost linkages are consultants and studentships. The most common large-scale linkage is the contracting of RD&D projects to academic or government laboratories; campus laboratories involve a substantial investment over several years. In ceramics most collaborative projects are supported by government (through U.K. Department of Trade and Industry or European Union schemes) and involve several firms as well as universities.

Informal linkage is often both precursor and successor of formal linkage. Indeed, formal linkages often flounder in the absence of friendly relations between research staff at the bench level. But informal interaction with personal contacts also takes place *quite apart* from any formal agreements—for instance, any time an industrial researcher picks up the phone to speak to an academic contact, or chats with them at a conference or meeting. In all cases, networks of academic contacts are actively pursued and maintained. In parallel computing and ceramics, this tends to be focused on a relatively small number of academic institutions working in specific areas, whereas in biotechnology researchers are actively encouraged to develop and maintain a strong network of academic contacts across a range of specialties relevant to their work. A general feature of links with academic researchers is the use of non-contractual *barter arrangements*: e.g., exchanging research materials or access to equipment in biotechnology[9] and ceramics, or discounting machines or maintenance in return for test or performance data in parallel computing.

2.2.2. Channels for knowledge from academia. Company researchers obtain knowledge from academia mostly by a combination of reading the research literature and interacting with personal contacts, and occasionally by directly recruiting academic experts. Published sources of knowledge from academia include abstracts, textbooks, and on-line databases as well as scientific and engineering journals. Personal contacts include consultants or other contractors and collaborators, former colleagues, or people met in the course of work. New contacts tend to be sought out very purposively—e.g., through reading and going out to conferences and visiting laboratories. There is some divergence in the amount of working time spent travelling away from the firm to network and gather information, even among large firms; researchers in smaller companies rely almost exclusively on existing personal contacts (or chance meetings) and on reading.

Table 5.2 suggests an interesting divergence in terms of the relative use of publications and personal contacts, with biotechnology researchers relying more on the literature and parallel computing researchers relying far more on contacts. The heavy use of publications by biotechnology researchers is probably general to pharmaceutical companies, which have highly developed

TABLE 5.2
Relative Use of Different Channels for Obtaining Knowledge from Academia

	Technology		
Channel	*Biotechnology*	*Engineering Ceramics*	*Parallel Computing*
literature	55%	42%	3%
contacts	36%	49%	68%
recruitment	11%	10%	10%

NB: these percentages are based on aggregated responses (60 interviewees) on the impact of knowledge inputs obtained from academic research by these main channels.

information services geared to making full use of the external literature. In addition, the volume of academic research in biotechnology is far greater than that in engineering ceramics (which is a relatively neglected area of research), and much of the emerging knowledge in biotechnology has been codified in the last decade. By contrast, researchers in parallel computing complained that the research interests of academia in this field (as reflected in the literature) are often too abstract or tangential to be of much practical value.

The literature and contacts provide quite distinct types of knowledge, and are often used in tandem. Publications are generally a vital initial source to scan for new developments or contacts, and to access relevant knowledge and information about specific research or test procedures. But industrial researchers tend in the second instance to approach personal contacts—for further information or clarification, or for an informed judgment, an outside reflection, or interpretation of the material read. Crucially, personal contacts provide tacit knowledge not available in research articles, which is essential if researchers wish to implement or adapt experimental practices and procedures specified in these articles (Senker 1993). In biotechnology especially, personal contacts also allow industrial researchers to find out about new techniques as they arise, through the "unpublished grapevine."

Recruitment of experienced researchers from academia is used only occasionally to acquire specific capabilities—e.g., in experimentation and testing, or in searching for future opportunities. Our evidence indicates an important relationship between recruitment and academic linkage, however. While the buildup of specialist RD&D teams in new or unfamiliar fields demands that firms bring in additional specialist staff at some stage, recruitment is rarely the first step by which firms acquire capability in a new technological field. Companies in both biotechnology and engineering ceramics have linked up with academic research in order to extend their *existing* knowledge base and learn something about the specialty before committing themselves in this way.

2.3. Why Do Companies Interact with Academia?

The crucial question of why companies interact with academia is approached by asking what it is that companies obtain from this source. Insight into the contribution of academia to innovative RD&D comes from investigation of: (i) evidence on the *benefits* resulting from specific linkages; (ii) a broad overview of the *types of knowledge* obtained from different sources; and (iii) analysis of the *impacts* of the knowledge from these sources on companies' innovative activities.

2.3.1. The benefits of linkage activity. Interviewees identified a range of benefits from formal and informal linkage activity, but academia is most commonly used and valued in four areas: networking and keeping abreast of academic research; general and specific assistance; access to specific expertise; and public relations and goodwill.

As noted above, personal contacts and the research literature are used to keep abreast of academic research. This emerged as a very important benefit of linkage in both ceramics and biotechnology though relatively less so in parallel computing.

The area of general and specific assistance includes general help, advice and information, and the opportunity for open-ended discussion; this was frequently reported as a major benefit of ongoing friendly relations with academic contacts. Nonetheless, academic or government researchers are more commonly approached for help with *specific* problems or queries. Very often the help provided by academia is in the area of assistance with experimentation. In biotechnology, where new enabling research techniques are emerging all the time, this appears to be the greatest single area of benefit on linkage with academia. In contrast, researchers in ceramics value access to new and expensive research equipment, and the related expertise needed to interpret results. This is because RD&D in this field focuses on understanding the behavior of individual materials under specific conditions. Significantly, academic assistance with instrumentation is negligible in parallel computing because companies use their *own* machines to test and develop new systems.

In general, companies only fund academic research in areas where they lack the expertise in house. This may occur because the piece of research is deemed to be peripheral to the company's RD&D interests, so contracting is cheaper than employing somebody on a permanent basis. Or, as noted above, linkage with academic research may be used strategically—to help companies build up capability in new or previously unfamiliar technologies, in advance of recruiting new staff with the expertise.

Public relations benefits were frequently cited in relation to low-cost linkages. For example, companies value hosting students (studentships), even though the scientific or technical contribution is usually marginal, because of the opportunity for the industrial researcher to test and build up a relationship with student's supervisor; they may also result in future recruitment. More generally, it is hoped that the goodwill developed in informal interaction, including barter arrangements, will encourage academic contacts to come to the company (rather than a competitor or not at all) if they come up with a good idea or relevant breakthrough, or wish to collaborate, at any point in the future.

In both ceramics and parallel computing, academic laboratories made notable material contributions to product development during firms' early involvement in the technology. More typically, academic contributions to new product development tend to be in providing indirect and instrumental inputs to problem solving. In this area and in the provision of strategic advice by academic contacts, company researchers value the assurance of the outside expert view or reflection.

In parallel computing, the largest number of linkage activities is with the strategically vital customer base in university and government laboratories, and the chief group of benefits flows from the crucial role played by these laboratories in the development of the technology. From the outset, academic users were able and willing to take risks and experiment on the early machines, and many companies still rely heavily on academic users for test data and feedback on system performance. Companies also benefit considerably from the publicity that results from having prominent academic users.

2.3.2. Types of knowledge from academia. Table 5.3 summarizes the responses of researchers in each technology on the relative importance to RD&D of four

TABLE 5.3
Types and Sources of Scientific and
Technological Knowledge Inputs to Innovation

Source of Knowledge (by field)	Type of Knowledge Input			
	Knowledge of Particular Fields	Technical Information	Skills	Knowledge Related to Artifacts
INTERNAL				
Biotechnology			**TACIT**	tacit
Ceramics			**TACIT**	**TACIT***
Parallel computing			**TACIT**	tacit
OTHER COMPANIES				
Biotechnology		formal		tacit
Ceramics		**FORMAL/ tacit**		tacit
Parallel computing	**tacit**	**formal/tacit**		**tacit/formal**
ACADEMIA				
Biotechnology	**FORMAL**	formal		tacit
Ceramics	**FORMAL**			tacit
Parallel computing	**FORMAL**	formal/tacit	tacit	

NB: Heaviness of types indicates the importance of the knowledge inputs in each box.
* This relates to production equipment; in the other fields, "arteficts" refers to research equipment.

broad categories of knowledge: knowledge of particular fields, technical information, skills, and knowledge related to artifacts (used in research or production).[10] It also indicates the degree to which these inputs are formal (i.e., codified) or tacit; and the general sources from which they are obtained.

The importance of different types of knowledge varies somewhat between technologies. However, virtually all of those interviewed claim to rely more heavily on tacit knowledge and related skills—the "learning by doing" acquired largely "on the job" and transferred as people change jobs. The importance of formal knowledge—acquired largely from academia, through education and reading the literature—was also acknowledged by all. Thus, the picture that emerges is one of tacit knowledge and skills building on and supplementing codified knowledge. Significantly, our evidence on knowledge flows between personal contacts reveals that, despite the emphasis on "on the job" learning, academia also contributes to the tacit knowledge used in RD&D (see Senker and Faulkner 1995).

2.3.3. The impact of knowledge inputs from academia. Data on the impact of knowledge from different sources on companies' innovative activities were compiled by asking interviewees to identify one or two sources of knowledge contributing most to thirteen different aspects of RD&D. The data show clearly that academia makes a major contribution to "scanning the research frontier" and "underpinning knowledge" in all three technologies.[11] This finding concurs with the importance attached to linkage for "keeping abreast of developments in academia."

In the activities associated with instrumentalities—"research equipment," "RD&D procedures," and "skills in experimentation and testing"—knowledge from academia appears to make a notable impact in engineering ceramics,[12] confirming our findings on the reported value of academic linkage in providing assistance with experimentation in this field. The academic contribution to instrumentalities is insignificant in parallel computing, reflecting our finding that parallel computers are themselves the main "instrumentalities" in this field. However, our data appear to understate the value of the academic contribution to research techniques and skills in biotechnology reported in both this and an earlier study (Faulkner 1986). Similarly, the reported benefits of academic research linkage in providing practical assistance with problem solving appears to conflict with our finding that internal sources contribute chiefly to "routine problem solving." This latter finding serves as a reminder that most problems that emerge in the course of RD&D are solved internally, and that academia help with specific problem solving is usually partial and indirect. Finally, the findings for parallel computing show a higher academic contribution to "articulation of user needs," "feedback on existing products," and, to a lesser extent, "scanning for new applications," which concurs with our evidence on the benefits of linkage with academic users in this field.

3. Analysis and Implications

The main similarities and differences between the technologies are outlined in Table 5.4. As expected, the strength and character of industry linkage with academic research does vary between the three fields studied, highlighting the need for more targeted policies. But our study also revealed significant areas of convergence. As we show below, some of these findings appear to challenge accepted wisdom in the area of policy for industry-academic linkage.

3.1. Cross-Technology Diversity in Industry-Academia Research linkage

Clear cross-technology differences emerged in the extent of formal linkage activity; in the relative significance of knowledge inputs from academia; and in some of the specific knowledge contributions from academic to industrial RD&D. There is no existing literature to guide our interpretation of this variance. However, analysis of our contextual data suggests that it may be related to a number of factors. Advanced engineering ceramics is illustrative. In this field, supply chain knowledge flows are more important to innovation than knowledge from academia. The level of industry-academia linkage activity is limited—and the future prospects made uncertain—by the generally lower level of academic research funding and dynamism in the field (compared with biotechnology) and by bottlenecks to the wider application of advanced ceramics caused by the lack of fundamental understanding about how they behave in different conditions. On the other hand, government funding supports a large proportion of formal industry-academia research linkage in ceramics, which counteracts to a considerable degree the barriers of size experienced by small U.S. parallel computing firms who do not benefit from government support for collaboration with academia.

We have developed a taxonomy of the factors that appear to underlie the cross-technology differences in the strength and character of industry-academia research linkage between the three fields we studied (see Faulkner and Senker 1994). The significant factors relate not only to issues of firm size and sector characteristics, identified above, but also to the knowledge base of both academia and companies, and to the character of the technology itself. The complex and interrelated nature of these factors defy any simple explanatory model of all diversity in industry-academia research linkage. We nonetheless believe that the taxonomy represents an important step toward more systematic understanding of these interactions and, at a minimum, is broadly applicable to other fields of advanced technology. Additional factors might prove important in other technological fields; geography and location, for example, are probably more important in established and traditional sectors than they appear to be here.

Our findings on the diversity in industry-academia research linkage confirm that policies to promote linkage which approach "industry" non-selectively, can only be partially effective. It is crucial that initiatives in this area be based on an understanding of companies' specific knowledge requirements in particular sectors and technologies, and targeted on those areas where linkage with academia is most likely to be appropriate.

The taxonomy developed in this study could be used as a tool to identify which sectors or technological fields might be appropriate targets for intervention; it highlights issues to be scrutinized in judging the chances of strong linkage in any one field and at any one time. Similarly, one could adapt the knowledge flow indicators used in this study to combine analysis of industry's knowledge requirements in a technology with audits of the strengths and weaknesses of academic and government research, in order to establish what specific knowledge requirements could be met from academia. Such an exercise could provide essential contextual information, both for intermediaries seeking to promote industry-academia research linkage locally and for the development of government policy to support strategically important new technologies.

3.2. The Knowledge Contribution of Academia to Innovation

Our exploration of the question, what do companies get from their interactions with academic laboratories, produced strong cross-technology convergence in terms of the *general nature* of the inputs obtained from academia , alongside the specific differences noted above. Thus, taking together the evidence on the benefits of linkage activity and on the type and impact of knowledge from academia, our study shows that academia contributes to innovative RD&D in three distinct ways: (i) in the training of qualified scientists and engineers, with formal knowledge of specialist fields; (ii) as a potent source of new knowledge in these fields; and (iii) as a source of practical help and assistance, including the area of instrumentalities (except for parallel computing).

Keeping abreast of the research frontier allows industrial RD&D staff to access new knowledge that underpins in-house RD&D efforts and, occasionally, offers new opportunities for exploitation. These findings emphasize the

TABLE 5.4
Main Similarities and Differences Cross-Technology

Questions	Technology		
	Biotechnology	*Ceramics*	*Parallel Computing*
1) what is the extent of interaction with PSR?			
1.1 extent of formal linkage	high	varied	low
1.2 extent of informal linkage	(extensive *in all fields*)		
1.3 future trends in linkage activity	continuing high level	limited prospects	mixed
1.4 relative contribution of STI sources	other companies < PSR (internal > external *in all fields*)	other companies = PSR	other companies ≥ PSR
2) how do companies interact with PSR?			
2.1 nature of formal linkage activity	some very large-scale linkage	facilitated by government programs	primarily customer links
2.2 nature of informal linkage activity	(*in all fields*: active networking; trust building is important, bartering common)		
2.3 channels for obtaining STI from PSR	literature > contacts	literature = contacts	literature < contacts

(continued on next page)

TABLE 5.4 (continued)
Main Similarities and Differences Cross-Technology

Questions	Technology		
	Biotechnology	Ceramics	Parallel Computing
3) why do companies interact with PSR?			
3.1 most common benefits of linkage activity	assistance with experimentation	keeping abreast of PSR	feedback on products and marketing
	(*in all fields*: keeping up with research frontier; general and specific assistance; access to expertise in strategic and peripheral areas; goodwill)		
3.2 types of STI from PSR	primarily knowledge	knowledge + skills and artifacts	knowledge + technical information
3.3 impact of STI from PSR	+ instrumentalities	+ instrumentalities	+ future innovation
	(*in all fields*: scanning research frontier and underpinning knowledge)		

general importance to industry of the basic research carried out in academia, and so flies in the face of calls for academia to move away from basic research in order to become more market oriented and more "relevant" to industry. Significantly, our data indicate that the flow of material inputs to new product development from academia into industry is negligible, despite the current policy emphasis on the commercialization of academic inventions (see 3.3 below). On the other hand, the practical assistance provided by academia in the area of experimentation and instrumentalities has been emphasized (at least in biotechnology and ceramics). This evidence provides further support for de Solla Price's (1984) contention that instrumentalities are a crucial area of overlap and interaction between academic research and industrial innovation, and his recommendation that capital equipment should have higher prominence in the allocation of resources for academic research.

Our overall assessment of the areas in which academia contributes to industrial innovation confirms that made by Martin and Irvine in 1981, but its conclusions are still to be taken fully on board in policy circles. Arguably the most crucial factor influencing the level of industrial interest in interacting with university and government laboratories is the extent to which relevant new knowledge and opportunities are emerging from within these institutions. Our findings lend weight to the concerns expressed by some academics and industrialists, that academia is being diverted from producing the types of knowledge most useful to it by the emphasis on specific products and commercializable results (see Dimancescu and Botkin 1986; Feller 1990; Senker 1991). What is important is that government and academia listen to industry's demand for academia to conduct basic research, and to target such research in areas of strategic interest to industry.

3.3. The Importance of Informal Interaction and Knowledge Flows between Academia and Industry

Two major areas of commonality emerged on the question of *how* industry interacts with academia. First, flowing from the discussion above, academia's contribution to innovation generally takes the form of indirect, intangible, and largely invisible flows of ideas, knowledge, and expert assistance; like Feller (1990) and Martin and Irvine (1981), we found the flow of discrete commercializable artifacts or patented ideas from academia to be negligible. A huge amount of effort has been channelled into commercializing and patenting research results emanating from university and government laboratories in the last decade or so. Like Feller, we believe that this effort may be disproportionate to the benefits that can realistically be expected to result. Yet it seems the message has still not got across. The heroic language of technology transfer, in which spectacular breakthroughs are almost instantly transformed into profitable innovations, is still widely prevalent in the discourse of policy makers, be they local economic development agents or central government advisers.

The other related area of commonality is that, while there is considerable variety in the range and scale of formal linkage activity, all companies benefit from strong networks of personal contacts in academia. Our analysis indicates that the overwhelming majority of the knowledge that flows from academia into industry does so via *informal* rather than formal linkage. This can be explained on three counts. First, most of industry's knowledge requirements are specific and small scale, and arise suddenly in the course of RD&D; in most cases such knowledge transfer simply does not lend itself to contractual agreements. Second, there are considerable tacit and skill-based elements in the expertise industrial researchers seek and obtain when they interact with academia, which cannot generally be obtained from the literature (Senker and Faulkner 1995). And third, trust building, mutual respect, and understanding are vital prerequisites to success in formal industry-academia research relations; and these are most easily built up informally—witness the importance of barter arrangements and the emphasis on positive informal relationships *at the bench level* that emerges from our and other research (e.g., MacKenzie and Rhys Jones 1985). Our findings on the combined importance of informal interaction and of reading the literature provide a much-needed perspective on the current preoccupation with formal linkage activity, especially large-scale collaboration. While such collaborations can have a considerable impact individually, we believe the emphasis on them is misplaced—just as the emphasis on technology transfer of tangible products is misplaced.

Such policy implications are unlikely to find a receptive audience in academic institutions that, without exception, are making strenuous efforts to increase their research revenues from non-government sources by formalizing industry relations and securing intellectual property rights. But informal interaction is of enormous economic significance *in its own right*, and much of this interaction simply could not be captured by formal agreements. Indeed, there is a real danger that attempts to formalize such interactions would merely inhibit them and, as a consequence, limit the scope for subsequent formal collaboration. Contrary to popular assumptions, our findings indicate that the scale of expenditure on industry-academic research linkage activities does not necessarily correlate with the benefits to industry. If the objective of public policy is to maximize the contribution of academia to industrial innovation, then it is clear to us that what matters far more than the number of formal research or licensing agreements is the number of "communication channels" at which the less "spectacular" flows of knowledge and assistance take place informally between academia and industry. We have called this a "dating agency" approach, in contrast to the current "marriage brokerage" approach (Faulkner and Senker 1995).

3.4. The Limited Role of Industry-Academia Research Linkage in Industrial Innovation

Our analysis of knowledge flows in innovation has proved useful in placing the contribution of academia in context. Our findings provide clear confirmation that company RD&D is the dominant source of knowledge to innovation, including new product ideas. Even in new technological fields, where external research linkages are likely to be stronger, firms still rely heavily on their existing knowledge base and in-house efforts. We have here a strong reminder (if one were needed) that external research linkage is no substitute for internal capability. For cost and capability reasons companies will generally only fund academia in areas complementary to their own efforts—a crucial point, often overlooked in discussions of the limitations to industry-academia research linkage (Fowler 1984). Companies interact with government and academic research when they have specific reasons for doing so, and not because in general "it is a good thing." This is probably the most intractable barrier to any sizeable increase in company links with academia, and has policy implications for both government and company strategists.

The case of engineering ceramics demonstrates that public-sector support can result in linkage taking place where (for reasons of size) it might not have occurred otherwise. But this technology highlights an important caveat, namely that the strength of the academia base is also a major determinant of the *scope* of public-private research linkage. So industry-academia research linkage is no substitute for government funding of academic research: public policy seeking to promote the development of promising new technologies must *integrate* the main instruments available—i.e., training and research support as well as collaboration—if it is to be effective (Senker 1991). Moreover, the importance to innovation of knowledge flows between other companies, especially those in the supply chain, and of market and production related knowledge as well as RD&D, reminds us that research or science policy is only one element in innovation policy. It is to be hoped that the current interest in understanding national systems of innovation will take on board the complex knowledge networks that characterize the innovation process.

With respect to company strategy, it is clearly difficult for companies to move into new or unfamiliar fields of technology. While external research linkage is no substitute for in-house capability, the picture that emerges from our study is one of innovation involving a *synthesis* of diverse types of knowledge inputs from a range of both internal and external sources (see also Gibbons and Johnston 1974; Pavitt 1984 and 1991). This reminds us that the role of company RD&D is not only to produce knowledge but also to access, absorb, and transform externally held knowledge. Several authors stress the paradox that firms' ability to monitor, evaluate, and utilize external knowledge is strongly dependent on the strength of their in-house expertise, or "absorptive capacity" in the field. In particular, basic research carried out in house gives companies the ability to recognize and interpret the potential value of the basic research conducted in academia, and to decide which areas they should move into (Nelson 1982; Rosenberg 1990; Gambardella 1992). The implication of this, confirmed by our field experience, is that the buildup of capability in a new and unfamiliar field must be an incremental and iterative process, carefully managed and monitored.

4. Policy Conclusions

In summary, the findings and analysis presented above point clearly to the following policy conclusions:

1. The potential for useful industry linkage with academic research varies considerably. There should be greater efforts to target industry-academia research linkage in areas of greatest scope and likely benefit. The potential for linkage could be assessed strategically in terms of companies' *specific* knowledge requirements in particular sectors and technologies.
2. Industry is helped to innovate most by knowledge and expertise arising from the basic research carried out in the public sector. Thus, the current concern of academic institutions to increase income from industry and/or to improve the commercialization of academic research should not divert their efforts toward short-term, applied research and away from long-term, basic research. Similarly, in selecting their priorities for funding, governments should take account of the *strategic* research needs of industry, rather than succumb to short-termism. Within this, funders of academic research should also bear in mind the importance of providing adequate resources for experimental facilities, including research instrumentation and technicians.
3. By far the greatest contribution of academia to innovation takes the form of indirect and intangible flows of knowledge, and the bulk of these knowledge flows occurs through the literature and informal interaction. The current policy emphasis on technology transfer efforts to commercialize academic "inventions," and on large-scale formal collaborations, is therefore misplaced and out of proportion with the benefits which ensue. The main way to increase academia's contribution to innovation is to increase the

number of communication channels (and thus knowledge flows) between academia and industry; a "dating agency" approach should replace the current "marriage brokerage" approach.

4. The majority of the knowledge used in innovation necessarily comes from in-house capability; and this is an inevitable limit on industry-academia research linkage. While such linkage can be a valuable stepping stone for companies moving into new or unfamiliar fields, it is no substitute for in-house capability; this must be built up incrementally. Similarly, government support for research linkage cannot compensate for a weak knowledge base in academia; public policy seeking to promote promising new technologies must integrate efforts in research funding, training, and collaboration.

CHAPTER 6

Science Parks and Innovation Centers

RIKARD STANKIEWICZ

Introduction

As measured by the rate of their diffusion, science parks and innovation centers are among the most successful institutional innovations in the field of science and technology policy. In recent decades, hundreds of them have been created throughout the industrialized and industrializing world. However, the enthusiasm that accompanied them in the 1970s and '80s has now been replaced by a growing skepticism. In fact, today many of them are experiencing a profound identity crisis. In this chapter I will try to sum up the experience to date and point out some implications for the design, management, and future prospects of science parks seen primarily in the context of promoting university-industry interactions.

Models and Expectations

The development of science parks and innovation centers constitutes an interesting example of institutional evolution where certain early, more or less spontaneous social innovations are "replicated" in new environments. In the case of SPs the original models have been provided by the agglomerations of dynamic high-tech businesses along Route 128 in Massachusetts and in Stanford, California. A similar model development has occurred in Britain around Cambridge. These original "phenomena" have been analyzed by a number of scholars,[1] who identified a range of factors contributing to their success. The lack of space precludes a detailed summary of their findings. However, the following factors seem to stand out as particularly important:

1. *Technology*: each of the developments has been riding on an "innovation wave" following the emergence of new major generic technologies. One essential features of these technologies was the fact that new technical ventures could be started with relatively modest inputs of capital.

2. *General economic climate*: in each case there was a favorable conjunction of economic and political circumstances.
3. *Demand*: in each case there was a massive demand pull from other high-tech industries (especially defense and space) localized in the area.
4. *Leadership*: in each case there was a clear commitment on the part of key actors within the academic infrastructure to the promotion of technological innovation.

The other crucial factors were:

5. *The quality of the R&D infrastructure*: the presence in the area of several outstanding R&D and educational institutions at the forefront of technological development.
6. *Industrial infrastructure*: the existence of a constellation of complementary industrial activities.
7. *Skilled labor*: a pool of technologically skilled workers at several levels of sophistication.
8. *Culture*: a general familiarity with and encouragement of entrepreneurial behavior.
9. *Institutions*: the presence of adequate economic, especially financial, infrastructure.

When most of these factors are present simultaneously in a given locality, a snowballing process of industrial innovation may be initiated. That process becomes self-sustaining due to "agglomeration externalities" (Dorfman 1983) manifesting themselves, among others, in the rapid diffusion of technical, managerial, and marketing skills and knowledge through personnel mobility, informal know-how trading, and through the mediation of public R&D and educational institutions.

The spectacular successes of Route 128, the Silicon Valley, and Cambridge were bound to set off attempts elsewhere to create similar developments. The process of social emulation, however, is far from simple. It involves the elements of abstraction, rationalization, and mythologization of the original models as well as their modification and adaptation to the specific circumstances under which they are being "replicated." This process of imperfect copying creates an institutional variety that while enhancing the process of evolution of an institution tends to confound its students.

Just what is abstracted and rationalized depends on many factors, among which interests and, in particular, action constraints are particularly important. Simplifying things somewhat, we could say that deliberate efforts to reproduce the original "phenomena" occurred at three levels:

1. On the one hand, attempts have been made in several places to replicate the gross features of the successful spontaneous "high-tech centers." The concept of *technopolis* has a strong urban/regional dimension and generally involves an attempt to simultaneously enhance as many as possible of the success factors identified above.[2] This may include regionally coordinated policies in education, physical infrastructure, transport and communications, R&D policy, science parks, and various procurement and business promotion schemes. Programs of this kind, if they are to be successful, require the command of considerable economic and political resources and can be successful only in the long run. The most famous of them has been MITI's program in the '80s involving setting up nineteen technopolises. The Japanese example has been emulated in many European countries that saw the technopolis approach as the means of vitalizing industrially backward or declining regions.[3]

2. At the second, less ambitious level, attention is focused on just a few factors which are regarded as strategic. The promotion of *science parks* belongs to this category. Compared with technopolises the parks are much more restricted in spatial and institutional terms. Some science parks such as, for example, the Research Triangle in North Carolina exhibit certain features of the "technopolis model," others are hardly more than glorified real property development schemes. Indeed, in most cases the concept of "science park" is an amalgam of several elements, which occasionally conflict with each other. It is therefore difficult to define them exactly. For our purposes, the best solution is to follow the definition proposed by the UK Science Parks Association, which requires science parks:

   (i)   to have formal and operational links with a university, other higher education institution, or research center;
   (ii) to be designed to encourage the formation and growth of knowledge-based businesses; and
   (iii) to have a management function that is actively engaged in the transfer of technology and business skills.

So defined science parks may or may not allow manufacturing operations on their premises. (In the latter case they are usually referred to as "research parks.") They may have among their tenants both commercial and non-commercial organizations. The firms may be business startups, established companies, or R&D departments and centers of companies located elsewhere.

The great advatage of science parks is that the policies involved are relatively straightforward and do not require massive use of economic and political resources. After all, what is proposed is an improved utilization of an already existing resource such as a university. The assumption is that a park, or a similar institution, will somehow be able to initiate a virtuous cycle of development, thus compensating for the absence or weakness of other factors normally associated with rapid development of high-tech industries.

3. By *innovation center* or *incubator* we will mean here a smaller development, confined to a building or a few buildings, often but not necessarily located within a science park and dedicated to providing fairly elementary support to small technology-based startups. The mix of services varies considerably from case to case, but it often includes the following elements (Stankiewicz 1986): (i) formal courses on various subjects relevant to entrepreneurship; (ii) assistance to inventors interested in carrying out a commercial/technical assessment of their ideas; (iii) assistance in the promotion of the necessary contacts with potential business partners, and financial institutions; (iv) provision of rudimentary facilities and technical expertise necessary for further development of the technologies involved.

In this chapter I will abstain from any attempt to evaluate the merits/demerits of technopolises and concentrate instead on science parks and innovation centers. The rapid proliferation of these schemes occurred in the United States in the '70s and in Europe in the '80s. Several factors have contributed to that development. The already-mentioned relative simplicity and comparative cheapness of the concept were important considerations. Others included the need on the part of the universities to look for alternative sources of funds for themselves and for employment opportunities for their graduates, the general change of climate regarding university-industry relations, the great hope for the technology-led recovery from the "stagflation" of the late '70s and early '80s and the upsurge of regionalism in industrial policy that followed in the wake of structural changes brought about by the IT-revolution and the globalization of the world's economies.

On a more conceptual level we can identify three types of rationale for the creation of science parks and innovation centers: (i) the expectation of improved knowledge and technology transfer from universities to industry, particularly through the creation of new firms; (ii) the hope that the development in the parks of "dense technical communities" would generate lateral flows of technical and commercial know-how among the tenant firms leading to creative chain reactions; and (iii) the belief that the existence of parks would result in long-term cultural and institutional changes in both the academic and industrial communities, making the interactions between the two easier. The last argument has been particularly important in Europe (Stankiewicz 1986).

The above three "rationales" rest in their turn on a number of other more general and, in themselves, highly plausible assumptions, including: i) *The interactionist theory of creativity*, according to which invention and innovations, especially radical ones, depend on interactions among heterogeneous bodies of knowledge and cultures;[4] and ii) *The proximity hypothesis*, according to which physical closeness is important for the creation and sustaining of such interactions.[5]

Recently, however, the ability of the parks to live up to these expectations and to vindicate the assumptions underlying them has come to be questioned. Let us therefore briefly review the current debate on the merits and demerits of the parks.

Performance

Despite a considerable literature on the subject, reliable broadly based assessments of the performance of science parks continue to be quite scarce. Many specific case studies, evaluations, and "lessons from experience" (see, among others, Gibbs, ed. 1985) are available and many more can be expected in the coming years. Perhaps the best systematic empirical effort to date has been the study of the British parks by Monck et al. (1988). A more comprehensive critique of the concept of science park has been attempted by Massey et al. (1992) and Quintas et al. (1993).

What sort of picture does emerge from this literature?

The General Assessments

General assessments of "science parks," while common enough, are rarely based on any systematic empirical evidence. Most of them are made in relation to the expectations concerning the parks. In most cases the conclusion is that these expectations have not been realistic. Cautionary comments started appearing in the early '80s when science park enthusiasm was at its peak (see, for instance, Segal 1982 and OTA 1984). The intrinsic difficulties of engineering a Silicon Valley phenomenon have been stressed by, among others, Miller and Coté (1987). In the same year, MacDonald published a paper in R&D Management which pronounced the parks a failure. An almost equally negative assessment was recently made by Van Dierdonck et al. (1991) and by Massey et al. (1992). They contrast with a much more positive conclusion drawn earlier by Monck et al. (1988), who stated that: "There can be little doubt that Science Parks have made a promising and useful contribution to economic development in the UK." However, even in that analysis there are many ambivalent findings.

Let us therefore briefly review the more specific results of these studies and relate them to the three types of rationale behind the parks, which we listed in the preceding section.

The Effects of the Parks on the Technology Transfer from Universities to Industry

Several studies report ambivalent findings regarding the ability of parks to enhance interactions between universities and industry. On one hand, it is clear that many parks have been quite successful in attracting tenants and that most of the tenants are quite satisfied with their locations in the parks. On the other, it is an almost uniform finding that the proximity to a university is rarely mentioned as a major motive for firms to move into a science park in the first place. The pattern of communication and collaboration between the firm and the university departments is also rather disappointing. Both Monck et al. and Van Dierdonck et al. find that direct R&D collaboration between the firms and the universities does not seem to be greatly enhanced by the parks. Both studies also report that the resident firms when recruiting their scientists and engineers do not seem to be biased in favor of the local university. Nor are there many other formal ties such as student projects, etc.

On the other hand, there is considerable evidence (see especially Monck et al.) that the informal communication and the use of university facilities are indeed enhanced by residency in a park. Furthermore, it appears that links to the university are the strongest among small startup firms, especially the spin-offs from the academia. Thus, there is evidence that the parks do play a positive role in encouraging and facilitating entrepreneurial behavior among academics. The ability of academic spin-offs to contribute to the development and diffusion of sophisticated technologies is also confirmed by the fact that they are often run by scientists and engineers with higher qualifications, and operate more closely to the leading edge of technology, than is normally the case among high-tech firms outside the parks. However, as has been pointed out by, among others, Monck et al., the firms started and owned by academia tend to grow more slowly than those owned "professionally." Consequently, the direct economic impact of the academic spinoff firms must not be overestimated. Furthermore, contrary to expectations, there is little evidence of the evolution of such firms from a predominantly "soft" orientation to the production of "hard" products and services.

Generating Dense Self-Sustaining Technological Communities

An important element in the lore of research parks has been the notion that the firms located in a park would interact vigorously with one another, thus creating a creative melting pot of technical, scientific, and commercial cultures. Another component of the lore has been the expectation that there would be a snowballing of new companies on the model of Cambridge or Silicon Valley. There seems to be little evidence that either of these phenomena occurs to any significant extent. Networking as such is a fairly common occurrence among high-tech firms, small or large, but it is hard to link it to residence in science parks. The general impression is that the hyper-creative atmosphere caused by intensive communication and collaboration among the residents of a park is rarely if ever realized.

The General Cultural Impact of the Parks

In this area there is a great shortage of systematic studies, and most of the evidence available is impressionistic and anecdotal. Some observers express the belief that the very presence of parks close to the universities affects motivations and perceptions of the academics and provides role models that enhance the propensity to collaborate with industry and the willingness of individuals to become entrepreneurs. Those are plausible observations but we still lack systematic assessments of the net effect of the parks on the universities in terms of the pattern of academic R&D, the motivations of scientists, and the general use of university resources. My view (Stankiewicz 1986) has been and continues to be that that impact is on the whole beneficial, in that it helps to achieve the necessary degree of cultural and institutional "interpenetration" between the scientific and commercial communities. Such interpenetration creates opportunities that can result in a wide variety of collaborations, only a fraction of which will take place in the parks themselves. However, this is not a universally shared view. MacDonald (1987), for instance, views the social costs of promoting academic entrepreneurship as greater than its potential benefits.

Interpretations

There are three main interpretations that can be assigned to the findings summarized above: i) a radical criticism of the very *concept* of science parks; ii) *methodological* critique of the studies and evaluations themselves; and iii) an institutional interpretation accounting for the putative failure of the parks in terms of the *organizational and managerial* practices involved.

The Radical Critique

The radical critique denies the validity of the earlier discussed rationale and assumptions behind the science parks. Thus, MacDonald (1987) and Massey et al. (1992) claim that, for intellectual as well as institutional reasons, the universities cannot play a direct role in the technological innovation process. Van Dierdonck et al. (1991), while attributing to the universities an important role in the generation of new technologies, criticize the notion that interactions in *local* as opposed to *international* networks are of crucial importance in the process of technological innovation. Still others, for instance, Jonsson et al. (1991), while emphasizing the impact of universities on the local economy, deny that there is any need for the type of arrangement represented by science parks and point to a large spectrum of alternative mechanisms facilitating high-tech entrepreneurship and transfer of technology from universities to industry.

These radical critiques do contain many important elements of truth. However, they tend to overstate their case. I do not think they have succeeded in seriously damaging the general rationale behind the research parks. Apart from often being mutually contradictory, they also conflict with accumulating evidence that the universities do indeed play a critical role in certain processes of technical innovation, that the transfer of technology from universities to industry (and the other way around) is hampered by a variety of institutional and psychological factors, that both local and distant networks are important in the process of technological innovation, etc. (SPRU 1996). Furthermore, the radical critics seem to overlook the fact that, after all, there exist science parks that by any set of reasonable criteria must be regarded as successful. Whether such success can be achieved in all, or even a majority of cases is another matter.

Methodological Factors

The evaluation of the performance and impact of science parks is an exceedingly difficult undertaking. The problems of measurement and of acquisition of relevant data are enormous. The intricacy of the causal relations is daunting and the risk of creating methodological artifacts considerable. Indeed, it is possible to argue that a number of methodological factors tend to produce negative biases. These are:

1. The tendency to use unique historical situations as a sort of benchmark for measuring the performance of the average research park.
2. The great difficulties of defining "control groups" for the firms operating in the parks.
3. The problems of controlling/accounting for a range of "contextual factors" such as general economic climate, unique features of the local industrial structure, and, especially, the particularities of different technologies.
4. The fact that many evaluations have been clearly premature; usually the parks studied have been in existence for only a few years.

Indeed, this last point is very important. Very few, if any, of the effects of parks on communication, collaboration, entrepreneurship can be expected to develop immediately. The economic impact on the region will often require a still longer time. Furthermore, despite some attempts in that direction (see for example Monck et al.), there are no well-developed dynamic models of the development of science parks. Consequently, the time factor rarely appears as a well-articulated dimension of the analysis—surely a major shortcoming.

Yet, no matter what their methodological failings, the studies discussed above do converge on certain major points which are consistent with the more informal views of many observers involved with the parks themselves. These points are:

1. The short- and medium-term performance expectations that provided much of the political motivation for the rapid diffusion of the parks have been far too optimistic.
2. In particular, the belief that physical proximity automatically leads to technological and economic synergisms has been naive.
3. Institutional and management factors appear to have played a major role in the success/failure of the parks.

I find the last point particularily important and will discuss it in some detail. Although comparatively few studies attempt in-depth analysis of the institutional structure and management of the parks, the importance of these factors is stressed by several authors. The appropriate infrastructure and managerial and financial services are often found to increase the attractivness of the parks to the resident firms, particularily small ones. The involvement of universities with the parks is likewise regarded as crucial for effective communication and collaboration between academic departments and the tenant firms.

Yet neglect or weakness among the leadership and management of the parks is a common feature. Monaco et al. find that most of the parks studied by them lack a proactive leadership and strategy. Managerial services are underdeveloped and the involvment of the universities low. In fact, only in four cases studied by Monaco and his colleagues did the university act as the principal in the development of the parks.

The role of institutional and managerial factors can be discussed under four main headings: i) the strategic vision/objectives; ii) the attitude toward spinoff companies and "proto-firms"; iii) the infrastructure; and iv) university-industry interface.

Structure and Strategy

Science parks are often an outcome of a complicated process in which a variety of heterogeneous interests and expectations intermingle. Not surprisingly therefore, the identity of the parks is often unclear, contradictory, and subject to disputes. In many cases there develops a profound ambiguity as to what the ultimate objectives are: a real property development, a means of attracting industry to a particular location, or a mechanism for stimulating technology development and transfer.

One area in which these conflicts are likely to be particularly serious is the recruitment of tenants. If the benefits of geographical proximity are to be realized and the potential of the university adequately used, it is important that these tenants have sufficiently overlapping interests and are active in those fields of R&D in which the local university possesses some strength. A degree of cohesion is furthermore important for the development of meaningful infrastructure and for interfacing the parks with outside scientific and commercial communities. Unfortunately, due to the lack of foresight, the wish to expand the park rapidly, the political pressures, or the requirements of profitable real property development, many parks fail to be sufficiently selective. As a result, many of them have the wrong composition and wrong culture.

Spinoff Companies and Proto-Firms

It is thus essential that the concept of science park be clarified and some sort of coherent strategy defined and systematically pursued. This is particularly important with respect to the support the parks render to new firms of various types. This is the area where the parks can and often do play an especially beneficial role, provided there is a strong commitment to technology development and transfer as the main goal of the parks. Also required is a sophisticated conception of technological entrepreneurship.

As observed by this author elsewhere, most students of academic spinoffs seem to rely implicitly on a quasi-Schumpeterian model of entrepreneurial activity in which the evolution of spinoffs proceeds through a number of stages, starting with invention, followed by development and prototype testing, to vertical downstream integration as successful generations of products are developed, manufactured, and marketed. In this process the new firms coalesce into an industry that displaces, or at least reshapes, the existing industrial structure (Stankiewicz 1994). Although it fits relatively well what happened in the emerging microelectronics and computer industries in the '60s and '70s, this image is based on a distorted interpretation of the nature of academic technological entrepreneurship.

The transfer of academic know-how and technology to industry can take a number of different routes depending on such factors as the field of technology, the ability/willingness of established industry to absorb/utilize new technologies, etc. Four such routes are particularly important:

1. The *first* is the direct transfer from the academic setting to industry of technological ideas and know-how, which are then developed within the established firms. Such a transfer may or may not involve the movement of individuals or groups of scientists/ engineers.
2. The *second* route involves the provision by academic scientists/technologists of certain highly specialized services based on the know-how that is best generated in the academic setting. This often leads to the emergence of small firms, mostly but not exclusively *consultancies* living in some form of symbiosis with the university. The founders of such firms are often reluctant to sever the relationship with academia. These firms, while important for technology transfer and diffusion, seldom grow large in terms of turnover or employment (comp. Jonsson et al. 1991). They are widely scattered among all kinds of technological fields, but particularly common in the areas where the rapid advance of generic technological capabilities creates temporary shortages of relevant competencies.
3. The *third* route goes via the spinoff firm, which has a well-defined marketable product and a genuine growth potential. Some of these firms may need an incubation period in the vicinity of the university. However, in the longer term, the quasi-academic culture of science parks does not constitute the best environment for such firms. Therefore, they should as soon as possible move to more normal industrial environments.
4. The *fourth* route goes via what I would like to call *proto-firms*. By this term I mean a commercially motivated activity in which investment is made in the creation of *technological assets* but which for a considerable time cannot generate the cash flow to be self-sustaining. Initially, a proto-firm is simply an R&D project that because of its size, interdisciplinary character, and the proprietary character of the knowledge it produces, cannot be accommodated within the academic structure; nor, for structural or managerial reasons, does it fit well into the framework of an established company. A proto-firm may eventually evolve into (i) a regular product-oriented firm or (ii) a mature development company. But it may also (iii) become absorbed into an existing firm, or in some form (iv) spun-in back into the R&D system. A major characteristic of a proto-firm is that while, from the conventional point of view, it represents an incomplete set of assets, an attempt to force it into a regular market regime may significantly slow down or arrest its technological development. Proto-firms are common in fields where new basic technologies are evolving rapidly, but where their effective commercial utilization requires very large resources and integrative capabilities. Pharmaceuticals and advanced IT technologies belong to that category. In these fields proto-firms play an important role of supplying radically new technologies to the established large firms,

which can combine these innovations with their awesome systemic/integrative, marketing and financial resources. I would argue that the high-tech industries today are characterized by a structure that fits neither the so-called Schumpeter Mark I model (stressing the role of small entreperenural firm) nor Schumpeter Mark II (emphasizing the innovative capabilities of large established firms). Rather, we seem to be witnessing the emergence of a new industrial pattern of technological division of labor characterized by a form of vertical disintegration along the R&D chain (Stankiewicz 1994, 1996; Whittaker and Bower 1994). The proto-firms are destined to play an important role in that emergent pattern.

The universities and engineering schools are particularly important as the source of such proto-firms. They are far less frequently capable of giving rise to regular product-oriented firms (Stankiewicz 1994). The latter are much more likely to be spun off by the already existing firms. On the other hand, the academic proto-firms often fail to develop and tend to degenerate into narrow niche activities. That depends as much on deficient financing and management as on various structural factors. Proto-firms need the support of appropriate infrastructure to offset at least some of their inherent weaknesses. The science parks, if appropriately organized and managed, can help this to happen.

Infrastructure and Management

In order to provide adequate support to fledgling firms and proto-firms, it is essential that the parks should be able to provide a set of integrated technical, managerial, and financial services as well as good information and communications infrastructure. It is not realistic to expect that these services can be provided by the existing university. The latter can and should serve as a backup and a general resource on which the firms in the park can draw when they need specialized support. The more routine functions, however, should be taken care of by the parks themselves.

Clearly, the support infrastructure should include those functions that normally are taken care of by "innovation centers" and other types of "incubators." However, that is not enough. The feature of science parks that makes them particularly suitable as the environment for proto-firms is that, because of their large scope and heterogeneous resources, they can create the "competence density" required for effective technological entrepreneurship. In particular, the parks should function as places where "competent teams" can be more easily formed. By enhancing the visibility and credibility of promising proto-firms, the parks can help to match technical and R&D skills with the necessary managerial and marketing skills. For these reasons, the presence in the park of a number of mature firms as well as a dense network of contacts in the local business community are crucial. However, in order to create the required "competence density" and to support the necessary specialized service functions, a park needs to have a well-defined technological focus and recruit its tenant firms accordingly.

All these things require proactive management and leadership of the parks based on considerable skill and resources. Those skills and resources take time to develop. They require a long-term orientation and a great persistency of purpose. They also demand "patient money." In the past decade there has been an excessive reliance on various types of "venture capital." That should be balanced by greater financial involvement by large established companies and governments.

The University-Industry Interface

If the function of the parks is to facilitate technology transfer from academia to industry, then the institutional interface between parks and the universities with which they are linked is crucial. In the absence of such interface, the parks are likely to be transformed into more or less sophisticated real property developments. This in fact has happened in many cases due as much to the absence of consistent vision on the part of the universities as to ordinary commercial pressures. The parks that evolve in that manner may still be beneficial, for instance from a regional point of view, but they can hardly be expected to have a major impact on the technology transfer process.

The strong link between the park and the university requires the latter's direct involvement in the development and running of the park. It requires a network of formal and informal relationships between the academic and the business communities. The presence of academics on the board of the park and, especially, on the boards of its tenant companies, as well as the participation of the members of the park in the affairs of the university, is one important method. The existence of appropriate formal arrangements facilitating the involvement of individual academics in the activities of the park, such as rules for part-time employment, leave of absence, consulting, etc., are also important.

However, it is also crucial that the universities see the parks as extensions of their own R&D organizations and plan their own educational and R&D activities accordingly. The universities should develop R&D strategies that establish them as centers of excellence in well-selected areas of basic technologies. They should seek to acquire a critical mass in these areas which can act as a magnet for industry and, at the same time, allow for a sufficient spillover of talent and ideas from academia to the surrounding economy. The parks should be a natural location of many "peripheral" R&D and educational activities, including major national and regional research facilities, technical consultancies, etc. In short, the parks should be strategic tools for universities to enhance the R&D and technological agglomeration around them.

The fact that the interface between parks and universities has been poorly developed can largely be explained by the institutional and cultural factors that have traditionally hampered the relations between academia and industry. It seems that in many cases support by the universities for the parks has been quite superficial and based on short-term, opportunistic motives. In such cases the prospects of success are of course very limited.

Conclusions

The emergence of science parks in the '50s and '60s and their rapid growth and diffusion in the '70s and '80s is a result of deep changes in the process of technological innovation, changes that are reflected, for example, in the increased importance of universities as the agents of the development and diffusion of new basic technologies. These general underlying trends are likely to continue to call for new institutional arrangements facilitating the interpenetration between the academic and industrial communities (Stankiewicz 1992).

Science parks are one among many methods of improving that interpenetration. They have, among other things, the advantage of promoting links between the industrial and academic communities in a manner that does not threaten the autonomy of the latter. However, since the early '80s, the parks have come to be seen mainly as the tools of promoting regional economic development. This was accompanied by a range of expectations regarding what the parks could accomplish in a comparatively short term. Those expectations have not been realistic, and depended on incorrect interpretations of what happened in the Stanford, Boston, and Cambridge (United Kingdom) areas. Predictably, this has led to disappointments and critical reactions. Many parks suffer today from a crisis of identity. It is not clear whether their primary goal is (i) commercial property development, (ii) attracting business to a given locality, or (iii) developing and transferring technology. Several of the recent assessments of the performance of the parks are negative and question the very assumptions on which the parks have been based. The present author's view is that the criticism has been exaggerated and, in some respects, premature. Nevertheless, it must be taken seriously. It is quite plain that the parks do not offer "quick fixes" for economic difficulties, regional or national.

Neither are they the only or necessarily the best ways of interfacing universities with industry. They are simply *one* among many alternative methods of doing those things. Their ultimate success depends on their being able to find their specific niche and function. To do so they will have to develop consistent strategies and pursue them with considerable persistence and managerial skills. Up to now, this has rarely been the case.

It is argued that the development and support of new technology-based firms (especially proto-firms) should be the main function of most university-affiliated parks. However, the parks should not merely function as "hothouses" or "incubators." They should also act as technology brokers who facilitate the formation of "competent teams" by bringing together people with complementary skills from the academic, business, and financial communities. In that sense, the presence of many different actors in a park confers considerable advantages, provided it does not compromise the clarity of its goals. The active involvement of the universities in the running of the parks and the support of science and technology policy bodies, particularly on the financial side, are also necessary for success .

The above observations need to be corroborated in further studies. Despite several recent efforts, our knowledge of the parks continues to be rather patchy and opinions about their success or failure too easily influenced by the mood of the day. We still know too little about the organizational and managerial aspects of the parks and about the nature of technological entrepreneurship. In particular, far too little is known about the developmental dynamics of parks and about their relative usefulness in different fields of technology. Another area of ignorance is the impact (scientific, technical, economic, and cultural) of the parks on the academic community. It would therefore be of great value if the studies based on statistical surveys were complemented by some more longitudinal in-depth analysis of parks that have either clearly succeeded or clearly failed.

III

International Comparisons

Academy-Industry Relations in Middle-Income Countries: Eastern Europe and Ibero-America

KATALIN BALÁZS and GUILHERME ARY PLONSKI

Although Eastern Europe and Ibero-America are far removed from each other in both distance and culture, they confront similar problems with regard to university-industry relations. Although they have great historical, social, and economic differences, there are common issues that need to be addressed by policy makers as well as the scientific community.

Both regions haved passed through a period of political, social, and economic change accompanied by economic crises and an increasing need to adjust to the world market. The previous protectionist economic policy in Ibero-America and the autarchic central planning of Eastern Europe had replaced the role of market competition. Protectionism and central planning produced artificial price systems that bore no relation to the wider real market nor to international standards of productivity.

Not surprisingly, in both regions the industrial structure itself was not conducive to innovation, although in certain sectors interest in research and development (R&D) grew in response to goverment-created islands of innovation. But these developments remained isolated, separated from other parts of the economy, and neither pushed nor pulled new technology into the wider national economic environment.

Political and economic changes over the past eight years, however, have been dramatic, opening up the national economies of both regions to world markets. Many firms have found it difficult to change their attitudes and strategies to keep up with the new reality. Thus, in this period of transition, both areas have found that their industrial structures are still not adequately innovative and are marked by a growing albeit insufficiently competitive capacity.

One important consequence of the industries' low level of interest in technical development during the earlier period was that universities and research institutes had developed a strong science base without strong links to the corporate sector. In response to the new circumstances of the transition, both regions are endeavoring to forge new links between academia and industry. In Ibero-America, there is a growing governmental attempt to build and strengthen university-industry cooperation through various initiatives in different countries. Typically, these involve investments, grants, tax and financial incentives, all of them designed to contribute to the creation of an attractive environment for promoting contracted and cooperative R&D. In Eastern Europe, it has been necessary for science and technology policy to be two-dimensional, first introducing reforms to R&D organizations, and then developing an economic and cultural climate more conducive to innovation.

Despite such ambitions, there is political resistance to bringing about these changes through a centrally coordinated policy; in both regions, the policies for economic stabilization now adopted put more stress on the market, with little role for government planning measures. Moreover, the political legacies of the past—the militaristic regimes of Ibero-America and the centralized states of Eastern Europe—have undermined any belief in the state's playing a full and benign role in society and the economy. Thus, S&T policy has needed to be nurtured and sustained by interest groups involved in R&D, the universities, research institutes and their S&T administrations.

Academy-Industry Relations

One striking difference between the two regions has been the scale, role, and development of the existing R&D system. In Eastern Europe, because of the political ideology of scientific socialism, the R&D system was developed faster than the economy itself, originally focused on basic research, and separated from education and industry. Unlike this situation, in which the R&D system seems to be overdeveloped, in Ibero-America the science base is still immature in most countries. Thus, the task in Eastern Europe is to reform and refocus R&D, to build bridges to industry, while in Ibero-America bridging to industry has to be accompanied by the continuous building of R&D capacity.

Whatever the different scale and focus of these problems, it will be equally difficult for both to build overall industrial capacity in different, but equally unfavorable, environments marked by shrinking markets and very limited interest in investing for innovation. Government can, of course, help here by providing the investment that links public and private sectors; hence the importance of academic-industry relations.

However, since most governments in both contexts are rather new to creating science policy, the development of specific programs for enhancing academic-industry relations have been initiated by research managers (including senior staff in universities). However, because of the limited local demand for S&T by an underdeveloped industrial research base, there has been a strong temptation to encourage linkage with overseas corporations, rather than building on local experience.

Models of academic-industry relations have also been imported, and the spread of science and technology parks, incubators, and technology centers is commonplace in both regions. Although these new bridging mechanisms and institutions are very progressive in making academia more flexible and more sensitive to economic needs, in practice the value of such initiatives as innovation parks and contract research organizations is rather uncertain. In an innovation-resistant environment, the content and context of their activities are different from those of the developed countries and thus their impact on the national economy is likely to remain small.

Academic-industrial relations (A-IR) are, of course, only part of any national system of innovation and play a special role in bridging primary knowledge-production and knowledge-use organizations. However, the scale of their economic impact should not be exaggerated. The new organizations and new mechanisms of technology transfer bring professional management and competitive business close to academia. However, they cannot change the wider innovation context of the national economy, in which industry itself needs to adjust to the world market, to undertake structural change and develop competitiveness. Let us now look more closely at each of the two regions.

R&D Transition in Eastern Europe[1]

Eastern Europe not only confronts its own political and economic transition from a centrally planned to a market economy but the transition of the world economy as well. Global structural change during the last two decades has challenged the advanced countries too, and required adjustment to changing circumstances. In the early 1970s the oil crises shocked energy-intensive industries, while during the 1980s the emerging new technologies posed new problems for the effectiveness of many industrial sectors. Despite making some adjustment, leading countries are still experiencing falling or static growth rates, and in mid-1992, renewed signs of economic crisis reappeared (World Bank 1992).

The collapse of the Soviet system and socialism has not made economic adjustment any easier for Eastern European countries. Centrally planned economies were rigid and lacked sensitivity and adaptability toward technological developments happening outside of the Soviet, COMECON, and CMEA theatre. While the Western economies made deep structural changes and sought to meet new technological demands, the Second World states were unable to respond effectively and as a result have, since the Soviet collapse, become economically very vulnerable (Maier 1991).

Nevertheless, since socialism gave a priority to science, the actual research system is relatively well developed. Up till the late 1960s, in most countries the growth of R&D expenditure was higher than that of GDP and compared favorably with countries elsewhere; in short, this well-developed R&D infrastructure provides a particular advantage for most Eastern European countries. What, then, is the role of science and technology in this context; is the widely developed R&D network equally valuable in all areas? How can R&D institutions, universities, and research labs be managed while the budget deficit has been increasing for years? Are there managerial patterns that might be copied from the developed countries, in order to draw on their experience for this region? Answers to these questions must be given at two, related, levels, one concerned with economic needs, the other with R&D capacity.

Economic Need

Firms in transition economies face crisis management problems as well as the transformation of their ownership, market sizes, and so on. There is little investment in physical assets and even less put into human resources. Industrial R&D expenditures are now declining rapidly. Generally, the further firms are from stabilizing their market position and formulating a long-run market strategy the less interest they have in technical change or demand for R&D activity and its results. The usual firm strategy is passive and conservative, relying on using accumulated resources rather than introducing new, more risky, technologies (see Török 1991; Laki 1993). The collapse of the integrated Eastern European "market" hit most firms very badly, and it has been virtually impossible to replace the secure contract system of the past with a market-led new-technology orientation. However, privatization, restructuring, and foreign direct investment is going to change firms' behavior as soon as they have passed their crisis and the market has started to expand. Competitiveness will become an important issue for companies that could be improved by new technology. The means will depend on firm size, strategy, and firm-to-firm relations as much as on academy-industrial collaboration. However, there is an academic network that has been seeking its own survival, as industry has, during the first years of economic and political transition.

Existing R&D Capacity

At the same time, although the extent and quality of Eastern European R&D systems are good, there have been growing institutional pressures to reduce the costs they incur. Since 1989, the R&D budget for research institutions has been cut dramatically, causing a deterioration in research capacity and a brain drain out of Eastern Europe. In addition, existing R&D capacity, crucial for future innovation in the region, suffers from major structural problems, which reduce the possibilities for building new links between academia and industry. The previous Soviet science system was based on a linear innovation model that was understood as a "technical development" model whereby centrally planned and procured technologies, unrelated to marketing pressures, were developed and deployed via a chain of separate institutions, each with a clear, simple purpose and organization and sharply separated from the others (Darvas 1988; Balázs 1988, 1990).

The National Academies of Science were organized with a brief to pursue basic research in discipline-based research institutes. The Academies in fact performed two functions, their assemblies acting as eminent societies for the scientific elite, while also being required to coordinate basic science for the nation as a whole. These two overlapping roles caused confusion and even conflict. Assembly members were selected on the basis of honors and reputational status rather than any managerial skills in policy making. Indeed, the academicians' status was guaranteed by the political *nomenklatura*. The institutes operated under government accounting rules with funding from the state budget to meet academicians' plans. Thus, "academia" had a specific meaning in Eastern Europe that excluded universities.

Universities were devoted to education and in principle basic research was not their responsibility. Thus, higher education and research were separate from each other. During the decades of socialist administration, an unhealthy rivalry developed between the two sectors as they competed for resources from government. In the universities, despite poorer physical assets and lower overall funding some research activity did in fact take place. Lecturers working for their scientific degrees often carried out research with their students. Today, university research is growing rapidly and its potential is considerable.

Industrial research—both applied and development work—had been organized in industrial research institutes under the auspices of branch ministries. These were also budget-holding institutes supporting and tied to firms within their branch. Later on in most countries the industrial research institutes were transformed into R&D enterprises, which began to have a marked impact as soon as planning constraints were removed and the market allowed to gain more influence. Nevertheless, firm-based R&D was still insignificant, having only marginal importance in the more science-based sectors such as pharmaceuticals.

Overall, the R&D system was seriously fragmented. The gap between academia and industry was reproduced throughout a range of institutions that had a research role to play. Funding was allocated to institutions rather than to individuals or research groups, while evaluation was weak and ritualistic. A wide range of research fields was sustained with little sense of priority setting by policy makers.

While this institutional inertia could be found throughout all Eastern European countries, and constituted the principal structural problem preventing change, there was considerable variation across countries with regard to local political circumstances, such that some countries could cope more easily than others with the demands of transition. In Hungary, for example, new economic policies and a consistently pragmatic political line after 1968 had helped to introduce a market-oriented society even though the institutional R&D system remained largely unaltered. Although science policy encouraged a greater move toward the exploitation of research results and forced some institutes to build closer relations with industry, the "shortage economy" meant that industrial needs were defined in very restricted terms: R&D contracts had more to do with solving everyday routine problems of firms than opening them up to new technologies (Balázs 1988, 1990).

In Czechoslovakia, by contrast, 1968 saw change go in the opposite direction, and the system came more strictly under central control. Polish economic problems eventually led to the political autarchy of the 1980s, falling living standards, reduced public expenditure, and an exodus of Polish intellectuals. And when the Romanian system reached its lowest point of political legitimacy during the 1980s, with an extreme political leadership and totally closed economy, basic research was abolished and academic research institutes marginalized. It is worth noting however, that industrial research here was actually strengthened to enable the imitation and adaptation of overseas technology in order to replace imports. In short, these national political differences had varying impact on their R&D systems: they were modified (as in Romania, where support shifted toward industrial research as part of an isolationist strategy of socialist self-reliance) or adjusted (as in Hungary, where contract research and some R&D within firms were encouraged) (Müller 1996; Jasinski 1996; Sandu 1996).

Reforms and New Academy-Industry Relations in Eastern Europe

In the past few years, shrinking funds and the end of traditional Eastern European secure markets have forced research institutes and their managers to find new ways of increasing income. New legislation and a more competitive market environment has brought the latent research capacity of these groups into the open. Given the discussion above, however, the ability to use this is hampered by structural problems, lack of critical mass, and severe restructuring problems for industry, not least caused by the pace of privatization, all of which encourage short- rather than long-term perspectives.

There is a pressing need, then, throughout all Central and Eastern European countries to develop more effective policies that sustain the science base while raising the industrial demand for research. Both can only be secured by improving the links between academia and industry. And here, four issues need to be addressed:

- How best to overcome the historical split between universities and the academies?
- The clarification of the shape and character of scientific activity over the medium to long term—what foci and priorities it should have, how best should disciplinary and interdisciplinary needs be met, and so on?
- Who is best placed to undertake the very different science-based activities that will be crucial to a changing innovation system—basic research, contract R&D, business and management development plans, and so on?
- Within this context, what are the appropriate forms of A-IR that can best contribute toward building that local technological capacity crucial to future innovation in Eastern Europe?

With regard to the first of these, an improvement in university/academy linkage depends in turn on broader higher-education reform. A first step would be to introduce properly supported postgraduate education, notably a full doctoral provision, while science degree training is given over to universities. This policy would encourage greater links between the two institutions, notwithstanding the legacy of past rivalries. It is noticeable, for example, that at the personal level there are already growing links, such as "double chairs," common projects, and specially co-designed courses. This suggests that for many individuals professional academic interests appear to break through institutional boundaries. Legal steps also have been taken in several countries improving university autonomy and initiating post-doctoral education. However, the division of interest and power on the one hand and limited financial sources on the other make fast development difficult (Balázs, Faulkner, and Schimank 1995).

Secondly, priority setting is a most critical issue. Currently, there is an acceptance of the view that basic research strengths are key resources for future competitiveness. While this is not in doubt, there is a need to focus existing capacity in more specific directions since, while of high quality, many research areas lack the critical mass to develop the work fully.

Such a policy move creates its own questions: Can money allocated to certain areas of science be clearly and unequivocally tied to defined areas and not leak elsewhere? how much overall expenditure can a government afford for longer-term investment? where cutbacks are deemed appropriate, how can the affected areas be nurtured for redevelopment at a future date? what kinds of academy-industrial relations will be best to develop both during and after economic revival—can the same mechanisms serve for both?

The first question can begin to be answered by changing the financial mechanisms in such a way as to give more responsibility to the grant system and transparent peer review, while reducing but still providing basic infrastructural support for science areas. Most of the post-socialist countries have taken steps in this direction and set up new funds for financing research on a project basis. There is a long learning process for the scientific societies and individual researchers about application, evaluation, and fair competition. The second question will only be resolved via negotiation regarding the structure of power within government as well as overall policy strategy. The argument to decrease expenditure to relieve the current budget deficit is strong, so the S&T community has to work hard to defend itself. Its position would likely be stronger were it to accommodate proposals for restructuring of the science institutions themselves. So these first two issues are related. However, negotiations on science and technology issues through the government departments has been very weak due to the lack of interest of most of them. Post-socialist governments have been overwhelmed by the key objectives of the transition and crisis management. In sum, this (more or less identical) government approach has had very similar impacts on the R&D sector in all Eastern European countries. The research system has been simultaneously abandoned by the state, by the market, and by industry (Balázs 1995).

Reform inside academia (universities and research institutes) means a reorganization of decision making on the one hand and the setting of clear rules for research and business management on the other. This would help to avoid further unhealthy overlapping institutional roles and responsibilities. Business and industry-oriented activities (including development or design-oriented contract research) can then be organized in a more appropriate way.

There are a number of possible ways to reform academia. As recent experiences and plans show, some countries have adopted Western countries' models for academic-industry relations. But simplistic copying in this way is dangerous, since social and economic environments are so different. One must consider these distinct contexts when designing new mechanisms and institutions. Although the Academy of Sciences in most countries plays a rather conservative role, in this or that way research institutes have themselves been prepared to carry out reforms ahead of policy makers (Balázs 1996). For example, some now undertake evaluation of which of their resources must be devoted to basic science needs and which can be released for business-oriented contract research. Moreover, research institutes might consider their scientific research as image-enhancing activity and acknowledge its role as such; such an image can be used not only to bolster the interests of science per se, but also can be sold as part of more business-related programs. There is therefore an opportunity here to harmonize the interests of researchers doing pure research and others "making" business.

One partly designed and partly "natural" outcome of these changes is the formation of spinoff firms from research institutes and universities. New legislation associated with the formation of private companies has encouraged this too. Small research teams, production units, or technical departments have experienced greater income generation as private firms. The spinoff firm was an entirely expected consequence of the Hungarian transitional experience. In one sense, its appearance was similar to that in developed countries, as it emerged in response to both falling budgets as well as new entrepreneurialism. Unlike those in the West, however, Eastern European firms are much less likely to be associated with high-tech generic science, since this type of academic entrepreneurship has not been a spur to economic progress but to economic decline. They are rather more likely to embody a strategy for personal and institutional survival. Nevertheless, small firms do represent a new economic potential due to their flexibility and science orientation. Many are, however, still tied umbilically to their research institutes and it would require policy decisions from the center to force them to go it alone. But there have been no supporting government policies in most countries. State policy has tended to play a neutral role in remodelling R&D institutions; fiscal policy that cut back expenditure has had a much more direct impact, challenging R&D institutions to exploit their capacities in order to survive. Thus, the role of the state has been replaced by local, organization-level decision-making bodies, such as associations and agencies (Balázs 1995).

There are examples in the region of emulating Western practice by establishing new bridging institutions, incubators, and more ambitious innovation parks. In Hungary, for example, the "Zoltán Bay Centres" have been established patterned on the German Fraunhofer Gesellschaft; the old industrial research institutes were unsuitable vehicles for such an initiative. Three Centres—in new materials, biotechnology, and engineering—provide new opportunities for linkage and the exploitation of research results. They are seventy percent "self-financed," with the rest provided by core government funding. At present, given the weak local demand for R&D, "self-financing" in practice means considerable reliance on securing state contracts and procurement rather than wider private market clients. However, in principle, they can grow to be important new vehicles for technology transfer, as long as government gives them the time to develop their potential strengths (Balázs 1994).

There are also attempts to create innovation parks in the region. For example, Romania's Incubator Centres are the focus of a new technology policy. However, it is clear that most of its elements and claims are, to date, more rhetoric than reality. In practice, the local universities and former research institutes are underfinanced, and the research capacity is idle. The Centre is an initiative to provide an umbrella for small businesses started up by departments, research groups in services, and small production units (Sandu 1996). In Hungary, there is a similar example of a park attached to the Technical University of Budapest. INNOTECH Innovation park, like other similar organizations, is an incubator for new enterprises, as well as offering management advice to university staff keen to exploit their work. The purpose of INNOTECH is then similar to that found among Western counterparts. However, like these others, it too has problems. Small firms that have located there are often unattached to the university so that linkage between the two is weak or nonexistent. The firms are small, often joint ventures with foreign corporations, and rarely focused on hi-tech R&D. Understandably, such firms are unlikely to leave the park since they are unable to accumulate resources to secure an independent existence. So, although INNOTECH represents a new approach to academic-industrial relations, it also illustrates that it is going to be difficult to realize its potential as a model for innovation in an unfavorable economic environment.

Many other examples in the post-socialist countries (see Webster, ed. 1996) show a tendency to adopt Western university-industry relations models. The closer analysis also led us to understand the limits of this application in the different economic and innovation contexts. We have suggested elsewhere considering these post-socialist economies as follower economies that face a long adaptation and learning process (Balázs 1995; Radosevic 1995, 1996). Under these conditions they certainly will require a different kind of research system and a strong knowledge industry. In this case, the emphasis may not be so much on basic research as on adaptability, transferable skills, knowledge distribution, technology transfer, information services, quality improvement, flexibility, and the like. The new technology centers, industrial and science parks, as well as the spontaneous spinoff activity, appear to be a good way of transforming the R&D sector in this direction. Although we recognize limits and constraints, these forms of academy-industry relations may improve followers' efficiency by producing the necessary recombination of existing skills and knowledge. As the transformation of the economy stabilizes, this activity will be curtailed. The value of any model is always context dependent. Similar problems can be found in the Ibero-American region, to which we now turn.

Cooperation in Ibero-America

The issue of academy-industrial relations has been present in the region (which comprises Latin America, Portugal, and Spain) at least since the late sixties, when two experts in science policy, Jorge Sábato (the former head of the nuclear program in Argentina) and Natalio Botana, proposed their model to insert S&T into the economic development process. They observed that each of the three main actors—the S&T infrastructure, the productive structure, and the government—must develop its particular strategies interacting with the others. This was not the usual practice. For example, universities are used to interacting with other universities or research institutes inside their own countries (establishing what Sábato and Botana called *intra-relations*), or with their equivalents in other countries (what the two authors called *extra-relations*). What has been missing were *inter-relations*, between the mentioned university and industry and also with government. A similar situation prevailed from the standpoint of the other two principal actors.

The building of the so-called Sábato's Triangle of interaction has taken almost a quarter of a century, especially with regard to the inter-relations between the S&T infrastructure and the productive structure. For some time, the main focus has been on the ideological discussion, potentialized by an academic sector that had suffered external intervention by the military regimes and wanted to assure that the universities would be protected from any unwanted outside influences. This ideological discussion has almost faded out. However, some distrust and criticism between the university and industry, and between the basic and applied research perspectives, remain; moreover, there is still a lack of criteria for academically evaluating applied research (Lavados 1994).

Just as in more advanced industrialized countries, there is an increasing interest in cooperation between industry and university in the Ibero-American region. This can be verified by the growth in the actual number of cases of links, the new fiscal and credit mechanisms provided by government funding agencies for cooperative academy-industry projects, the number of conferences and events debating this issue over the last five years, the increasing number of master's theses and doctoral dissertations dealing with aspects of academic-industry, and the rise of multilateral organizations' interest in promoting such linkage.

According to recent in-depth studies (Plonski 1993 and 1995), there are several aspects common to the majority of the countries reviewed (Argentina, Brazil, Chile, Colombia, Costa Rica, Cuba, Equador, Mexico, Peru, Portugal, Spain, Uruguay, and Venezuela). One aspect is the policy of substitution of imports, promoted by the United Nations' regional economic and planning office in Latin America (known by its Spanish/Portuguese acronym, CEPAL). The basic idea was to promote local industrial development, to overcome the deterioration in trade balance. This was understood to be an unavoidable consequence of the tendency to reduce the international prices of the natural commodities exported by these countries (agricultural and mineral products), in comparison to the prices of manufactured products that had to be imported. Therefore, special measures were taken by most national governments to help these new industries, including stringent protection against imports and subsidies for locally producing products that had been imported, even if the local cost was higher or the quality was lower.

Cooperation has to be understood according to the peculiar characteristics of the region. For instance, in Argentina, as in other countries, several difficulties interpose themselves on the development of an innovation culture, all of them consequences of the peripheral nature of the country in the world economy. These include protectionist policies that have been applied for several years, the need for recessionary adjustment, the technological dependency of local firms, low rates of investment in R&D, the scarcity and/or high cost of credit, and the chronic structural weight of external debt. Compared with Eastern Europe, the last two items particularly restrict the innovation system.

The above-mentioned protectionist policies have allowed each actor to accommodate to its own traditional niche. For example, strong links between the university and the productive sector could not be expected in Colombia, which had a closed industrialization model. In Spain, the study found, until at least the mid-1980s, interaction between the two sectors was sporadic, reflecting a context in which businesses were protected from foreign competition and universities worried more about teaching than creating research and knowledge.

Furthermore, when universities in Ibero-America did create knowledge they did so with state funds. In Brazil, for instance, the participation of the private sector in S&T expenses has traditionally been about twelve to fifteen percent, much lower than in the United States (fifty percent) or in Japan (eighty percent). The S&T policy supported the supply of potential technology, and paid little attention to the need for innovation in the productive sector, reflecting the gap between university and business. This separation was only possible in an environment of protection against competition for both sectors—the former by the criteria through which public funds were allocated, and the latter by tariff and non-tariff barriers for imports.

The fact that almost all of the research universities or research institutes in Ibero-America are public is relevant to the discussion. There are no tuition fees (with the pssible exception of continuing education programs), and all of the salaries and other basic expenses are paid with government resources, with no strings attached. There is no culture of private philanthropy, a common practice abroad, especially among university alumni. Additionally, there are administrative restrictions regarding the use of private income from contracted research or other projects, due to the regulations that affect all of the public sector. These restrictions have caused some universities or research groups to create private not-for-profit organizations to manage those funds and expedite the day-to-day activities of privately sponsored projects. These organizations pay a fee for the use of university assets, but not for the use of staff time.

Stronger Linkages

Major changes in economic policy throughout the region during the past ten years have, however, led to recognizing the need for a stronger technological and science base, and consequently for improved links between academia and industry. In Spain, for example, the economic environment has changed dramatically as a result of open border policies demanded by the regional agreement that resulted in the establishment of the European Union. In Costa Rica, as the productive sector has become more involved in international economic activity and the removal of import duties has opened up markets to greater competition, industry has sought improvements in its competitive capacity through stronger links with universities.

It is evident that the push for linkage has traditionally been stronger from universities than from industry as the latter has struggled with the short-term problems of survival in a turbulent macroeconomic environment. However, the reduction of the endemic very high inflation rates to "civilized" levels in recent years should allow companies more time to consider strategic policies for technology development, including new modes of inter-institutional collaboration.

A common characteristic of Ibero-American countries is the importance of favorable legal mechanisms and the role of the state as a stimulator of business-university cooperation. Thus, three instruments enacted in the early 1990s—Law 23.877 (Law of Promotion and Stimulus of Technology Research) in Argentina, the Program to Support Industrial Technological Capability in Brazil, and the Frame Law on S&T in Colombia— seem to be a watershed in each country, marking a new stage in the effort to encourage academic-industry relations. They establish one or more of the following elements, all favorable to collaboration: tax incentives, soft loans for joint projects, the possibility of adding private income to the salaries of academic staff and researchers (which had been virtually impossible, because of the restrictions affecting public servants), guidelines for sharing profits derived from intellectual property, and many other initiatives to promote linkage.

Brazil has been one of the countries in which most of the above-mentioned elements have been put into practice. For example, there are two laws to promote industrial R&D. Law 8248, enacted in 1991, provides tax incentives for the information technology industry, providing that five percent of the gross income is invested in R&D or in quality programs; there is also a provision in the law that forty percent of the amount spent in R&D (i.e., two percent of the company's gross income) must be outsourced to universities, research institutes, or similar institutions. Law 8661 enables companies to use R&D expenses to deduct eight percent of their income tax. A sizable amount of $1.3 billion of R&D has been proposed by industry and agribusiness under this Law, with a ratio of 3:1 of additional money spent by companies to tax incentives given by government. Law 8661 does not require companies to outsource any of their R&D activities; however, dozens of agreements between industries and universities are being voluntarily established in this context.

FINEP, the national agency for financing S&T in Brazil, established FINEP-TEC in 1995, a line of credit of US$ 60 million to support industry-university R&D projects. Industry gets a loan considerably softer than the usual credit lines for R&D. University gets a non-refundable grant for ten percent of the amount borrowed by industry, in addition to the amount of the research contract. The first project supported by FINEP-TEC was the development by the University of São Paulo's Engineering School for Pirelli (a transnational company with headquarters in Italy) of a simulator to test the resistance to mechanical stresses of energy cables at 1,000 meters below sea level. The US$ 2.4 million project is necessary in order for Pirelli to provide those cables to Petrobrás, the national oil company, which undertakes the most advanced offshore operation in the world. The idea to develop this joint R&D effort materialized through an employee of Pirelli's Technology Center in São Paulo, who was undertaking his master's degree at the University of São Paulo's Engineering School, and knew both his company's problem and the core competences of the faculty in the Department of Naval and Oceanic Engineering.

Several other initiatives to promote industry-university cooperation have been put forward by Brazilian governmental agencies. They include grants to academic researchers on condition that there is the participation of industry in the R&D effort (by FAPERGS and FAPESP, respectively the Rio Grande do Sul and the São Paulo state agencies for supporting science). There are also non-refundable grants given by the Ministry of Science and Technology, through a program to support university-industry cooperative research projects involving at least two companies.

As is to be expected, it is the research-intensive universities and those with larger postgraduate programs that have developed the more extensive links with business, rather than those oriented toward teaching as the sole or main priority. Clearly, the capacity to engage in knowledge and technology transfer is directly related to the available knowledge base.

In terms of modes of collaboration, almost every variety can be found described in the specialized literature, including incubators, science and technology parks, and technopolis areas. They are put into operation by transfer offices (known in Spanish by their acronym, OTRI), university companies and foundations, and international technical cooperation programs and projects.

A recent innovation model is the UNIEMP Institute in Brazil (UNI for university and EMP for *empresa*, which means company in Portuguese). Its principal role as a national NGO is to promote the concept of linkage between the two actors.

Cooperation with small business is another area that is extremely relevant to Ibero-America. The activity of SEBRAE, an NGO established in Brazil as a joint effort of private sector and government focused on very small and small businesses, is remarkable in trying to focus universities on the smaller side of the business spectrum.

One successful example of such an initiative is a hotline called Dial Technology, which developed a user-friendly interface for small businesses and potential entrepreneurs. Pioneered in 1991 by the University of São Paulo, it completed 10,000 supports in September 1996, developed channels to the community through the radio, newspapers, and magazines, and also established a training program focusing on the most demanded requests for support. Similar initiatives were adopted by fifteen other organizations (mostly universities) in Brazil, and also in Argentina.

Finally, it is noteworthy that a growing focus on innovation, rather than just developing scientific capability, became an explicit condition of recent significant World Bank and Inter-American Development Bank loans to the national S&T sector of several countries in Latin America.

The Role of International Cooperation

Despite a relatively low level of R&D compared with industrialized countries, and an even lower proportion of private-sponsored research, the countries in the region have encouraging areas of scientific and technological achievement, and a wealth of valuable scientific and professional resources. "These are, however, caught in the traps of scarce funding, large inefficient bureaucracies and the absence of strong research tradition" (Vessuri 1995). Therefore, the issue of international cooperation becomes vital in order to promote the efficient use of these resources, for economic and social development.

One of these efforts is the Ibero-American Program on S&T for Development (known by its Spanish acronym, CYTED). It encompasses circa 8,500 researchers in twenty-one countries, focusing on hard areas such as biotechnology, food treatment and conservation, and mineral technology, but also on the issue of technology R&D management. It also promotes joint ventures, similarly to the EUREKA Program (this is called IBEROEKA).

As part of CYTED, a Network of Industry-Cooperation Management, the CYCOOP Network, was created, with the main goal of exchanging information and experience among the academic and practitioner communities. The network focuses on management because this is a critical success factor in any cooperation. In fact, an evaluation of the twenty most promising cooperation projects supported by the United Nations Development Program—UNDP during 1987–1991 in Chile showed that almost all of the problems found were related to the projects' management rather than to scientific or technical issues.

The CYCOOP Network has already published two books, promoted several training programs on University-Industry Relations (with participants coming from nine countries in the region), developed communications among the interface organizations, and facilitated the study and diffusion of good practices.

There are several other initiatives in the region trying to promote university-industry relations, such as the Columbus Program, Eural Program, and CINDA. The establishment of a "network of networks of academy-university cooperation" to focus in an articulate manner on relevant issues for the region is being tackled, with the support of the UNDP and UNCTAD (under the so-called Latintec Program).

Conclusion

This paper has reviewed the circumstances facing two regions experiencing major social and economic change, and how this change impacts on their local academic-industrial relations capacity. Clearly, though there are important cultural, political, and material differences, it is apparent that both have experienced difficulties in the transition toward more competitive economic contexts. Moreover, the institutional structures that have prevailed in the past have not been conducive to the formation of strong academy-industrial links. Legacies of the past continue to be felt today even though new initiatives are breaking down some of the structural barriers.

Models from more advanced states have been taken up at both the national and the international level in both regions, and these efforts are noteworthy. However, local contexts make their implementation problematic, in the short term at least. It is likely that academic-industrial relations will only play a growing role in promoting the innovation capacity of both regions where wider macroeconomic changes take place too. There is still too much that is precarious on this count in both regions for us to be confident that collaboration will grow at the pace it needs to if locally driven economic growth is to be achieved.

Although the R&D sector and the universities had been more developed in Eastern Europe than in Ibero-America, the shift from a closed to an open economy and all the difficulties of the transition have led to similar problems. Uncertain industrial interest keeps the demand side of the technology market still very weak in both regions. The industrial structure has been increasingly fragmented since the large firms in Eastern Europe were broken up, the majority of industry is made up of small and medium-sized companies. However, the structure in Ibero-America is even more extreme. Neither multinationals nor small entrepreneur entities are expected to become knowledge buyers. Thus, in both regions emerging academy-industrial relations still show a "science push" model. However, the content of the cooperation is far from basic research in most cases. What we recognize in both regions is the changing character of the academia and R&D sectors. Universities and public research laboratories become more entrepreneurial, as do small research units and individuals. Academy-industrial links in the form of research contracts or more business-oriented forms are both important channels of knowledge from academia to industry and channels of information from the international knowledge pool.

Governmental commitment differs between Eastern Europe and Ibero-America. The new post-socialist countries are far from recognizing technical development as a major tool for improving their own competitiveness. National states in Latin America are taking more small steps toward reliance on their—still underdeveloped—science and technology resources.

The globalization of science and technology issues and the integration process both regions undergo in the 1990s will force national governments to pay more attention to academic-industrial relations in order to make more efficient use of their capacities on the one hand, and to learn about their needs and opportunities on the other hand.

CHAPTER 8

Academic-Industry Relations in Russia:
The Road to the Market

MIKE BERRY and LIOUDMILA PIPIIA

For Western science, the "second academic revolution" of recent years has been characterized by increasing links between science and economic policy and the greater commercialization of fundamental—mainly university—research. The first of these was not something new for the Soviet Union, which over seventy years had seen a systematic attempt to subordinate science to economic policy. This had led to periods of tension between the two as the state had attempted to impose greater control over science in the interests of the economy and also from political motives. At the same time, some scientists had sought to reject the excessive role of the state in determining their work. In the late 1980s, however, the second of these processes developed in the Soviet Union, as commercial relations began to play an increasingly important role in science.

In the period between August 1991 and January 1992 the situation changed very rapidly. In fact, it was probably true to say that the whole of Soviet science was in the melting pot; the breakup of the Soviet Union had swept away many of the old central structures and the individual republics had begun to develop their own scientific agencies and policy. All of this led to enormous problems in the funding of science; the pay of scientists had been disrupted and with the rapidly increasing inflation those salaries, even with substantial increases, were no longer enough, the brain drain of scientists to work abroad had reached worrying proportions and many others sought to go if they could.

Before going on to discuss the impact of these changes on Soviet science it is important to stress two major features of the R&D system in the former Soviet Union. Probably the most important feature of Soviet science was its domination by the defense sector, which was even more complete than in the United States and other leading Western countries. Almost everything in science was subordinated to the military potential of the USSR and only at some of the peripheral parts was it free from its influence. What we see and discuss about Soviet science in terms of its staffing, finance, facilities of research, etc. is but the tip of an iceberg, the rest of which has been largely out of sight and is only now coming into view. Most of the best scientists and the best facilities and equipment were to be found in the defense sector. Secondly, it is important to remember that, unlike most Western countries, the universities contributed only a very small part of fundamental research in the former USSR, since that was a prerogative of the Academies of Science.

From the point of view of the average scientist, the system of centralized planning had one advantage—it was not very efficient. In practice, the plans of research institutes consisted to a large extent of their own proposals, which were simply amalgamated into the plan of the next level up—in the ministry or in the Academies' departments. There were some projects that came from the top down but again particularly in the academy these often reflected the interests of the major scientists involved in the institutes, and it was only perhaps in the defense sector that the instructions from above took the form of unavoidable orders. There were few penalties for failure and projects and their funding tended to carry over from year to year. In the market situation, however, the penalties for failure are more serious and the pressures different.

In the late 1980s, however, thanks to the gradual introduction of a contract system for research, institutes began to face some of the features of a market system. Contracts had existed in the past but these were usually formal arrangements, often with the ministry—in the case of industrial research institutes—playing an intermediary role. Following a decree in 1987, some 2000 R&D organizations were transferred to *khozraschet*, a system of commercial relationships under which expenditure had to be met out of income. This was followed by a further decree in 1988, according to which institutes of the Academy of Sciences and higher education establishments also had to switch over to the new system from the beginning of 1989.

Under this new system, industrial R&D organizations had to build up a portfolio of orders to finance them throughout the year. Leading institutes would receive some major orders directly from the ministry but had to find the rest themselves. This was a traumatic change for the institutes accustomed to simply receiving funds without much effort. As one commentator pointed out, the new situation would require a complete change of thinking both for ministry officials, who were used to stopping the research organizations from doing anything without detailed instructions, and for heads of research organizations, who had lost the habit of working independently (Ivakhnov 1987). Some optimists welcomed the new independence while pessimists were afraid that they would be unable to find sufficient orders to cover the costs of their organizations.

In practice, however, many R&D organizations adapted rather quickly to the new situation, but not in the way that government expected. They concentrated on easy short-term projects—often recycling work that had already been completed—that would bring a good profit. As a survey in 1989 by the Committee for Popular Control concluded, "the workforce of research institutes put in the first place obtaining profit at any price" (Anon 1989). This meant that major projects declined, particularly those with a long lead time. Despite these drawbacks, the introduction of *khozraschet* did play an important role in beginning to release some initiative among R&D organizations, although from the point of view of the long-term scientific development of the USSR it brought little benefit.

Similar tendencies developed in many higher education establishments when their work was transferred to the new system—in the view of one writer, in higher education, "the desire to earn money is beginning to overtake the desire to work creatively" (Lavrov 1990). There were even reports that students were excluded from work on lucrative research contracts to leave more for the staff (Lavrov 1990).

The position was somewhat different in the Academy sector. In the USSR Academy of Sciences, contract work in the 1981-85 period had reached twenty-one percent and this was felt to be damaging to the development of fundamental research. As a result, according to the decree of 1987 this was to be reduced to fourteen percent in the period 1986–90 (Berry 1988). Not unexpectedly, the attempt to switch Academy institutes to commercial relations failed to find much enthusiasm. When the new system was introduced in 1989 there should have been an increase in contract research, but in practice this did not happen. This was partly because the Academy received an increase in budget funding of some thirty percent, so there was less pressure to respond to the new decree (Lavrov 1990). In addition, the transfer of industry to *khozraschet* and self-financing tended to reduce the amount they had available to spend on contracts. Even more important for the Academy was the reduction in funds available from contracts for the defense sector because of the increasing importance of conversion (Nikolin 1990). In the Academy, base funding made up a significant part of income and additional income was available from competitive tendering for research projects financed from various levels of research programs, National, Academy, and Academy Department. As a result, there was less incentive for them to make an effort to obtain contract research, particularly as wages in the Academy were increased significantly in 1990.

This does not meant however, that there was no entrepreneurship in the Academy, but it seemed to have found its outlet through the creation of other bodies, such as temporary research collectives, small enterprises, and cooperatives, rather than through the formal institute structure. Thus, there were a number of cases where institutes had set up successful organizations to capitalize on their research results. There were, however, complaints that the activities of many of these new organizations were poorly monitored and that they were frequently being used as a means of siphoning off state funds by charging excessively high prices.

Some scientists welcomed the new opportunities, while others saw the dangers as being more significant than the short-term benefits. As we have seen above, many organizations developed an entrepreneurial approach in the changing situations and it is difficult to escape the impression that some leading scientists welcomed the challenge. As one Academician, an institute director, pointed out: "the market economy requires a scientist today to be not only the creator of a useful commodity, but also an entrepreneurial businessman, expanding his contacts and with a feel for market conditions" (Pan 1991).

Many scientists, however, were less happy with the prospect of domination by market forces. Thus, Academician Afanas'ev pointed out, "The approaching market conceals a certain, I would say, serious danger for Academy science. The Academy investigates basic rules and principles, which at the present moment and sometimes for many years and decades do not give any practical result, while the market weighs everything on the scales of profit, measures things in money especially hard currency. Academic science is little compatible, if it is not completely incompatible with entrepreneurship, commerce, the game of the market forces of supply and demand" (Afanas'ev 1991).

It is also necessary to bear in mind that in practice science began to operate in market conditions ahead of other parts of the economy. The reason for this is that at that time there was no market mechanism operating to encourage technical progress in industry. As one writer put it: "Why invent new medicines, when the chemist does not even have the old ones?" (Nesvetailov 1990). Where there was no competition among producers for customers, one of the most important levers for speeding up scientific and technical progress was missing. There was less reason for industry to develop links with science than in the West because many factories were still in a monopoly position and in the absence of convertible currency there was no competition from abroad. Cooperatives and other small enterprises had begun to develop, but for that period they made very little contribution on the production side.

In science, by contrast, the various kinds of small organizations began to make a significant contribution to some aspects of research. There were three main types of organizations involved in that. The best known of these were probably the cooperatives. These were most successful in areas where little equipment was required, such as, for example, programming. As Table 8.1 shows, the number of cooperatives increased sharply after they first appeared in 1987, though the rate of growth slowed down subsequently. Although the

TABLE 8.1
The Development of New Organizational Forms in Science

New Organizational Forms	1988	1989	1990
Scientific and Technical Cooperatives:			
Number (at end of year)	2,100[1]	10,393[2]	12,562[3]
Workers (x 1,000)	55.0[1]	321.5[2]	312.6[3]
including part-timers		215.6[2]	196.7[3]
Output (x million roubles)		3,151[2]	4,503[3]
Centers of Scientific and Technical Creativity of Young People:			
Number (at end of year)		500[1]	750[4]
Output (x million roubles)		1,000[4]	(2,000)[5]
Total Output All Types:			
(x million roubles)[6]		4,700	(>6,000)

Notes: (   ) estimate.
Sources:
(1) Narodnoe khozyaistvo SSSR v 1988 g., M. 1989, 281.
(2) Narodnoe khozyaistvo SSSR v 1989 g., M. 1990, 274.
(3) Narodnoe khozyaistvo v SSSR v 1990g., M. 1991, 64.
(4) B. Saltykov, Nauka i rynok. Proverka na sovmestimost', Kommunist 1990, No. 14, 26.
(5) According to V. Tsybukh (Zavtra budet pozdno, Pravda, 9 April 1990, p. 2), the Centers had contracts to the value of 3,000 million roubles in 1989. This would suggest that the 1990 figure would be at least 2,000.
(6) B. Konovalov, Put' nauki cherez rynok (interview with N. P. Laverov), Izvestiya, 16 September 1990.

majority of cooperatives had a guarantor in the form of a state organization, R&D organization, or enterprise, it is clear that in some cases this growth was at the expense of existing organizations—there was a noticeable brain drain from institutes to cooperatives, because of the higher level of pay that could be obtained. As the table shows, however, a large number of scientists worked for cooperatives part-time, while keeping their main employment, often using the facilities—and the work—of the institute in their commercial work.

This highlights one of the most important problems of the pre-transition situation—the lack of any clear legal framework for R&D. As a result, there were no clear legal owners of existing work and work was often stolen or pirated without any penalty (Nikolin 1990). The Chief Academic Secretary of the USSR Academy of Sciences criticized this state of affairs at the March 1991 Annual general Meeting of the Academy, pointing out that many cooperatives continued to receive a considerable income, using results and facilities of the Academy institutes. He called for the presidium to discuss relations with the cooperatives, small enterprises, and joint ventures (Makarov 1991).

The other major form of small organization were the curiously named Centres for Scientific and Technical Creativity of Young People. These were initially set up as contract research units under the auspices of the Komsomol, the Young Communist League, and acted as intermediaries between customers and performers. They had some advantage over the cooperatives in that they were official organizations and did not suffer from the bad reputation that the cooperative movement rapidly acquired. By the beginning of 1991, there were 750 of these bodies. Assessments of the amount of work they performed vary somewhat but suggested that they had reached about 1,000 million roubles in 1989 and probably exceeded 2,000 million roubles in 1990. This already exceeded the largest R&D expenditure by a civilian ministry, which, in 1988, was 862 million roubles by the Ministry of Instrumental Industry (Perminov 1990). These organizations on average handled a much larger amount of work than the cooperatives.

Among the other new organizations in this field were the innovation organizations under the All Union Society of Inventors and Rationalisers and the Council of Scientific and Engineering Societies, but these lacked the flexibility in the payment of staff of the two bodies described above and as a result had not been able to keep up with them. Lastly, following a decree of August 1990, "small enterprises" with up to fifty workers (in industry—up to one hundred workers) could be established in the area of science and scientific services, and could enjoy a number of financial and other privileges. There were said to be more than 1000 small enterprises in the USSR in 1990, of which one-quarter were involved with innovation projects (Lynnik 1990).

In 1989–1991, it could be also seen that the emergence of links between Soviet organizations and Western firms generated new research results (Berry 1991). Thus, at the 1989 Annual General Meeting of the USSR Academy of Sciences it was announced that the Academy had set up the Department of Foreign Economic Links, and also that a commercial Foreign Economic Association had been set up to carry out import and export operations for the Academy. At that time, nine joint ventures had been set up involving Academy institutes and eleven were in preparation. By 1990, this had increased to thirty-three registered joint ventures with twenty-five in preparation. By the beginning of 1991, there were seventy-nine joint ventures specializing in R&D, which were already operating, probably about one-third of those actually registered (Nevzorov 1991). Academy institutes and other organizations were also being used by some Western firms to provide scientific labor much more cheaply than would be possible in the United States (Holusha 1990).

With the financial problems that sharply appeared at the end of 1991 and the increasingly important role of hard currency in the former Soviet Union, those trends seemed to increase. Moreover, some institutes set up their own departments of International Economic Relations to develop such links.

At the end of the pre-transition period the development of alternative forms of science was seen as an urgent priority in view of the prospect that a large number of scientists would be made redundant in the next few years. This was likely to apply to both the defense and the civilian sectors. In practice, however, the more enterprising members of the scientific community were already getting involved in cooperatives on a part-time basis. At the same time, it was not so easy for other scientists to find jobs if they were made redundant. The other key role of those new types of organizations was to provide for the first time some genuine competition for R&D, but progress was too slow. Research on the cooperatives showed that their main competition came from the other cooperatives. The only field where competition was particularly widespread was in the preparation of software (Perminov 1990).

Although the higher education sector played a less important role in research in the former Soviet Union than in most Western countries, it too had begun actively to involve itself in the application and production of its research results. New bodies had been created to do this, combining the resources of groups of higher education establishments. Thus, in 1990, forty higher education establishments combined to form an association for the production of small bath and small tonnage products, while forty-six joined forces in the Association of Scientific Instruments, offering 293 different instruments that were not produced in the country. These developments had in the past been held back by the absence of a legal and financial framework (Anisin 1990).

The former Soviet Union has also shown interest in western developments, and this has seen a surge of interest in science parks, technoparks, and other kinds of incubator activities to promote the use of R&D results. Science parks have been set up or planned in a number cities such as Tomsk, Cheliabinsk, St. Petersburg, Tallinn, Saratov, in some cases linked to the Academy institutes and in some cases to higher education establishments or both (Bobylev 1990). The first of these was set up in Tomsk and was controlled by a limited company founded by seven higher education establishments and two Academy institutes and other local bodies (Shukshunov 1990). Also, a Russian Science Park Association had been established, and in autumn of 1991 an international accord was signed between that and UK Science Park Association. It was expected that that agreement would help to provide advice and training for the growing science park movement in Russia. At a conference on "science and technology parks" in St. Petersburg in October 1991 there were said to be twelve parks in existence. However, the first experience of the market reforms showed that the process of imitating Western development in this area was not so easy. Under conditions of the liberalized economy the cost of services provided by established Russian science parks was too high, so that only a very small portion of the potential innovators could develop their ideas within science parks.

Nevertheless, some scientists believed that the advent of the market would save science in the former USSR from its many problems by providing improved pay for scientists who otherwise might leave the country as part of brain drain, and generally would reward the good scientists instead of providing largely equal pay irrespective of work, as had occurred in the past. Before crossing the Rubicon of the market, there were at least two polar expectations among scientists. On one hand, some of them welcomed the opportunity to make money for the first time whatever the source, and had no real objections to devoting their time to it despite the long-term consequences. On the other hand, some members of the scientific community followed a more idealistic line and stressed that science might be seen as a part of the grand intellectual development of mankind, and therefore should be unsullied by commercial considerations. Such people considered that the situation in science in the United States with its frequently cutthroat competition for posts and grants was not really what science was about.

The end of the time of "perestroika" and the collapse of the USSR had led its science to two possible scenarios. In the worst-case scenario, Russian fundamental science would be completely undermined by lack of finance and scientific instruments and the loss of its best scientists to foreign laboratories and to cooperatives and other business enterprises (Dickman 1991). Its best ideas would be developed abroad and Russia would become a second-rate scientific power.

In the optimistic version, Russia would manage to stabilize its economy and through improved conditions and greater democratization would manage to retain many of its leading scientists. The new small firms and cooperatives would bring flexibility in innovation and provide the basis for the rapid expansion of high technology industries in Russian economy.

Russian Science in Transition: Old Problems and New Conditions

Russia inherited the overwhelming part of the R%D sector of the former USSR. Indeed, 56.6 percent of scientific organizations and 67.4 percent of scientific research staff of the USSR were located on Russian territory in 1991

(Centre for Science Research and Statistics 1992). The "shock therapy" measures of 1992, used in the hope of a quick transition to the market, put the R&D sector under conditions much closer to the worst-case scenario sketched out above.

Financial support for R&D fell dramatically in both industrial and government sectors. During the entire Soviet period the state had set the rules of the game, and now it found itself without any clear strategy toward the restructuring of R&D. Ad hoc governmental measures aimed at "rescuing the Russian R&D potential from disintegration" were inconsistent and had insufficient financial resources behind them. In fact, both government and the research institutes were forced to improvise.

The unstable financial position of the research institutes and the low level of salaries paid to R&D specialists testify to underdevelopment of the R&D sector in Russia today. Employment in this sector continues to decrease and the demographic profile of R&D personnel is distorting, given the unattractiveness of scientific work for talented young people.

In these circumstances, it is not surprising that, in a context where government is encouraging market reform, and where the state is unable to sustain the R&D sector, the privatization of some considerable part of public research institutions becomes an attractive, and perhaps inevitable option. However, the privatization of R&D units has been neither easy nor consistent in its operation. Two points are worth making here.

First, it was initially suggested that the logic of market relations would lead to a situation where industrial enterprises would be interested in merging with research institutions. As a result, the industrial R&D sector would be deinstitutionalized and converted into company-based R&D within restructured large industrial enterprises. However, the economic situation in the country not only failed to encourage this process but even prompted enterprises to curtail their own R&D activity and to reorient their R&D units to other kinds of activity. From 1990 to 1994, the number of enterprises performing R&D declined from 449 to 276, i.e., by more than one-third (Centre for Science Research and Statistics (CSRS 1996, 8). Integration of research institutions with industrial enterprises took place only in a few cases in the most prosperous export-oriented industry sectors (oil and gas) and did not become a common tendency.

Secondly, given the drastic decrease in and for R&D, the privatization of the R&D sector could lead to a loss of important areas of R&D at the national level due to a change in the scientific activity of newly privatized research institutes. In order to limit the possibility of this happening, the relationship between the government, research institutions, and potential customers of privatized activities in the R&D sector was regulated by Government Decree

No. 870, adopted in July 1994. This introduced a number of R&D institutional categories, the first of which would secure the longer-term R&D potential required at national level. The categories are:

- R&D institutions, the privatization of which is forbidden;
- R&D institutions that are to be transformed into budget-center establishments;
- R&D institutions that are earmarked for transformation into joint-stock companies with 100 percent shares in state ownership.

Those R&D agencies that fall outside of this list are to be privatized by one of the methods stipulated by the Governmental Program of Privatization—the sale of institutions by a commercial or investment tender.[1] All intellectual property rights in the production sector and other intangible assets used in business activity that generate profits are included in the privatization cost of any entity to be sold. According to the government documents relating to the privatization process, the following terms must be observed:

- maintaining the manufacture of specific kinds of products, goods, and services, as well as preserving the R&D profile of the entity for a period stipulated by the privatization plan;
- preserving the actual employment of R&D specialists for one year;
- maintaining a level of investment that would meet existing customers' requirements during a period determined by the privatization plan, including the first year after the point of sale (in the case of commercial sale), and prohibiting any actions addressed to the R&D entity's property that could change its functions (in case of sale on the investment tender).

Since the beginning of privatization in 1992, most attention has been given to the sale of R&D institutions engaged in applied projects as well as the R&D units of industrial enterprises. In the period 1992–93, about 500 R&D entities were privatized, including a number of institutions in the defense sector. According to data of the Ministry of Science and Technological Policy of the Russian Federation (MSTP), in 1995 there were about 1,400 privatized R&D institutions, i.e., forty percent of the R&D institutions in the country. Just over 6006 institutions are on the list of organizations not liable to privatization.

The principal form of privatization in R&D has been the conversion of state owned research institutes into open joint-stock companies. Forms of privatization such as commercial and investment tenders, auctions, and the redemption of leased property are not commonly used. The available statistics can serve as a sort of estimate of the first results of privatization. The overwhelming majority of privatized R&D institutions is based on joint property. In 1994 such institutions in the R&D sector amounted to twenty percent. This figure corresponded approximately to the share of R&D institutions privatized during that year. The number of private research organizations was insignificant—only four percent of all R&D institutions (Table 8.2).

The majority of privatized R&D institutions are not allowed to state that they have become equal participants in the R&D market and can play the role of some alternative to the public R&D sector. First, the government has retained control over the majority of privatized institutes through securing blocks of shares or the Golden Share in federal property. According to data from the MSTP, the maintenance of governmental control was stipulated for sixty-seven percent of those institutions in the industrial R&D sector that were turned into joint-stock companies.

Second, the economic conditions of these institutes continues to be critical: the portfolio of orders for R&D activity remains incomplete, financial resources are not enough to complete most existing projects, and the salaries of R&D specialists are much lower than in industry and in the country in gen-

TABLE 8.2
R&D Institutions by Type of Property

	1993	1994
Total	4,269	3,968
Russian property	4,267	3,968
Public property	3,597	2,999
of which:		
federal	3,385	2,801
provincial	212	198
Municipal property	21	10
Property of		
voluntary associations	8	13
Private property	116	150
Joint property		
(without foreign		
participation)	525	796
Foreign and joint property		
(with both Russian and foreign		
participation)		2

Source: Centre for Science Research and Statistics 1996, 10.

eral (in many institutes salaries are paid late because of a lack of money in bank accounts).

Third, newly privatized agencies failed to maintain adequate experimental and testing facilities; this has since limited their ability to build and exploit applied projects for local and national markets.

Under these conditions, it is quite understandable why, besides regulated privatization, the adaptation of the R&D sector to market reforms is accompanied by so-called spontaneous privatization, where some elements of R&D institutions' property are taken in ownership by various categories of employees (Tambovtsev 1995). Most state-owned research institutes have become surrounded by numerous small enterprises using the equipment and intellectual property of those institutes. The results of a sample survey have shown the existence of some informal contracts between the administrations of institutes and associated researchers: "in exchange for non-conflict obtaining of possibilities of keeping their posts (offices) and take part in the receipts from spontaneous privatization of the institutes' immovables, the highest link gives researchers possibility of spontaneous privatization of the equipment and intellectual property" (Tambovtsev 1995, 81).

It is difficult for the government to direct these developments since it chose to adopt a policy of minimum intervention concentrating its efforts on the support of R&D institutions and paying much less attention to R&D activities as such. So far, the problem of a transition to a more effective form of budgetary management and resource distribution based on competitive research grants has remained of secondary importance. Competition-based support of research projects executed by purpose-oriented budgetary funds accounts for only five percent of the R&D budget (Table 8.3). The share of the federal S&T programs and other governmental priorities financed by the MSTP on a tender basis amounts to only twenty percent of the federal R&D budget. As a rule, even within the limits of this small share, the sums allocated are spent on the organizational support rather than on the project accomplishment.

The major part of the R&D budget is distributed through ministries and departments who use these funds to support associated R&D institutions. The funding mechanisms used here are very similar to the approaches to R&D funding used during the planned economy. Therefore, the problem remains of introducing new mechanisms that will bring effective federal support of R&D institutions.

Among the more successful measures concerning applied research should be mentioned the Decree of the President that was signed in May 1992. According to this Decree, industrial enterprises were obliged to assign 1.5 percent of the prime cost of products to sectoral R&D funds for the support of

TABLE 8.3
Percentage Distribution of the Federal Budget Appropriations on Civil R&D

	1992	1993	1994	1995*
Total, of which:	100	100	100	100
1. Russian fund for basic research	3.0	2.1	3.9**	7.2**
2. Academy R&D and higher education institutions	27.9	24.1	31.0	27.8
3. Governmental programs and priority objectives	17.8	14.4	14.0	20.3
4. Defense industry R&D institutions	37.8	48.5	40.5	35.7
5. R&D institutions of other ministries and departments	13.5	10.9	10.2	8.5
6. Fund for promotion of small enterprises in science and technology	—	—	0.4	0.5

Source: Centre for Science Research and Statistics 1996, 39.

* Plan
** Data for the Russian Fund for Basic Research include appropriations of the Russian Humanities Research Fund: 1994 - 0.2%, 1995 - 0.5%.

applied research. About twenty percent of these funds are allocated to the budget of the Foundation for Technology Development, which is now providing tender-based support of applied research projects on a repayable basis.

It should be noted that this document has had a positive effect on the intensification of competition in the R&D sector. It gave birth to tender-based financing of applied R&D projects from non-budgetary funds. As a result of its implementation, seventy-one non-budgetary sectoral funds are now in operation transacting about 800 billion rubles. However, it is still rather difficult to estimate the real influence of these funds on industrial R&D in general.

It is very difficult to convince a common taxpayer of the value of R&D if the practical implementation of results of scientific research is insignificant and the economic situation does not favor an intensification of the innovation activity. Market conditions require radically new approaches to the stimulation of innovation in comparison with the conditions of a directive economy.

During the Soviet period, innovations were the product of a planned procedure. A planned innovation was safe from any resource shortfall since it was supported by a directive decision with the appropriate concentration and centralization of money, facilities, and personnel. Besides, the product of an innovation or a new technological process was not oriented to customers but was pressed on them. The overwhelming majority of innovations were somehow or other performed in the defense complex. New products of civil destination on a mass scale were typically only foreign analogs performed by domestic manufacturers (Mindeli, Pipiia 1995).

Parallel to the shift towards market, the government also had to develop the institution of intellectual property and to improve patent and license relations. At present, the following laws have been adopted and are in effect: Law on Copyright and Adjacent Rights, Patent Law, Law of Trademarks, Law on Legal Protection of Software and Databases, Law on Legal Protection of Integrated Circuits Topology, Law on Arrangement of Works and Provision of Safety in Gene Engineering. The following draft laws have been prepared and are being discussed and standing in line for adoption: Law on Science and the State's S&T Policy, Law on the Status of Research Institutes, Law on In-Duty Inventions, Utility Models, and Industrial Prototypes, Law on the Patent Court.

Under conditions of total state property it was impossible to talk about respect for property in general and still less for the property comprised by the products of intellectual labor. At the present stage the problem is not just adoption of corresponding laws but also creation of a real mechanism to secure protection of intellectual property rights.

The government tries to influence innovation activity in the country not only by establishing an appropriate legal base but by methods of indirect regulation as well. For example, there are tax exemptions available to firms for production investment and R&D. But the imperfections of the taxation system as a whole do not facilitate large-scale investments in the country. Small and medium-sized enterprises find themselves in the most difficult situation. Even with a successful use of investment, it is very difficult for small firms to consolidate their position in the market since the taxation pressure that falls upon them within the very first year of production brings to naught the successes achieved during the previous stages of the innovation cycle.

According to the available statistics, in 1994 there were 3,319 innovative enterprises, or 22.4 percent of the total population of firms. Among them, 25 percent were private enterprises, 54 percent were enterprises with combined (public and private) forms of property, and 18 percent state-owned enterprises (Centre for Science Research and Statistic 1996). The indicators of specific shares of innovation enterprises by sector of industry, presented in Table 8.4, are distributed in such a way that higher values correspond to more prosperous sectors (oil extracting and refining, gas extracting, non-ferrous metallurgy, chemicals, and petrochemistry) and those sectors specifically oriented to high technologies (microbiology, medical equipment, and pharmaceuticals).

TABLE 8.4
**Share of Innovative Enterprises in the Total Number
of Enterprises by Sector of Industry: 1992–1994**
(percent)

	Total	22.4
1. Oil extracting and refining, gas extracting		48.1
2. Coal, slate, and peat		12.3
3. Ferrous metallurgy		34.2
4. Non-ferrous metallurgy		48.7
5. Other metallurgy, n.e.c.		26.2
6. Chemical (excluding pharmaceuticals)		42.5
7. Machinery and metal-working (excluding medical equipment)		37.6
8. Wood, pulp, and paper products		18.3
9. Stone and clay products		12.6
10. Glass, porcelain, and faience products (excluding medical articles)		20.9
11. Textiles, clothing, and leather		17.6
12. Food products		17.7
13. Microbiology industry		40.5
14. Medical equipment and pharmaceuticals		47.9
15. Other sectors		14.0

Source: Centre for Science Research and Statistics 1996, 75.

The data above should, however, be treated rather carefully, as they do not exclude cases of firms dependent on imported technologies. Nevertheless, the indicators suggest that an enterprise's intention to innovate to a considerable extent depends on the existing economic conjuncture. On the one hand, the stable financial position of enterprises strengthens their interest in new products and technologies. On the other hand, most enterprises in crisis-affected sectors are passive, do not look for new ideas, and prefer to wait for better times.

In general, the relations between R&D and industry are still problematic inasmuch as the transition toward market has yet to be properly achieved and so the supply-demand relation between innovation and industrial need remains underdeveloped and distorted. Under conditions of the planned economy this contradiction was smoothed by directive methods of management. In the transition to the market economy the disharmony between knowledge producers in research institutes and users in industry has revealed itself completely. The government has underestimated the scale of this disharmony and reforms in the R&D sector continue to lag behind the economic conditions of the business enterprise sector. Declarations about the strategic importance of R&D, which appear in great number in the media and official documents, fail to take account of the realities of the situation today. In fact, uncertainty within government about which R&D road to go down and how support for R&D is to be provided meant a qualitative deterioration of R&D potential between 1992–1995. The market of potential customers for S&T products is insufficiently known and science-based estimates of the real demand for R&D results are absent.

Isolated attempts by governmental bodies charged with R&D management to become intermediaries between researchers and industry are doomed to failure when they ignore the real level of demand from the business sector. In order to become an effective intermediary between R&D and industry, governmental bodies of R&D management must direct their actions toward closer collaboration not only with other federal ministries and departments, but also with those who in practice are shaping the economic situation in the country, i.e., financial and industrial groups, leading industrial enterprises of the country, concrete representatives of big business, and so on. In spite of the difficulty of this task under the present socio-economic situation, the interests of Russia's long-term development require its solution. Similar tasks face other Central and East European countries (Webster 1996).

If we return to the pessimistic and optimistic scenarios sketched out at the end of the previous section, the first of them is the more likely if the existing trends in Russia's S&T policy continue. The quantitative characteristics of the national S&T potential will continue deteriorating, research institutes will try to preserve themselves primarily through government support, and any radical changes in the relationship between the government, R&D, and industry will not happen.

Parallel to any improvement in the economic situation in the country, industrial enterprises are likely to display more interest in R&D, but then a paradoxical situation may emerge: the rise of unsatisfied demand for R&D coupled with a wide range of S&T products on offer from research institutes. In fact it means a divergent development of R&D and industry which pays little attention to understanding mutual interests.

The more optimistic version of the scenario may come true if the government changes its approach to R&D support, sufficiently increases selectivity of its S&T policy, raises the social status of researchers, and tries to find convergent interests between the academic R&D sector and industrial enterprises. However, such governmental S&T policy will stimulate an organizational reduction of the national R&D potential. (In this paper we do not examine the problem of reforming defense-related R&D institutions performing R&D of strictly military orientation, since this sphere is very specific and reforms in it must be coordinated with the objectives of military policy and the interests of national security).

The second scenario will require from government not only new approaches to R&D support but also the development of social programs for the employment of discharged R&D personnel. Providing that a thorough elaboration of the measures undertaken within these programs by government officials and representatives of the research community is given, the social tension that is to emerge with reorganization of this or that institute can be reduced to the minimum since the high qualifications of redundant researchers should enable them to secure work elsewhere in teaching, consultancy, and so on.

The problem for the second scenario is that the government has not ranked R&D among its priorities and is hardly ready to conduct the reforms that will be needed more generally. Therefore, if the situation described in the second scenario were to emerge, such an "evolution" would cost much to both government and society.

Universities in Scotland and Organizational Innovation in the Commercialization of Knowledge

MARGARET SHEEN

Introduction

In the mid-nineties, U.K. universities are facing a number of major challenges. The shift toward mass higher education and the continuing requirement for efficiency gains are stretching institutions financially. Higher student staff ratios are putting additional pressure on human resources and the time staff can allocate to research (most public-sector research is university-based in the United Kingdom). Research quality assessment depends on how "basic" the research is, yet, at the same time, there are new pressures for relevance and for wealth creation.

The importance of innovation as a stimulus to economic growth and wealth creation is now accepted. In those complex and diverse process we call innovation, technology and scientific knowledge are often key factors. So, institutions of higher education are now encouraged to engage more actively with industry. Thus, some of the money spent in public-sector research may have to demonstrate a more direct impact on wealth generation. Along with these changes there is a desire on the part of government for greater accountability of how public funds are being used. Public funding of research is increasingly being made dependent upon partnering with industry.

Over the past few years, industry, also, has experienced major changes through a process of downsizing and restructuring. While this, supposedly, has left firms "leaner and fitter," corporate restructuring has disproportionately reduced the size of the research function. The reduction of R&D capacity in many firms has led to more contracting out of research. In some industry sectors, e.g., pharmaceuticals, the opportunities for universities to engage in collaborative research with companies has never been greater.

All these changes in the United Kingdom have been nationwide. The focus in this chapter, however, is on Scottish universities. This interest is not merely parochial. Universities operate in an international and national, as well as local, arena. Rather, the intention is to differentiate between the regional and national and to examine what challenges arise for institutions located in regions at the periphery of much larger and more prosperous economies. Scotland is of particular interest not only because it exhibits some characterisitics of disjunction between higher education and its manufacturing base but also because the central belt is an area where once the educational, technical, and industrial were much more deeply entwined. As industries die, change is inevitable. The important question may no longer be, Why did those industries decline? but, How best to exploit the advanced knowledge base in universities for the purpose of regeneration?

This chapter considers the factors shaping relationships between universities and industry and discusses some organizational structures that are evolving in universities as a response to these new imperatives.

The Universities and Economic Environment in Scotland

This section describes the historic background of Scottish universities and the recent changes in university governance and funding. This is combined with a brief overview of the prevailing regional economic and industrial conditions.

From their inception in medieval times (Aberdeen, the first of four ancient universities, was founded in 1495), the Scottish university system has possessed some distinctive elements, resembling more the European tradition of governance (Carter et al. 1992). This distinctiveness derives from institutions that combined the responsibilities of college (the community of teachers) with the powers of the *universitas* to grant degrees. Authorities agree that unlike the

> grudging and minimal view of the state's role in education which had prevailed in England, there was a collective perception that it was the duty of the State to maintain universities in "full efficiency," not for the advantage of the individual, but for the advancement and good of the community as a whole. (Anderson 1992)

In fact, universal access and high standards in education from the primary school upwards have been a matter of national pride. Scotland today has a higher proportion of the population attending university than England. However, while primary, secondary, and further education have remained under Scottish control, the universities have, for the greater part of this century, been part of a wider national (U.K.) system of funding arrangements.

In Victorian times, universities were not the only institutions offering advanced instruction, and many new institutions were set up reflecting the huge expansion in commercial activity. At the height of the Empire, Glasgow, in the West of Scotland, was the second city in the Empire. It was not only the hub of commercial activity but also a great center of manufacturing including steel, heavy engineering, and shipbuilding. Many technical institutions were set up to train apprentices. Anderson's Institution, having been established by the will of John Anderson as a "place of useful learning" in 1796 (the period of the Scottish Enlightenment), grew by accretion of these institutes to become, in 1912, the Royal Technical College. In 1964, the College amalgamated with the Scottish College of Commerce and by royal charter was instituted as the University of Strathclyde. Not long afterwards Heriot Watt in Edinburgh, which had grown similarly from technical institutes, also received its charter as a university. Today, the University of Strathclyde educates more engineers than any other institution in the United Kingdom. However, policies to give special funding support to technological institutions never matured and the United Kingdom is unusual among other European countries in having no officially designated technological institutions. Whereas in England the university system is more differentiated in terms of status, Scottish universities, whether ancient or "modern" have maintained a greater homogeneity in spite of their hugely differing origins.

Two recent changes are destined to have a major impact on the future shape of the university system. In 1993, throughout the United Kingdom, the binary divide was abolished, thereby upgrading polytechnics in England and centrally funded institutions in Scotland to university status. Thus, an elitist system has ostensibly become one of mass higher education. Glasgow now has three universities, with another, Paisley, just outside the city boundary. Edinburgh also has three universities, and there are thirteen universities in Scotland.

Second, there have been changes in the way research and teaching are funded. Scotland has once again regained control of her universities through the establishment of the Scottish Higher Education Funding Council (SHEFC). The greater proportion of this funding is for teaching and, under the new system, less will be for research. These rather complex arrangements leave Scotland in a more autonomous position with regard to the rest of the United Kingdom but bound to compete on a national, i.e., U.K.-basis for money to support project-based research. Broadly, the effects of the changes will be to reward "excellence" in research disproportionately. Already the effect is being seen where research strengths are becoming more concentrated, if not always throughout an institution then at least in some departments. A league of institutions has emerged where "top institutions" have top-graded (category 5) research in most departments. New universities, which up till now have had little research capacity, will find it increasingly difficult to get a foothold on the research ladder without finding non-traditional sources of revenue to invest in research.

Overall, Scotland is perceived to have a very strong higher education sector both in terms of quantity (concentration) and quality (research activity is higher than in England). However there is little direct evidence of the higher education sector's acting as an "engine" for innovation in regional manufacturing. Indeed, Scotland's industrial fortunes have fallen as education has expanded and the "system," if there ever was one encompassing universities, appears to be uncoupled. But to ascribe a direct causal link is dangerous; the impact of higher education and research capacity is much more indirect, as we shall see.

Regarding the economic fortunes of the region, Glasgow, has suffered disproportionately in terms of industrial decline. The shipbuilding on Clydeside, along with many of the heavy engineering industries, has been reduced and of the few firms remaining, some are now foreign-owned. Textiles and whisky are still important sectors of the country's traditional industry base, but many food processors have not survived as consumption patterns have changed. On the positive side, fish farming (mainly salmon) has shown enormous growth over recent years and Scotland is one of the main suppliers of shellfish to Europe.

North Sea oil and gas is a major factor not only in the economy of Scotland but the United Kingdom as a whole. The challenge for Scotland is to move from an extractive industry using turnkey operations to an internationally competitive oil and gas service industry. However, the general picture is that, despite the number of small companies engaged in supplying this sector, only low levels of investment have been made in development. There is an Offshore Technology Park based in Aberdeen and a Petroleum Science Institute in Edinburgh. Both facilities are said to be underutilized (Scottish Enterprise 1992), although a number of universities have significant interactions with the sector.

Scotland's major manufacturing base now resides in electronics. In 1993, seventy percent of employees worked for about forty firms—most of them foreign-owned OEMs (original equipment manufacturers). Altogether there are more than 300 firms engaged in equipment manufacture with electronic components; especially telecomm equipment. The central valley between Glasgow and Edinburgh, where most of the plants are located, has become known as Silicon Glen but with scant resemblance to the innovative activity of Silicon Valley. These are branch plant manufacturers, and few companies have established close linkages with local suppliers, which might stimulate another layer of growth in the economy (Turok 1993). Not surprisingly, therefore, these companies have had few research links with universities. The picture is of screw-driver plants and an economy based on branch plant manufacturing.

In other ways, the Scottish economy reflects the larger U.K. picture (Scottish Enterprise 1991). As in the United Kingdom and other advanced economies, jobs in manufacturing have been replaced by jobs in services. What does cause concern, however, is that Scotland's rate of innovation, once the highest in the Empire, has now fallen below the national average. Some have put this down to the loss of entrepreneurial spirit in the nation, perhaps born of attitudes of dependency and a culture of social assistance payouts as the economy has declined. Significantly, there are also fewer head offices of medium/large-sized companies located in Scotland than a decade ago and dis-cernible anxiety about peripheralization.

The Scottish Development Agency (now reorganized as the Scottish Enterprise Network) is considered to have had a positive impact in stimulat-ing the development of the region. Much of their work has been in infrastruc-tural improvement and their "Locate in Scotland" campaign was, in fact, responsible for attracting much of the new manufacturing base to Scotland. The Agency has now been replaced by a small central unit, Scottish Enter-prise, networked with more locally-based LECs (Local Enterprise Compa-nies) which are roughly equivalent to the Training and Enterprise Companies (TECs) in England. The new system has still to prove itself; one of the disad-vantages now becoming evident in this new system is that too many interme-diaries have been set up to support enterprise, each operating under different sets of rules and causing confusion for potential customers. Regional assis-tance is both piecemeal and ad hoc; it is heavily bureaucratized to the extent that the administrative burden may now be disproportionate to the funding disbursed. There is also the question as to whether the new layer of adminis-tration in LECs will soak up a significant portion of budgets that previously might have been invested in projects. The university experience of the new system is patchy; some universities have received considerable support from their local LEC for initiatives to do with exploiting their ideas. Others have been less fortunate. Since universities receive no central funding to help them with exploitation and there are no funds for market research or for promo-tional activities, the LECs are an obvious agency to approach. If Scottish uni-versities are to access sponsorship from firms south of the border, they need resources to do so. With a local industry base with little internal resarch capac-ity, Scottish universities are disadvantaged by their location.

In order to explore more about the relationship between the universities and wealth creation we need first to turn to the broader national (U.K.) con-text of which the micro-environment, i.e., regional/Scottish, that we have briefly described is part.

The Failure to Develop a Technology Policy in the U.K.

The hypothesis put forward in this section is that while Britain appreciated the unprecedented fertility of modern science and its wealth-creating aspects in the postwar years, this distracted attention from other aspects of technological innovation underpinning much of the manufacturing base.

Since World War II it has become evident that countries have pursued very different policies with regard to science and technology. Several typologies have been identified (OECD 1991) but all are based upon the proposition that there have been two main strategies for gaining competitive edge in international markets.

Mission-oriented policies are conceptually rooted in the science push models of radical innovation. Science is at the front end of innovation and delivers revolutionary new products, and supernormal profits are appropriated at the early stage of the product life cycle. If the discoveries are of great significance, then this type of innovation can lead to whole new industries based on the new technology. Countries that follow this pattern are the United States, the United Kingdom, and France. Only major economies with an advanced research base under public control have pursued this strategy.

By contrast, *diffusion-oriented* policies rest on alternative conceptual thinking. Competitive edge is gained at the mature stage of the product life cycle through overall cost leadership and improving product quality. Greater emphasis is placed on incremental innovation in low-risk fields; technology plays an enabling role and enhances the productive capability of firms. Innovation thus is more *process-based.* Countries who have successfully pursued this strategy are Japan, Germany, Sweden, and Switzerland. As a rule, countries that have adopted "diffusion-oriented" policies have exhibited faster economic growth in recent years than countries that have adopted *mission-oriented* policies.

Although mission-oriented policies may have been to the advantage of the pharmaceutical industry in the United Kingdom, Britain's patchy performance in manufactured products has undoubtedly been affected by the lack of investment and insufficient attention to incremental product improvement achieved by enhanced technical performance and process innovation.

What is now becoming clear is that, for advanced economies, these are not alternative strategies; both are important but the impact will be different in various industry sectors, or even different functions within the same manufacturing firm. So there is a need to reevaluate the role of science in technological innovation.

The science push model of innovation may be a suitable paradigm for drug discovery but it is entirely inappropriate for the bulk of manufacturing industry. This is not to say that science is irrelevant to technological innovation; its relevance is not necessarily at the front end. Increasingly, technological innovation is drawing upon the science base. This puts science underneath technology; a different relationship entirely (this will be discussed more fully in the following section).

The Japanese have appreciated that science has another role to play. Japanese policies are founded on the broader hypothesis that there is a development cycle, which has four recognizable stages (Niwa 1992): manufacturing production; technology innovation; scientific discovery; and then scientific infrastructure.

This policy puts technology improvement in between manufacturing and the science base. It is the critical link that holds the science base in readiness to be available for enabling technical advance. Without this link the science base cannot be utilized by manufacturing. It is why the Japanese, after having imported and then improved on existing technology, are now building up their scientific infrastructure. Much of this new scientific capability is within the firm (Niwa 1992) and so will be brought into closest contact with technical expertise. (Whether a large in-firm scientific capability is viable within the more stringent economic climate now prevailing in Japan remains to be seen.)

It is the technological innovation and infrastructure that are lacking in the U.K. Britain no longer creates her own technology, she imports it. A highly significant survey carried out in 1990 by CEST (Centre for Exploitation of Science and Technology) compared the attitudes of German manufacturing companies to British manufacturers. Whereas British companies are very open in their approach to sourcing technology, the Germans are very cautious and committed to the long-term buildup of internal capabilities through research (Cheese 1991). Cheese (1993), who carried out this study, suggests that withdrawal from industries like textiles, machine tools, and motorcycles is evidence that the U.K. has lost her competitiveness and that at the root of this is the lack of ability to develop in-house propriety technologies (whether this is done in partnership with others or alone).

The corollary to this is that in the United Kingdom many of the linkages between suppliers and manufacturers have been lost. The United Kingdom as a whole, and Scotland in particular, no longer have the clusters of small and medium-sized firms that Porter (1991) suggests are at the heart of thriving regional economies. It is the vital customer-supplier linkages that von Hippel (1986) sees as a frequent stimulus to innovation.

This is not the place to explore such concepts in depth. The important point is that the United Kingdom has only a few world-class companies that are highly research intensive. Most of the manufacturing base consists of medium and small (even large) companies that have no research function and a relatively slim development function. Given the science and technology policies that the United Kingdom has pursued, this is no surprise. Also, it is equally revealing, perhaps, that the United Kingdom's most successful sector, speciality chemicals and pharmaceuticals, is precisely where the science-push model of innovation and policies based on it would be expected to be most effective.

The picture that this paints of the United Kingdom in the '90s is unquestionably one of great concern; the loss of an innovative manufacturing base has become a focus for concern at the Department of Trade and Industry, but nowhere is this problem more acute than in Scotland. The problem is that, put crudely, the United Kingdom now has a technology gap, and the question is how can that gap be plugged at a time when there are increasing calls on the public purse for social welfare needs. It is why the university-industry debate is particularly relevant in the British context, because universities are a major repository of scientific and technological expertise in comparison to the slender research base in the broad company sector. Unlike other European countries, who have developed a technology infrastructure, a layer of organizations to facilitate the diffusion of technology, in the United Kingdom this function is left in the main to independent consultants and contract research organizations. Nor have there been such structures as the Fraunhofer Institutes in Germany active in technology development. Most independent contract research organizations in the United Kingdom are not in receipt of any public moneys and have been unable to refresh their technology base to the degree of their European counterparts. There is no applied research organization such as TNO in the Netherlands. Moreover, most contract research organizations and other professional services are concentrated in the southern half of Britain. This again leaves the north of England and Scotland at a disadvantage.

In fact, as implied, the problem is two-fold. There is the issue of technology diffusion; getting companies to adopt new technology and then to develop it in order to innovate incrementally. The evidence is that British companies, over recent years, have not been sufficiently profitable to allow them to invest in new equipment and technology; and the lack of this technology has made them less able to compete, which has caught them in a vicious spiral downwards (Financial Times 1993). This is where diffusion-oriented policies would normally be directed but it is far from clear how far universities, with tightly constrained resources, will be able to divert attention to non-core activities.

Second, there is the issue of radical new technology development. Universities could have a significant input here but first one needs to understand more about the nature of technological innovation.

New Technologies and Innovation

The main purpose of this section is to understand the process of technological innovation and why the science and technology base in universities is so important.

Technology is such a complex and variable phenomenon that it is not easily captured by a single definition; the Collins Concise English Dictionary advances three interpretations:

1. the application of practical or mechanical sciences to industry or commerce;
2. the methods, theory, and practices governing such application;
3. the total knowledge and skills available to any human society.

Here, therefore, is an immediate distinction between science and technology. The aim of technology is purposeful while the objectives of science are to understand that which is different and not predicated on the former. What is especially useful about these definitions is that they embody concepts that help to unravel the role of technology in commercial production:

i) *empirically-based technology:* technology develops by a set of codified rules and tacit knowledge that is passed on mainly through people and is skills- or practice-based. How these methods are arrived at does not matter; what matters is that they work in a given situation.

ii) *application of science (theory):* empirically-based methods often fail when the context changes. Scientific theory is universal and can be applied over a wide range of situations. In a constantly changing environment (flexible manufacturing, for example), fix and mend methods are inefficient; scientific methods are superior. In a manufacturing climate, which continually demands higher performance criteria beyond the limits of practical experience, the scientific approach is essential.

iii) *technology as an aggregation of skills, methods and theory:* increasingly, new technology requires a fusion of competencies; information is being coalesced in novel ways.

In the development of a new technology, the bringing together of knowledge bases is often a key factor—multidisciplinary expertise is required to solve complex technological problems. For firms that do not possess a complete array of skills and technical expertise, this can be a problem. This difficulty is compounded by the insufficient and uncoordinated support for the development of emerging technologies. Why support should be necessary for developing new technologies is not so much a dereliction on the part of companies but a failure of the market economy. Every firm has a wide number of options it could follow but is limited, for economic reasons, to developing only those new technologies in house that will give it a unique edge in the market. Most technologies do not confer this singular benefit; there is a problem of appropriability. Hence, firms are unwilling, on their own, to support development of emerging *generic or enabling* technologies, which could also be used by their competitors.

The Japanese have recognized this problem for some time and have evolved a system of inter-firm collaboration to develop technology during the early phases and shadow the developments of their own research laboratories. It is less common for such collaborative agreements to develop in the Western competitive culture, but here too "needs must." General Motors, Ford, and Chrysler, the three U.S. car makers, have recently been awarded their first joint patent for a process that allows them to manufacture vehicle components from liquidmoulded composites. Together the companies have formed USCAR—the US Council for Automative Research—to work together to develop basic technology that will lead to better, more efficient products and enhance competitiveness. The cooperation works because each company receives due return out of the joint venture and, by developing only the raw, basic technology, each partner has the opportunity to customize the raw technology to serves its own individual requirements. After fifty years of intense inter-firm competition in the pharmaceutical industry, nine companies in Europe together with six firms in the United States are collaborating together for the first time to develop better medicines to combat AIDS. In the last decade there has been a rapid increase of inter-firm collaborative research (Watkins 1991). Only technology-intensive companies, or those with a deep enough pocket for development expenditure can afford to go this route to develop generic technologies.

But, as noted, a great preponderance of technologies *are* generic and how to resource their development is a problem for market economies. Furthermore, other factors like scale and scope, already mentioned, which are making the development of technologies more difficult for firms to go it alone are:

- a multidisciplinary input that may be required beyond the capabilities in house
- tacit knowledge, which requires access on a personal basis to those with the skills sought
- underpinning from the science base

Input from the science base is becoming a critical factor in more than a few new and emerging technologies. This, together with the breadth of skills available in many universities, is the reason universities are increasingly becoming involved with the early stages in the development of new technologies.

To give but one or two examples to illustrate this point: in the semiconductor sector, miniaturization is reaching its technological limits. Top-down techniques suitable for manipulating bulk materials will become too crude and bottom-up methods which involve molecular manipulation will be required. Hence, the skills base will move from engineering to the chemistry and the molecular sciences. Another example involving materials and a move from empiricism to science-based techniques is in drug formulation. Here, it is becoming increasingly important to understand the properties of materials, for example the excipients used to bind active chemical entities in tabletting, and the need to produce crystalline forms of greater purity. This work involves the physical chemist.

In the Technology Audits we have conducted we have come across many examples of the science base, chemistry especially, underpinning the development of new technologies. Much of this scientific work is applied in nature, putting scientists in a reactive mode; conceptually, it is technology that is pulling science and not science pushing on innovation.

Recognition of difficulty in resourcing generic technologies is reflected in the growth of government-funded schemes to lower the financial barriers to developing generic technologies. This is the main emphasis of the European Community Framework IV programs. In the United Kingdom the DTI (Department of Trade and Industry) LINK initiative has been set up to encourage firms to collaborate with universities on the early development of new technologies. It is one of the 50/50 contribution schemes, but made more flexible by the fact that companies are allowed to contribute in kind and not in cash. Even so, the scheme still has considerable drawbacks; few small firms can afford this type of commitment, and for universities, trying to get a group of companies together can be very costly in itself. Although the EC programs have been enormously helpful in bringing firms and universities together, the actual cost of submission to success ratio is getting so high that some potential applicants cannot afford to put together a bid, especially when this involves coordination with foreign partners.

Another main problem for developing new technology is the so-called predevelopment gap. This is a well-recognized phenomenon on both sides of the Atlantic (Wooton 1992). The problem is that while there is funding (typically on a 50/50 public/private basis) to develop the early stages of an emerging technology, there is nothing to support the next stage of early prototyping. This is vital if a new technology is to gain acceptability by industry and is all the more difficult if the new technology disrupts existing ways of doing things. For universities, there is also the expense of maintaining patents—sometimes a whole bundle of patents—and not knowing when to let go or whether to hang on.

There is no doubt that the culture of universities, while it may be inventive, is not educated about the barriers to successful innovation that await the intrepid inventor. IP (intellectual property) is frequently squandered because academics rush to publish their findings. A notable instance where academics could not wait for industry and went ahead and published their findings was at Dundee University. Their research on hydrogenated silicon and the subsequent development of LED (light emitting diode) technology was world-beating but their hurry lost them a patent that would have earned the inventors and the university many millions of pounds. Sometimes, academics imagine that they can do more than they are capable of when it comes to turning an invention into an innovation. Magnetic resonance imaging was developed in prototype form at the University of Aberdeen, but the technology was ahead of its time and the market was not ready for it, nor was there the faintest chance that a development company set up through the university would be capable of developing the degree of sophisticated equipment required. It was only when the technology was licensed on to General Electric that the technology found expression in the marketplace. Therefore, important as intellectual property is, it is the complementary assets that are often the determining factor in market success or the failure of technology derived from university laboratories.

Furthermore, there is not the supportive climate for spinoff companies as in the United States. The chief difficulty is the lack of seed capital enabling a new startup to develop to the stage where venture capital would be interested. In the majority of cases institutional policy is well advised to encourage the academic entrepreneur to licence on inventions to suitable partners who are far more capable than academics are of making a successful innovation out of an invention. This policy has served Strathclyde University well; in respect of IP earnings it is the leading U.K. University, revenue received annually amounts to £2.8 million, the highest in the United Kingdom, and significant even in terms of leading North American institutions. Nevertheless, some academics *will* always want to go one step further toward the marketplace and in order to do so, the University has a Business Ventures Group which operates a small fund to help new ventures with early-stage development. In doing so, the University may take notional "shares" in the embryonic venture which can be bought back at a later stage. For such entrepreneurs, Strathclyde has a small incubator unit on campus housing around thirteen small companies (not all spinoffs). There is also the West of Scotland Science Park, which can accommodate new technology-based firms (NTBFs). On the Science Park, a small company, Targetting Technology, has recently been established by Glasgow Development Agency (the local LEC) using European Regional Development Funding whose mission it is to assist NTBFs.

This form of assistance is thought to be necessary because, at a regional level, Scotland has a lower than average rate of NTBF formation. Why this should be so is not altogether understood. Some evidence suggests that Scots are risk averse because of the social stigma attached to failure. Also, there is a perceived lack of business support services available to entrepreneurs. A recent survey of small biotechnology startup companies in Scotland highlighted the need felt by companies for additional expertise in marketing and finance (Leaver 1992). Clearly, there is a lot of support of this nature around, but whether it is tailored to fit client needs is another issue.

To sum up, universities in the United Kingdom are increasingly involved with commercial sponsors in the development of new emerging technologies. As technology becomes more science-based, this trend will undoubtedly continue. But not all emerging technologies will necessarily be the springboard for new company formation. Most of the time, "raw" technologies will be licensed on to commercial partners. For researchers in Scottish universities, the links at national and international level are very important because they enable academics to collaborate with leading-edge companies beyond the regional industry base. Such links do not, however, directly benefit the local economy, to which we now turn.

Universities' Role in the Diffusion of Technology

It is an interesting question why universities should become involved in the diffusion of technology and the application of knowledge for private benefit. The arguments against universities' involvement have been rehearsed frequently and run like this: universities' mission is teaching and research; when institutions are funded by public money, accountability requires that public moneys are not diverted for private benefit. This argument appears quite clearcut and straightforward; but how does this apply to training, consultancy, and contract research?

Many business schools are heavily involved in all of these activities because, it is claimed, it is vital for their members to interact with the real world in order to have a grasp of the context of their expertise and, through consultancy, to practice their profession and establish credibility in the field. If their institution also benefits through additional income, and normal responsibilities are not neglected, real benefits can accrue to the institution. The same argument is put forward for professional engineers who are actually required by their professional organizations to carry out a certain amount of field work in order to retain their professional status.

This point about learning in context is crucial for technology. Technology advances either by the application of new theory to improve control over existing processes or by using known technology in novel contexts. Teachers and researchers of technology-based subjects in universities therefore need to keep in close contact with industrial practice. This need has been officially recognized in the United States: the NSF report (National Research Council 1991) on the competitive edge in manufacturing speaks of "the factory as the laboratory" and emphasizes that new learning must be linked with industrial practice.

However, much contract research offers no opportunity for new insights. By far the greater proportion of work where companies require external expertise is not novel. Nor are academics the best people to conduct work requiring routine problem solving but high throughput and process skills, to give a low cost service. It is for this type of service that the contract research organizations are in business.

In the United Kingdom, the history of the contract research organizations has, in the main, been of organizations set up to serve the research needs of specific industry sectors and of small companies, in particular, who could not afford to support their own R&D function. Over the years and with the prevailing philosophy of a purely market-driven economy, these research organizations have had little assistance from government to improve their own technology base. Unlike their European counterparts they have been remote from academia and many have failed to keep themselves at the forefront of latest practice. This situation has only served to widen the gulf between industry and academia and is very different from that in many other European countries where the research, technology, and innovation centers act as intermediaries.

Scotland, perhaps more than any other region in the United Kingdom, could benefit from the implementation of "diffusion-oriented" policies. As indicated at the beginning of this chapter, many of Scotland's SMEs are technology followers, not leaders. That most of the contract research organizations are located in the southern half of the United Kingdom is an additional barrier for many smaller firms seeking assistance.

Hence, some will and do turn to universities. But universities do not necessarily seek this kind of relationship. Small companies are all too often cash poor and want their problems solved at lower than market rates. Universities, on the other hand, are either looking for exciting research opportunities out of industrial links or they are wanting income that can then be ploughed back to support other research. Neither is normally forthcoming from small companies. Understandably, industry liaison officers in universities are reluctant to take on a plethora of very small contracts that involve a high transaction cost for little benefit and, in addition, run a higher than average risk of termination by the firm in mid-contract, leaving research students stranded with no income support to complete their research theses.

Therefore, helping companies to "catch up" with their technology is not an option that universities normally find attractive. With increasing competition for research funds, it remains to be seen whether the former polytechnics will be willing to pick up more of the applied type of work. By doing so and diverting energies, they could well place themselves even further out of reach of central funding which follows "quality," i.e., basic, research. Given the difficulties described, it is only logical that if universities are to become involved in any large way with technology diffusion, then they will need different structures and systems, which we go on to discuss later.

What we have only hinted at so far, is that the type of structure or posture that a university—or academic group—develops in relation to industry is contingent upon the function that the knowledge/technology performs in the firm. These differences become very apparent when we begin to examine institutional links on a project-by-project basis as they vary across a single institution.

A Typology of University-Industry Links

A few years ago, ETRAC at the University of Strathclyde carried out a survey of all the university's links with industry in one academic year. To our knowledge, it is the only survey of its type. So, while the study was undertaken mainly for internal purposes, it does happen to demonstrate very clearly how academic disciplines differ in their relationships with industry. The findings also probably reflect some more general lessons about university/industry relations.

This survey has been reported more fully elsewhere (Sheen et al. 1992) and only the main findings are described here. To give a little background: the survey (a census) profiled all the contracts with industrial companies during one academic year. It does not cover undergraduate projects with companies unless these were drawn up by the R&D Office as an official contract.

Figure 9.1 demonstrates very clearly that by far the greater proportion of links are at a national, not regional level. There is a very important message here. Many policy makers expect that universities will contribute to the regeneration of the local manufacturing base, without thinking through the problem. They fail to appreciate what universities seek in their industrial links. Where the industry base is not advanced and not receptive to new technology, universities have little to gain from such links. As discussed in the previous section, universities' interests lie in working at the frontiers of knowledge and this leads them to cultivate relationships with world-class companies. Increas-

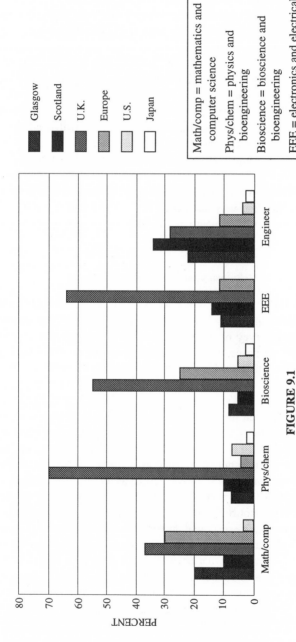

FIGURE 9.1
Distance of Collaboration

From ETRAC survey of interactions between University of Strathclyde (Science and Engineering Faculties) and Industry 1990/1991. Distance of Collaboration.

Glasgow
Scotland
U.K.
Europe
U.S.
Japan

Math/comp = mathematics and computer science

Phys/chem = physics and bioengineering

Bioscience = bioscience and bioengineering

EEE = electronics and electrical engineering

Engineer = all other engineering including mechanical

ingly, those links could be at an international level. In fact, one indicator of the quality of research in a university could well be the links with world-class companies. Most of the research-intensive universities therefore can be expected to have many more links nationally and internationally than they will have regionally.

Another point to note from our survey was the difference in distance of collaboration of different academic disciplines with different industry sectors. These links reflected the important role that universities play in research activities of the national pharmaceutical and chemicals sector; again, these activities are increasingly becoming global, and links with American and Japanese companies are expanding. This is in marked contrast with engineering (excluding electronic or electrical), which is the only sector where local and regional links outweigh national links.

Figures 9.2a and 9.2b illustrate some further important points. They show what benefits different industry sectors were getting from their partnerships with the University. (Note that this was a multichoice question so that the responses add across to greater than 100 percent.) The results are really no great surprise if one considers the national industry picture that was sketched out earlier. In fact, all our findings indicated how adept the research-intensive science-based companies were at finding collaborative partners and in utilizing schemes such as SERC's (Science and Engineering Research Council) CASE funding. As shown, it is those sectors that are the most highly research intensive that are extending their research base by either keeping a watching brief or supporting strategic research. It is the engineering sector that is looking more for problem-solving types of skills.

Our findings also indicated that it is the smaller companies who, in general, are seeking assistance at a much more practical level either about existing products or processes. We found that the majority of links that Strathclyde has with small companies are regional, not national, and, significantly, that it was small companies that made the first move to contact the university for assistance. This is evidence for the point made earlier that universities will not go out of their way to cultivate relationships with smaller companies. But where does that leave the smaller company or the company that has only a development function and no significant research facilities?

Regional authorities, we think, tend to take a far too simplistic view of how a university creates wealth at the local and regional level. Universities' contribution, we believe, is more indirect than indirect. In fact, universities contribute to the regional (local) economy in no insignificant way. A recent report demonstrated that Strathclyde University (McNicoll 1993) contributed an estimated £230 million to the Scottish economy in 1991–92 and generated an estimated 5380 full-time equivalent jobs and a spending power of £94.5

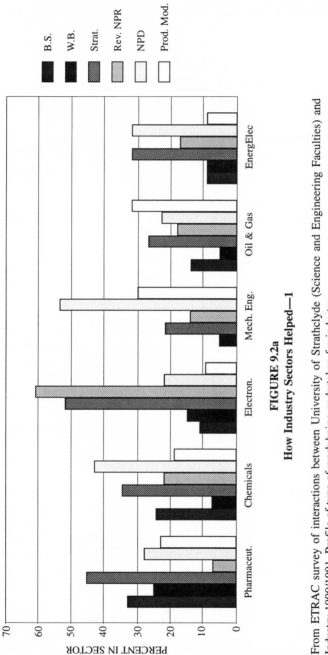

FIGURE 9.2a
How Industry Sectors Helped—1

From ETRAC survey of interactions between University of Strathclyde (Science and Engineering Faculties) and Industry 1990/1991. Profile of type of work being undertaken for industry.

B.S. = Blue Skies Research Rev. NPR = Revolutionary New Product Research
W.B. = Watching Brief   NPD = New Product Development
Strat = Strategic Research   Prod. Mod. = Product Modification

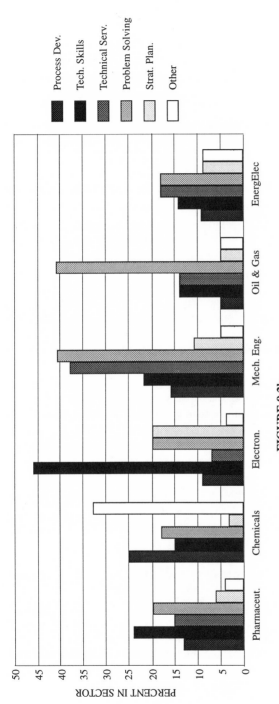

FIGURE 9.2b
How Industry Sectors Helped—2

From ETRAC survey of interactions between University of Strathclyde (Science and Engineering Faculties) and Industry 1990/1991. Profile of type of work being undertaken for industry.

Process Dev. = Process Development   Problem Solving = Problem Solving
Tech. Skills = Technical Skills   Strat. Plan. = Strategic Planning
Technical Serv. = Technical Services

million. That would be much the same for any university, but this does not mean that universities necessarily contribute directly to the industrial base around them. Regional authorities would do well to view universities as a business in themselves because in all the major cities in Scotland they are wealth generators.

The fact that government is exhorting universities to see *industry as a research opportunity* needs some qualification. This section has demonstrated how diverse those needs may be across different sectors. That more academics are beginning to see *research as a business opportunity* suggests that we may be beginning to move into a new phase which will radically challenge the way that universities conduct research. This leads us on to the next section considering the types of organizational innovations found in institutions of higher education as they adapt to their changing task environment.

Institutional Policies, Departmental Strategies, and Organizational Innovations

The department-based structure organized along disciplinary lines has traditionally served universities well in their teaching commitments and, where research was undertaken to inform teaching, there has been no reason to question such arrangements.

New factors are now emerging, including the exploitation of research, that raise questions about whether the department is still the most appropriate configuration when it comes to the research function. Not all of these factors are externally determined; some are internally generated by the nature of the research itself.

First, the ratio of research funding available in relation to those applying for public-sector support has declined. There is more competition. Thus, to be successful requires more concentrated effort and, in a positive feedback system, success breeds success. This increasingly competitive environment favors the establishment of more independent research centers and leads to a concentration of research. Some Research Councils actively promote this organizational configuration.

Second, as we move further away from the model of a university where knowledge is for the sake of knowledge toward the concept of creating potentially useful or relevant knowledge (what the French call finalized science), then universities need to have much more understanding about the *value* of the knowledge they create. Academics will have to become more market aware and understand the rudiments of intellectual property law so that intellectual property is protected before it is published. That way, new information can be exploited, value is not dissipated, and if the university retains ownership, then intellectual property can be used to generate further sponsored research from industry. Universities who are actively and increasingly engaged in knowledge trading all now have a central service unit, or trading company to deal not only with the management of intellectual property, but also with negotiation of contracts and marketing of the knowledge base of the University.

Third, because funding is increasingly competitive (the "well-found" laboratory has gone under the new dual-funding arrangements), academia is turning to other organizations to fund research. As Research Councils are now also requiring academics to find industry partners, that implies a considerably increased marketing effort to find industry sponsors. There is no budget that universities receive to fund this type of activity, nor is it something that most academics have any experience of. So we begin to see the establishment of centers that will market the research of a group of academics into target sectors. The Strathclyde Institute of Drug Research was established along these lines as a marketing platform that would promote the research of academics from a number of different departments who are involved in drug research.

Fourth, as is well known, real-life problems and phenomena are interdisciplinary and do not fit readily into academic disciplines. More sponsored research is requiring a multidisciplinary approach and thus poses a threat to departmental fiefdoms. Centers of excellence increasingly cut across disciplines. There may even be parallels here with business transformation where businesses have had to re-engineer themselves and modify functional organization. Universities have sometimes been characterized as *professional bureaucracies*. Many departments are highly resistant to structural innovation which might threaten their autonomy. The research institute is a useful mechanism for bringing together multidisciplinary groups. The Interdisciplinary Research Centres set up by the Science and Engineering Research Council in the 1980s had precisely this aim of getting academics to work with colleagues with different disciplinary backgrounds. This is therefore a further challenge to academia to broaden their outlook horizontally. Indeed, this challenge does not need to originate externally because of commercial interests. Any subject whose focus is systems based may need to integrate disciplines or specialties. In the biosciences, the divisions between cell biology, biochemistry, molecular biology, etc. are increasingly anachronistic. At Dundee University, the Department of Biochemistry, of international reputation, has merged these sub-disciplines to form one entity. Certainly, in biomedical research the multidisciplinary research institute is becoming the way that research, in our experience, is most frequently organized in Europe. That is true whether or not there is a teaching capability alongside the institute. The marketing platform model may thus be superseded by other more cohesive structures.

Inevitably, one would expect to come across many organizational variants that fall in between these structures, but, as far as one can see, the trend is increasingly toward focus, e.g., smart structures or industrial control systems and away from discrete disciplines, e.g., electronics.

These new configurations are particularly well suited to collaborative research of a precompetitive nature where the collaboration includes a developmental agenda. Collaborative research is research undertaken in partnership with commercial sponsors where the research is speculative, open-ended, and with a high degree of uncertainty as to the outcome. Any potential benefit to the firm is in the long term. Only research-intensive companies undertake this type of research. Few U.K. firms have this capacity; most are in the chemical and pharmaceutical sectors where sponsors have been interested in a single research specialty.

However, European Union funding under the fourth framework program strongly promoted collaborative research in interdiciplinary areas, helping to establish new partnering arrangements across Europe. As technologies become more complex and require articulation (i.e., technology fusion), so some universities have established key centers of expertise to exploit fourth framework opportunities. These partnerships are typically in engineering and entail working to much tighter specifications and deadlines. Such centers, however, can prove much more difficult to manage than the more simple one-on-one collaborative agreements. The root of many problems, again, lies in the disciplinary structure. Responsibility for project management usually lies with a manager of a key technology center which may at times run counter to the wishes of a head of department. Where staff have their time split between departmental duties and obligations to the key technology centers, they may experience a conflict of priorities.

Some of the most challenging opportunities can arise in the type of contract research where novel high-technology solutions are being sought. Academics may be attracted by the intellectual stimulation such work provides, but the need to deliver results to strict deadlines means can become the cause of conflicting priorities. There are some areas in technology-based subjects, such as engineering, where it really is not possible to be at the leading edge of research without becoming involved with industry directly. The Petroleum Engineering Department at Heriot-Watt University in Edinburgh is one such an example; it is one of the highest revenue earners per capita in the United Kingdom. Such departments may well become much more like the consulting partnership firms one finds in engineering firms undertaking advanced consultancy. Because, however, academics career progression depends on the contribution of the *individual,* there is more danger of internal competition for clients and maybe also, confusion on the part of industry. Furthermore, such departments may experience some difficulty both in managing their internal interface with the rest of their institution—universities, as professional bureaucracies, may not appreciate the commercial imperatives that drive such groups or understand why such groups can only extend themselves as far as a postgraduate teaching commitment. Although such groups may be high revenue earners they are not necessarily highly profitable. In always seeking out the novel problem to solve, industry may only pay enough to cover costs. Where profit could be gained is in selling the same solution, perhaps customized, to a different client. However, this would often be considered not appropriate to an academic institution. Nor would it be legal, given the charitable status of all public-sector universities.

A few universities occasionally engage with the world of contract manufacturing; albeit in very specialized and small niche markets. Speciality research compounds and fermentation processes, and small-scale formulation of pharmaceuticals would be examples. Here, the interest for the university may not only be the opportunity for learning and acquiring new skills but can actually be the revenue such activities generates which can be reinvested in research. Spare capacity in, for example sterile suites for small-scale manufacturing, can create additional revenue. Or novel techniques can be used to offer industry novel compounds which are not normally commercially available. The boundary between what is a product and a service can become highly blurred. Legally, universities are charitable insitutions and are permitted to undertake commercial activities on a very limited scale. Where these commercial activities become significant revenue earners, to keep within the legal boundaries a way round these rules and regulations is for the university to hive off the commercial activity as a separate company, owned by the university, but then to covenant back the profits to the university.

Sometimes it may suit an institution to establish a commercial operation, and, where there is associated research of a more academic nature, this may be manifested in the form of a dual organizational structure. Although equipment and capital resources may be shared, there are two distinct organizations using them—one an internal research unit; the other a commercial undertaking. This form of bifunctionality may take various forms. These alternative forms of organizing for research are not especially novel (Sheen 1993). What makes them more appropriate now is where contract research falls in between the mundane and the challenging; where on occasion a more advanced problem-solving capability is required; or where academia is generating new technologies, which can be offered as a technical service. Many academics have no interest at all in the commercial side nor, indeed, are many well suited to setting up the type of routine standardized procedures necessary for delivering cost-driven technical services.

We have observed several such experiments with dual-structure organizations. Some have flourished for a short time and then died, others have failed to reach their full potential. Two problems seem to beset such organizations. The first can occur when academics fail to distance themselves from the commercial operation. The second, often called "academic drift," is where those on the commercial side hanker after an academic approach. Applied research for commercial purposes must understand when to draw the line to further enquiry. A dual-structure organization needs to be just that—two organizations—one with a market orientation, the other with an academic orientation in order to avoid internal competition and confusion about who is serving the client.

The best example of a dual-structure organization that we know about is at the Technical University in Denmark (Sheen 1993). This configuration has been in place for about forty years, where both commercial capacity and the level of academic research have grown significantly from a local competence to an institution that has gained international recognition. The key to success is in the design, creating a symbiotic relationship between the commercial operation, which passes over novel problems for academics to look at, which then eventually get transferred back as new skills and capabilities to the commercial arm so as to keep them ahead of the competition. The Institute of Product Development works closely with Strathclyde University.

A further strategy for mixing commercial and research activity under the one roof is a joint-venture operation. Dundee Biotech is a joint venture involving the University of Dundee and Scotia Pharmaceuticals. The pilot scale fermentation facility is the largest independent unit available in any Scottish institution. The Unit can provide a confidential range of contract services to industry. The major advantage of this facility to commercial users is that the commercial viability and potential of novel processes and products developed in the laboratory can be evaluated on a pre-production scale without the necessity to invest in fermentation and trained staff.

Over recent years, as we have carried out research and consultancy in a number of universities in Scotland, the United Kingdom, and other European countries, we have observed an increasing number of opportunities for organizational innovations of this type. Many of these opportunities arise out of biotechnology, new materials and manufacturing processes, information technology, analytical and environmental science, where research and applications are advancing rapidly.

Compared to the United States, academics in U.K. universities are far less likely to become involved in spinoff companies. In Scotland, Scottish Enterprise have been keen to address this issue. After having conducted a lengthy and costly enquiry into the problem, they concluded that while the country has excellent institutions of higher education, these institutions have not spun off many companies. They may be premature with their judgment; what may be hindering this process is the culture, which is now changing fast in universities and not least because public-sector funding makes academics get out and talk to industry. But industry is unresponsive and research grants become too competitive, so entrepreneurial academics will inevitably find other routes to fund their research, including trading activities.

However, it is all too easy to make the case for more applied research and exploitation. The fact is that if too much research becomes derivative, then the quality of the research base can suffer. That is not to decry applied research but the need is to differentiate between routine problem solving and more advanced problem solving. A greater proportion of the knowledge we now require both for commercial and social benefits is context-related. Only those institutions that have the capacity to learn about the environment into which emerging new technologies are to be utilized can hope to particpate in the shaping of these new technologies. Institutions that understand this message will also appreciate that contextual learning will mean new collaborative mechanisms will have to be set up. Where more substantial relationships are envisaged this will manifest itself in terms of new organizational innovations and even in institutional transformation.

Conclusions

The exploitation of scientific and technical knowledge produced by public-sector research is now a main strand of government policy in the United Kingdom. The Foresight Exercise has consulted widely, bringing academics and industrialists together to identify key areas where more research is needed. Greater linkage between university research and industry is to be achieved by funding public-sector researchers who have co-sponsorship from industry.

These policies are being implemented at a time when even greater changes are taking place in the way universities are funded. Indeed, the whole higher education system in the United Kingdom is still in a period of transition. Public-sector funding is increasingly becoming concentrated in fewer institutions. The system would appear to be becoming rapidly differentiated. The infrastructure for research has declined and the "well-found" laboratory has been abolished. Thus, breadth and scope of research are being reduced and research and teaching are becoming more separate.

Greater accountability for all public expenditure is encroaching upon the established rights of autonomy of universities. Bureaucracy is increasing.

There are seveal contributing factors, such as the way resources are devolved to departments and the way research excellence is judged as discipline-based. All have tended to enhance the compartmentalization of knowledge at a time when the exploitation of knowledge requires the very opposite.

Efficiency gains and cost-cutting measures cannot continue indefinitely if quality is to be maintained. So institutions are turning their attention to greater income generation and additional sources of revenue, including the exploitation of their knowledge base. However, universities are extreme complex and diverse organizations, as are the individual academics they employ and the types of knowledge they create, so there will be many routes whereby new knowledge finds ultimate expression in the marketplace.

The universities in Scotland are regarded by regional authorities as an asset that can contribute to the economic redevelopment of the region. Understanding of how this process can be achieved is still at the formative stage. There are no simple answers. With a technology gap wider than in other areas of the United Kingdom between the manufacturing base and public sector research located alongside, better linkage seems the obvious solution until the roots of the barriers are understood.

The fact is that universities are themselves one of Scotland's largest "industry" sectors. That they stay at the forefront is important for their sustained level of activity. Scottish universities may be disadvantaged by their location in building industrial links and may have to seek more distant markets for the knowledge they create. But, in the long term, most advanced technologies are not dependent on local links, so early experience in accessing these more distant markets can be a competitive advantage.

The manufacturing base in Scotland incorporates many of the very latest manufacturing technologies. The disadvantage is that multinational firms control these factories so the value-added does not flow to the region. That, in time, may change, especially if we believe that spinoff developments are possible and institutions of higher education begin to address the negative attitudes to entrepreneurs.

It is unrealistic to expect that NTBFs from university spinoffs will give rise to new industry sectors. Such firms need encouragement as they will add to the technical diversity of the region, which can make a region more attractive for inwardly locating companies. The dual-structure organizations, described earlier, are one of the better ways to bridge the university/industry gap.

It is interesting to speculate that as the constraints upon universities are increasing, and autonomy of the institution being circumscribed, so to survive in an increasingly competitive climate requires extraordinary measures. Those already most successful will want to keep the rules the same. But for others, the majority not in that fortunate position, the need for experimentation and innovation has never been greater, so the propensity for organizational innovations may increase. That appetite is already apparent in the new universities; the commercialization of knowledge is one strategy they are bound to embrace with relish.

CHAPTER 10

Inching Toward Industrial Policy:
The University's Role in Government
Initiatives to Assist Small, Innovative
Companies in the United States

HENRY ETZKOWITZ and ASHLEY J. STEVENS

Introduction: Indirect Industrial Policy

The U.S. Government has promoted small innovative technology firms by coupling the funding of basic research at universities, teaching hospitals, and research institutes with policies to encourage the use of research results. These policies have favored small companies and have been accompanied by government initiatives to stimulate the availability of high-risk venture capital investment in new companies. Moreover, improvements in the system of intellectual property protection have reduced the risks of these investments. Government funding of research at companies has been of less importance. Until recently, such direct intervention was confined to technologies considered vital to the military. Indeed, an "indirect policy" to encourage technology transfer from academia to industry was in part created in response to ideological objections to governments intervening more directly in civilian industrial innovation.

The Bayh-Dole Act, originated by university officials and legislators to encourage technology transfer, moved the university toward a more central location in the economy.[1] The marketing of R&D, through offices located in the university's central administration, became an overlay on (and, according to some industrially active professors, an interference with) the university's traditional industrial role of supplying trained personnel and basic research knowledge through individual relationships of professors to companies. Technology transfer from academia developed in several stages; perhaps the most important was the creation of a system of federally supported research in the universities. Government funding, though, led to the emplacement of barriers

215

between academic research and industrial usage as an unintended consequence of federal policies to ensure fair access to a taxpayer-supported activity. Policies intended to make publicly supported research equally available
created a "free rider" effect, as companies were unwilling to take the risk of
developing such intellectual property, fearing that another firm would lay
claim to their work on the grounds that it had, at one time, been supported by
tax revenues.

These barriers were inconsequential impediments in an era when U.S.
industry maintained world technological leadership through R&D conducted
by firms themselves. In a new era of increased international competition,
external sources of R&D became more important, offering a potential competitive advantage. The buildup of government-supported intellectual property in the universities thus became more salient to industry and led to efforts
to take down the inadvertant barriers between the spheres. With more direct
routes to government intervention in the economy at the micro-level ideologically foreclosed, technology transfer from academia to industry became the
industrial policy of choice in the United States. The development of university technology transfer as an indirect industrial policy, in contrast to more
direct approaches taken in Japan and Europe, is our topic in this chapter.

The Road to Technology Transfer

The necessary condition for the creation of technology transfer from universities was the development of an extensive academic research base. The transformation of teaching into research faculties, the "first academic revolution,"
is still under way in many universities throughout the world. In the United
States, it occurred in the late nineteenth and early twentieth century, giving
academic institutions a new mission beyond education and training (Jencks
and Riesman 1968).

Prior to World War II, the government's role in the funding of research at
universities had been confined to specialized purposes at a relatively few
schools. The Morrill Act of 1862 [United States Statutes at Large, 503–5.] had
established the Land Grant Colleges, whose mandate had been to assist the
development of the U.S. agricultural economy and "the mechanic arts" (Hofstadter and Smith 1962). Today, the Morrill Act is mainly remembered for its
impact on agriculture. Some of the funds were turned over to expand existing
schools with a practical orientation, such as Cornell University, while other
funds went to start new schools. It is important to remember that the Massachusetts Institute of Technology (MIT) was originally established as a Morrill
Act institution, and its experience has been instrumental in the shaping of U.S.

policy on the interface between government, academia, and industry (Etzkowitz 1993, 1994b). Indeed, thirty percent of the Massachussetts moneys were used to help found MIT in 1864.

The Land Grant institutions later became the nexus of the agricultural extension service, which radically transformed the U.S. family farm, the center of the U.S. private sector in the nineteenth century. This policy was extremely effective. Universities became the major crop-breeding centers in the United States and bred seed lines suitable for the soil and climate conditions of their particular locality. This relationship changed in the 1970s, when changes in intellectual property laws pertaining to crops (the Plant Variety Protection Act and the Plant Variety Certificates that it allowed) resulted in a gradual movement of this activity into private seed companies such as Pioneer Hybrid in Des Moines, Iowa. Privatization was associated with scientific developments in genetics that potentially universalized plant improvement research, an activity that had formerly been local and regional (Kloppenberg 1988).

With the notable exception of agriculture and related activities, prior to World War II the bulk of academic research funding came from industry, and university research, of course, was at a much lower level of activity than we see today. For example, the entire research budget of the Columbia University physics department in 1929 was $10,000, and that was an exceptionally large figure at the time. In particular, foundations, the philanthropic extensions of corporations, played a significant role in encouraging academic research of both a theoretical and practical nature and in creating the project grant system which has become the hallmark of U.S. academia and much imitated worldwide in recent years.

Moving from general grants to support the development of research in broad fields at particular universities, leading foundations, exemplified by the Rockefeller, soon honed their approach by supporting particular investigators and projects in emerging research fields such as molecular biology (Kohler 1979). Among the notable projects of this era were the support given to Vannevar Bush to develop the differential analyzer, an early computer, at MIT, and to Lawrence at Berkeley for the cyclotron, both in the 1930s. Innovative interdisciplinary collaborations, such as those between MIT mathematician Norbert Wiener and the Mexican cardiologist Arturo Rosenblueth in the 1940's, were also supported and gave rise to interdisciplinary fields such as mathematical biology.

The Rockefeller Foundation was especially enabled to develop this targeted approach through its development of a staff of professional grants officers who visited universities worldwide, making their own assessment of individual researchers and their research projects. Proposals flowed in to these professionalized staff and were evaluated by them for recommendation for funding. A system of grants for discrete projects was further encouraged by the financial exigencies of the 1930s Depression, which placed severe limits on the ability of foundations to support the earlier model of broader research support. Much of the current system of basic research support was adumbrated in the actions of the foundations in the early twentieth century. Foundation programs in support of research persist to this date but with the notable exceptions of the Hughes Foundations in the United States and the Wellcome Trust in the United Kingdom in support of medical and biological research, they have become minor players in comparison to support offered by the federal government during the postwar era.

World War II

The next major intervention of the state in R&D took place at the onset of World War II. The government intervened to improve the technical base of military research by connecting it to the universities. Although the armed forces were satisfied that they could meet their own requirements for technological innovation, just before the U.S. entry into World War II academic scientists and engineers who had worked for the military during World War I convinced President Roosevelt that the armed forces needed assistance. Leading academics, including the president of Harvard, James Conant, and Vannever Bush, quondom vice president and dean of Engineering at MIT and then head of the Carnegie Institute of Washington, convinced the government that academic science could be used to develop technology for the military. These academics successfully lobbied the executive branch of the federal government to found an agency to support research on military problems. The Office of Scientific Research and Development (OSRD) was placed under the direction of academics rather than government officials or industrialists.

Universities were not the obvious choice for locating such research. With only a few partial exceptions, academic institutions lacked large research centers with the ability to carry on research and development. Industrial research laboratories at major corporations had greater R&D capabilities that could potentially be quickly turned to military use. But industrial scientists and engineers had not taken the lead in approaching the government. Industrial scientists such as Frank Jewett, the head of Bell Laboratories, took part, but in a secondary role supporting the lead taken by academics such as Bush and Conant. Since the research leaders who took the lead in this initiative were from the universities, they were placed in control of the agency established to carry out their plan and thus had the responsibility to dispense the funds allocated for the task.

Academics had to be drawn together from campuses across the country to establish large-scale research centers at a relatively few universities: MIT, Johns Hopkins, Berkeley, Chicago, and Columbia. The so-called Rad-Lab at MIT and a few other laboratories were established in electronics, nuclear physics, and other scientific and engineering areas relevant to solving military problems. This resulted in a concentration of research in a few institutions, against the ideology both of government and of universities. The American academic system is highly decentralized, with a multiplicity of institutions competing for funds of all kinds. Under conditions of military necessity, a few academic leaders were able to persuade their fellow academics to accept a concentrated system. Academics also agreed to accept federal research funds that they had refused during the 1930s Depression, fearing that research direction might be affected. An overriding purpose, the exigencies of war, changed academics' actions and then their beliefs.

The emergence of contradictions between academic research and its industrial use in the postwar era. The successful R&D effort coordinated by OSRD, largely on a few university campuses, suggested to Bush that the Federal Government could promote the development of new technologies by funding basic research. A vigorous debate ensued as to whether this research should be done in the context of national laboratories, as had been done in the wartime effort, or of universities, which were also involved in war time research. The question was whether civilian research should be located in the universities and military research in government laboratories, or was it more efficacious to keep university scientists, many of whom were determined to leave the wartime labs immediately after the close of hostilities, involved in defense research from their academic bases.

Also at issue were the boundaries between military and civilian research and the question of where the locus of control should be placed (Owen 1994). Much of this controversy was played out in the debate over the control of atomic research, which was eventually placed apart from the military in a new civilian agency, the Atomic Energy Commission, but under strict security controls. The closure of the wartime OSRD had given rise to separate research agencies in each military service who were now convinced, after the wartime experience, of the efficacy of the contribution of basic research to military goals and wished to maintain ties to the civilian basic research establishment, much of it located in the universities (Etzkowitz 1994).

In the interim, while the issues of how to organize government support of research were debated, a military agency, the Office of Naval Research (ONR), stepped into the breach and offered support for basic research, albeit with long-term military implications expected. The outcome was a compromise. The National Laboratories were funded directly and focused on defense related work, while the National Institutes of Health, tracing their origins to the mid-nineteenth century, were given the mission of health research.

In parallel with the expansion of research activity within government, the peer review system of federal funding of research at universities was established. The key element of this approach is that ideas for research are developed by scientists and the validity of these ideas is determined by committees of other scientists who work in the field. The separation of science from politics was made compatible with the expectation of government that research was useful through a peer review system, largely turning disbursement decisions over to academics within the confines of grant programs. Just after the war, the National Institutes of Health, in addition to being expanded from a small intramural research institute, was also given the mandate to manage extramural research in the medically related biological sciences. The National Science Foundation was established in 1950 to fund the physical sciences, the non-medical biological sciences, and soon thereafter, the social sciences and engineering.

Outside of defense needs, more basic research has been funded at universities than at National Laboratories. Medical research was also supported to meet military needs during World War II but the major impetus to the development of medical and biological research at universities in the past several decades has come from social movements and lobbying groups directed toward the cure of diseases. The health social movements to cure diseases, from cancer to heart to Alzheimer's, support voluntary associations that fund research. These associations typically feel they are not able to raise sufficient funds to accomplish their goal and thus exert political pressure to expand the federal role in health research. As a result, the National Institutes of Health grew through the efforts of social movements interested in using research to solve health problems. Most of the diseases that the NIH was funded to cure are still with us but the United States has a biotechnology industry as an unintended side effect of the generous support of basic research.

Management of Intellectual Property
Generated Under Federal Funding

Bush was aware from his interwar experience at MIT that an expansion of research would generate intellectual property and that patentable research would have to be managed if conflicts were to be avoided and rewards from research returned, at least in part, to their originators. Otherwise, emoluments would go to opportunists who viewed the university as a site of research results to freely draw upon and patent as their own. This was the view from MIT, and it led to the formation of committees to develop an academic patent policy at the Institute as early as the 1920s (Etzkowitz 1994b). Naturally, when OSRD was established there were provisions made for the patenting of research (Purcell 1979). Even during war there was a view toward peace when, with the lifting of wartime constraints, arguments would likely ensue over property rights in research if precautions were not taken. One of the prices that was paid for the provision of federal funding of research was strict controls over the use to which the results of the research could be put. The basic philosophy was that no company should be able to generate large profits at the expense of the public by the exploitation of patents that had been publicly funded by the taxpayer.

The result was that, during the early postwar era, only non-exclusive licenses could be obtained to exploit the results of academic research. The thought was that by licensing more than one company to practise a given invention, competitive forces would keep prices "reasonable." Licensing was centrally managed by an organization called the National Technical and Information Service (NTIS), located in an agency of the Department of Commerce, with traditional responsibilities to conduct scientific research in support of precise weights, measures, etc., since renamed, expanded, and given new responsibilities for support of industry. This approach was reasonably effective in managing patents in fields in which product development times were reasonably short and hence the development risk that a company took on was not excessive, in such fields as mechanical devices, electronics, chemical processes. However, the approach completely broke down in areas with long development timeframes such as the pharmaceutical industry.

In 1968, the Johnson administration conducted a study that found that no pharmaceutical to which the Government owned the patent had ever been developed for commercial use. Companies were simply not prepared to make the investment required to develop a drug, a cost that could run into many millions of dollars (even then, before the pasage of the Food, Drug and Cosmetic Act of 1973 raised the cost of obtaining marketing approval for a new drug substantially), without the guarantee that they would be able to recoup their investment through exclusive marketing rights.

The first response to the Johnson Administration's study was the development of Institutional Patent Management Agreements (IPAs). These were first implemented by the Department of Health, Education and Welfare (HEW) and later by the National Science Foundation. They allowed institutions to negotiate title rights to inventions made with federal funding. The process was long and arduous, typically taking three years. An institution starting down this road in response to a specific invention would probably have found the potential licensee's interest had lapsed by the time the agreement was in place. There were restrictions on the period of exclusivity under IPAs, to ten years. However, they provided a valuable precedent for the ability of academic institutions to successfully and responsibly manage their technologies.

Industry's view of academia as a source of intellectual property at this time were exemplified in a 1980 survey (National Science Board 1982) in which fifty-six firms were asked why they funded research at universities. Multiple answers were possible. The reasons cited are shown in Table 10.1.

Legitimizing Academic Technology Transfer: The Bayh-Dole Act

Officials from a few academic institutions, typically with a "land grant" tradition and/or extensive capabilities in biomedical research with commercial implications, took the lead in getting legislation passed to establish a new framework for technology transfer. These efforts took place in the context of increasing international competition for U.S. companies and the failure of the Carter administration's "reindustrialization" proposals to directly assist companies. Thus, there was a receptive atmosphere for ideas to assist industry indirectly with the results of government-supported research.

In many respects, the chain of events that led up to the passage of Bayh-Dole started at the University of Wisconsin in the late 1950s, when Professor Heidelberger, with funding from Bristol-Myers, discovered the anti-cancer drug 5–fluorouracil (5FU), which remains a cornerstone of chemotherapy to the current time. After Bristol-Myers started commercializing the drug, cer-

TABLE 10.1
Reasons Cited for Sponsoring Academic Research in 1980

	%
Gain access to manpower	75
Window on science and technology	52
General support of technical excellence	38
Gain access to university facilities	36
Obtain prestige; enhance company's image	32
Good local citizen; foster community relations	29
Make use of an economical resource	14
Solve problem; get specific information unavailable elsewhere	11

The last of the reasons cited is a good working definition of a proprietary advantage; in 1980 it was the last reason that companies looked to universities.

tain congressional staffers claimed that the patents should have been assigned to the federal government because federal funds had supported part of the work. Various investigations ensued, but extensive audits revealed that the extent of federal funding was minuscule and, while the government did not eventually pursue taking title to its ultimate conclusion and license the rights to another company, the result was that companies started to regard research as being "contaminated" if it had been supported in any way by federal funds (Latker 1996). This erected a Chinese wall between academic and industrial researchers that would not be finally torn down until the passage of Bayh-Dole in 1980.

In 1978, Purdue University wanted to negotiate an IPA in order to commercialize promising medical device technology but was told that HEW had stopped granting such Agreements (Personal communication from Howard Bremer, Wisconsin Alumni Research Foundation, to Ashley Stevens). They approached their Senator, Birch Bayh, to protest what appeared to be an arbitrary decision, and found a sympathetic ear. Bayh found that the Department of Commerce was starting to have concerns about the United State's international competitiveness and felt that the barriers that had developed between academic and industrial R&D was contributing to the problem. In turn, Purdue found support for a change in the current system from other leading universities such as Wisconsin, whose discovery of vitamin D and warfarin had put them at the forefront of developing the academic technology transfer paradigm, starting in the early 1930s; and Stanford, whose origins in industrial research mirrored those of MIT and, at the time, was preparing to found the biotechnology industry through the Cohen-Boyer patents on recombinant DNA technology.

Bayh, a Democrat, found a bipartisan co-sponsor in Republican Robert Dole, and in 1979 serious consideration started of the Bayh-Dole Bill. The bill came under the jurisdiction of the Senate Judiciary Committee, chaired at the time by Senator Edward Kennedy of Massachusetts. The enormous importance of higher education to the economy of Massachusetts insured a sympathetic hearing for the bill. The Senate Judiciary Committee found that in 1978, the government owned title to more than 28,000 patents and had licensed fewer than four percent of them, glaring evidence of the lack of success of the then-current approach. In addition to the restrictions on license terms, other factors responsible for the lack of success were the bureaucratic difficulties of working with a government agency and the separation of the inventor from the invention. Academic technology is so embryonic that the active involvement of the inventor is usually essential to its further development. With the University controlling access to the inventor, but NTIS controlling the licensing rights, there was a fundamental disconnect between the two required elements.

The Bayh-Dole Act, PL 96–517, formally known as the Patent And Trademark Amendments Act, was passed. It applied to not-for-profit institutions and small businesses (defined as those with fewer than 500 employees). It contained six important provisions:

1. Universities could elect to retain title to the results of federally funded research.
2. Universities were required to share proceeds with inventors. This was a most important aspect of the Act. The concept of patenting was foreign to most academics. Their academic reputations, under conditions then current, would not be enhanced by adding patents and licenses to their curriculum vitaes. In contrast to corporate R&D scientists who typically are required to sign away their patent rights as a condition of employment, academic scientists and engineers were given a tangible incentive to expand their purview to include the commercialization of research. U.S. academics joined German workers as beneficiaries by law in the fruits of their creativity.
3. Restrictions on licensing terms were removed. Licenses to small businesses could be for the lifetime of the patent. Licenses to large businesses were still limited to ten years.
4. U.S. manufacture was required for products to be sold in the United States. This requirement was to ensure that a reasonable share of the benefits flowed into the U.S. economy. Waivers can be obtained if the licensor can show the agency that funded the research that the licensee cannot economically develop the product if this requirement is enforced.
5. Small businesses receive preference. This was one of the most debated aspects of the Act. There remained considerable concern in the Senate about handing monopoly power that had been created with government funding to large corporations. It was felt that small companies would be less able to exploit that monopoly power at the expense of the public than would large companies, so a preference for small companies was incorporated into the Act. The meaning of the requirement has never been seriously tested. If an institution received equal offers to license a technology from a large and a small company, then clearly it would have to accept the small company's offer. However, this is never the case. Licensing proposals always differ, so the overall economic attractiveness of the competing offers must be compared and weighed.

   Also, in practice, small companies have found themselves best able to work with academic institutions and have emerged as the main licensees of academic technologies. Congress appears comfortable with looking at the results of university licensing in total, not on a case-by-case basis, and interpretation of this issue has therefore never been rigorously challenged.

6. The government retained a non-exclusive license to use the technology and march-in rights. The government's license is for its own use only. This therefore primarily impacts technologies for which the government is the primary consumer and has not been a major factor. The march-in rights give the government the right to take back title if it believes that an important technology is not being properly exploited. The authors are aware of at least one instance where this has happened, but it is certainly not a widespread practice and has not been an important factor in technology commercialization.

Another of the issues that was intensively debated at the time was whether the government should receive a share of the results of licensing the technology it had funded. The Senate Judiciary Committee decided that the government's return would come not directly from a share in the proceeds, but rather from the increased taxation that would result from the increased economic activity that would be a consequence of the Act's successful implementation. The federal legislation assigned ownership of knowledge to the university in which the discovery was made, if the research had been supported financially by the federal government. The purpose of the new federal legislation was to speed the transfer of technological knowledge from university to private industrial firms by eliminating governmental restrictions on the private use of the results of governmentally supported research. It was left to academic institutions to decide how to accomplish this goal.

Technology Transfer As A University Mission

Universities that were previously little involved in the transfer of technology quickly established administrative offices in the wake of the federal decision. Universities with some experience either on their own or through arrangements with the Research Corporation soon expanded their efforts to take out patents on the commercialisable research of their academic staff. By the late 1980s, virtually all research universities had established a technology transfer office. Following upon the growth of these offices, a membership organization, the Association of University Technology Managers (AUTM) was established to represent the emerging profession. AUTM membership has since risen to 600 full and 600 associate members and the organization runs its own training programs.

All major, and many minor, academic institutions, as well as an increasing number of government laboratories in the United States, now have technology transfer offices. Some, such as the National Institutes of Health, Stanford, MIT, and the University of California system have offices of 30–50 people. A smaller, less research-oriented medical school, New York Medical College, has a staff of a single person. Awaiting a buildup of research with commercial potential, the Westchester-based medical school is at the stage of developing its policy documents and seeking partners in the pharmaceutical industry to become a site for clinical trials.

There are two essential elements to academic technology transfer: the ability to license established technologies for which patents have been applied; and the ability to collaborate with the inventor of the technology to further develop it. While the first of these two steps in fact constitutes the actual transfer of the technology, because of the very early stage of academic technology, it is not worthwhile doing so unless the second option is also available and the cooperation of the inventor also achieved.

Some universities extended their efforts from the taking out and licensing of patents to produce income for the university into a portfolio of measures designed to establish new firms and thereby promote regional economic development. All of these efforts depended upon research staff and students bringing their commercialisable ideas to the attention of a university technology transfer office. In part because the taking out of patents was expensive, patents were often only sought when a prospective licensee could be identified. Universities had the reputation of being conservative patent takers. There was either an immediate sale or a long-term prospect of significant gain, with little middle ground.

The issue of the disposition of the returns from intellectual property rights derived from government-supported research continually reappears within and without the universities. The most contentious internal issue within the universities appears to have been settled with a more or less equal three-way division of proceeds among the university administration on behalf of the institution as a whole, the faculty members' department, and the individuals themselves. Student-generated rights were traditionally left entirely with the individual, perhaps on the grounds that they paid tuition and did not have employee status. However, since most graduate students in the sciences are on fellowships, often from a government or university source, graduate students have increasingly been defined as "officers of the university" subject to the same intellectual property rules as faculty.

A below-the-surface issue that rarely comes to light, given faculty members' near feudal power over their students in assessing progress toward the Ph.D. and in granting degrees, is claims made by faculty members to credit, both intellectual and pecuniary, for graduate student research. The academic system has virtually accepted a system of authorship by status in which provision of resources to conduct research carries with it an entitlement to credit of all kinds. As intellectual property rights become more salient it can be expected that relations among teachers and students will have to be more clearly defined. In U.S. academia such redefinition of roles typically takes place in the context of "conflict of interest and commitment" disputes over the propriety of individual actions when pecuniary self-interest or competing responsibilities are involved. A series of such disputes in the 1980s led to the clarification of the relationship between faculty and administration, discussed above, in the context of an overall redefinition of the mission of the university as one that encompassed economic development as well as teaching and research.

Etzkowitz has called this change "the second academic revolution," following upon the first academic revolution of the late nineteenth and early twentieth century in which research became an accepted academic mission, along with teaching, after resolution of a series of conflict of interest disputes, over the proper balance between these two activities during that earlier era. Indeed, tension still persists over the issue of whether too much attention has been given to research at the expense of teaching and calls for redressing the relative emphasis periodically occur. There is also a wide range of compromises among these different activities of teaching, research, and economic development in the 3,500 institutions that comprise the U.S. tertiary education system. It can be predicted that economic development as an academic mission will follow a similar course as the tension-ridden relationship between the two older missions, even as it becomes embedded as a taken-for-granted part of the academic structure (Etzkowitz 1990).

The actions taken in response to the passage of the Bayh-Dole Act produced, over the next decade, a profound attitudinal shift in U.S. universities on the role of academic research and the contribution it can make to economic development. Other countries are only just beginning to attempt to emulate this role in their own universities, for example, by introducing centers into the academic structure in Sweden and science parks in Finland (Etzkowitz 1995). Academic scientists in the United States are entrepreneurs. Under the peer review system, they must raise the funding for their research activities themselves. A large research division at a university or teaching hospital can therefore be regarded as a quasi-business with from $1 million to $10 million in annual revenues. The Bayh-Dole Act allowed these natural entrepreneurs to apply their talents to the benefit of the for-profit sector.

The Extension of Academic Technology
Transfer Models to Government Laboratories

In the Stevenson Wydler Act, (PL 98–620) passed in 1984, Congress mandated the national laboratories to play a technology transfer and cooperative research role with industry. Laboratories typically had one customer, a particular department of the government, for example, Los Alamos in nuclear weapons research for the Department of Energy, or Livermore, to do similar kinds of nuclear and Star Wars research. National laboratories were instructed that, in addition to what you normally do, if things come up in the course of your research that would be useful to civilian industry, some of your engineers and scientists should transfer that work to industry.

The Stevenson-Wydler Act extended Bayh-Dole (e.g., to include the results of research conducted at government-owned, contractor-operated National Laboratories, such as MIT's Lincoln Labs) and removed many of its remaining restrictions (e.g., on the length of exclusivity of licenses that could be issued) to further make explict the technology transfer responsibilites associated with all government research funding. Thus, the national laboratories soon began to establish technology transfer offices, often modelled on those existing in the universities, and to conduct joint research with companies through CRADA's (Cooperative Research and Development Agreements).

The National Laboratories had always had the same right to apply for patents on the results of their research as had the universities. The licensing of the patents was traditionally handled by the National Technical Information Service (NTIS). This organization operated under the philosophical perspective described under the earlier discussion of academic licensing, that companies should not be able to gain a competitive advantage from government-funded technology. There was therefore a requirement that any exclusive license of technology contemplated by NTIS first be advertised in the Federal Register. Companies that thought they might be harmed by such a transaction then had sixty days to register their concern and either compete for the license or persuade NTIS to grant non-exclusive licenses instead. This made licensing a technology from NTIS a more daunting process than licensing from an academic institution in the post-Bayh-Dole era.

However, even if a company successfully negotiated this hurdle, there was still no way for it to interact with the inventor to further develop the technology if the inventor worked at a National Laboratory. This imposed a further handicap on federal scientists. The Federal Technology Transfer Act (PL 99–502) was therefore passed in 1986 in response to the success that was almost immediately seen from the Bayh-Dole Act. It was intended to allow scientists at government owned, government operated ("GOGO") National Laboratories to interact with industry in a manner analogous to that in which universities, teaching hospitals, and independent research institutions are able to under the Bayh-Dole Act. In 1989, as part of the National Competitiveness Act (PL 101–189), authority for these collaborations was extended to government owned contractor operated ("GOCO") labs.

Its most visible effect has been the establishment of Co-operative Research and Development Agreements (CRADAs). Less visible but perhaps even more significant in the long term, was the emergence of a commitment to transfer technology at the laboratory level. Each department has set up its own technology transfer office—NIH's has forty-five employees, making it as large as the largest academic office of technology transfer, that of the University of California's office, and each laboratory has set up technology liaison officers to act as a focus for its own technologies. An association to represent these professionals—the Association of Federal Technology Executives (AFTE) was founded in 1993, modelled on the Association of University Technology Managers.

CRADAs have become a well-established feature of the technology transfer scene. To develop a CRADA, the laboratory and the company jointly develop a research program. One of the important considerations is that the company must contribute to the scientific program. This is in contrast to many typical university-sponsored research agreements, in which the company's role may be limited to providing funding and no scientific help. As a tradeoff for this contribution, the laboratory is not required to seek the full cost of the research from the collaborator. Indeed, the laboratory is not allowed to apply corporate funding to support its base operations. Corporate funding may only be used to expand operations—to add additional post-doctoral fellows or technicians to work specifically on the project. This may have led to some abuses, with companies that were planning to work in an area anyway offering up their efforts as their contribution to a CRADA. In addition to the benefits of the technology developed, a major benefit of entering a CRADA is that the company can exclusively license the results of the CRADA without the government's intention of granting an exclusive license being advertised in the Federal Register in order to solicit competing bids for the technology.

Second Thoughts: The Critique of Academic Technology Transfer

What is the future of academia as the traditional basis for research support, the so-called contract between university and government, weakens (Guston and Kenniston 1994)? The dimunition of federal research support could also affect the ability of the universities to carry out technology transfer. But are the universities ready to accept contribution to economic and social development through technology transfer as an explicit mission and justify receipt of public resources on this basis, directly rather than as an afterthought?

Some universities, those close to the MIT/Stanford and "land grant" models have eagerly taken up the challenge of regional economic development.

For example, in 1985, the state legislature asked Iowa State University to review its management contract of a federal laboratory, suspecting that the university (and the state) was losing more than it was gaining from the relationship. The university found, on the positive side, that the laboratory was supporting the research infrastructure of several departments including physics, chemistry, and engineering. On the other hand, the intellectual property emanating from the laboratory was primarily being licensed abroad rather than contributing to local economic development. The university began the process of founding startup firms to develop research locally, successfully creating jobs and economic activity in Iowa from the intellectual property of the university and the federal laboratory during the past decade (Personal communication from Michael Crow, Columbia University, Nov. 29, 1995).

At other universities, as the technology transfer profession generates ever more glowing reports of its ability to generate returns from federally sponsored research, skeptics contend that academic attention to technology transfer is misplaced on the grounds of wasted effort that will not produce significant results. To this day, there is a division of opinion among university faculty, especially at elite universities oriented to the liberal arts and basic research, over whether patenting or indeed any attention to the commercial implications of research is appropriate. Indeed, it was at these same universities that government funding of research was severely questioned and ultimately rejected during the 1930s. At Columbia University, as late as 1952, a faculty member in biochemistry in the Medical School viewed government research funds as "tainted" (Personal communication from Seymour Lieberman, Nov. 29, 1995).

Since that era, government funding of research has become academic orthodoxy. Ironically, as it is currently under threat of reduction; that dimunition is viewed as an attack upon academia. In the face of this decline, a parallel system of generating funds from academic research through technology transfer has been created. Nevertheless, this system is still in its infancy and many question whether it can ever become a signficant source of resources for academic research let alone a serious input into the economy. In addition, some critics hold that technology transfer detracts from academia by deforming the university from its traditional missions of research and education, their unique function (Feller 1990).

Others argue that moving more closely to industrial research interests smacks of "short termism" and will be duplicative of industrial research laboratories. A focus on technology transfer makes the university into a barrier between university and industry. It displaces the free flow of knowledge, through publication and informal discussion, with a wasteful effort to capitalize knowledge and reap a return for the university. "Technology transfer efforts which focus on industrial development of PSR [public sector research, i.e., university and government laboratories] 'inventions' are misplaced and out of proportion; by far the greater contribution of PSR to innovation lies in the less direct and intangible flows of ideas, knowledge and expert assistance" (Faulkner and Senker 1995).

Questions of whether the university should engage in technology transfer are confounded by calls for redistribution of these publicly originated benefits. For example, in the 1993 hearings held by the U.S. House of Representatives Small Business Committee, Representative Ron Wyden, the Chair of the Comittee, called for some of the profits from "taxol," a pharmaceutical derived from tree bark, to be returned to the public in the form of lower drug prices. There was also a proposal made at the Cold Spring Harbor conference held later in the year to discuss the controversial relationship between the Sandoz Company and Scripps Institute that some of the profits from university technology transfer be directed to a "trust fund" to support NIH and NSF research. Such a proposal would replicate, on a more massive scale and in a public format, the model of the Research Corporation, discussed above. Naturally, individual universities, especially those that are generators of significant royalties, prefer to keep the profits in house and make their own research investment decisions rather than turn them over to these redistribution schemes.

As we have seen, there is an additional issue related to the question of whether the university should sell its intellectual property to the highest bidder. Although the official injunction to favor small firms has no enforcement mechanism, there are pressures on universities from local authorities, especially those that have subsidized universities to develop technology transfer capabilities, to see that the intellectual property rights that they generate are developed locally. This can take the form of licensing to a local startup with little or no royalties in the short term as opposed to selling the rights, often to a larger firm elsewhere, with an immediate return. This issue is often played out in cross-pressures of a university president pressed to seek maximum returns in an era of academic financial stringency and a local government agency seeking to create jobs in the region, with the university technology transfer office having to balance between these two masters.

Earning money from technology transfer has to be balanced against competing academic goals as well as the regional interest in using the university's research results to establish new firms locally rather than marketing intellectual property to the highest bidder among established companies elsewhere. A policy of licensing technology to local startups, promoted by the provisions of the Bayh-Dole Act also creates an incipient conflict between universities and large corporations over technology transfer. While some technology licenses go to large companies, new competitors are also created. The University-Industry-Government Roundtable in the United States, strongly representing major corporations, has called upon universities to encourage the free flow of knowledge from academia to industry, intending "free flow" to mean both "without impediment" and "without cost."

Measuring the Economic Impact of Technology Transfer

The establishment of technology transfer offices and the array of mechanisms, including incubator facilities and science parks, gives hope (some say, false hope) to regions that have not yet seen a glimmer of a high tech valley, coast, or corridor. In the face of injunctions to give up the protection and marketing of intellectual property, AUTM has attempted to justify the contribution of university-originated technologies to the U.S. economy and, by implication, the utility of the technology transfer profession. These reports justify the expense that universities have undertaken in subsidizing technology transfer offices, patiently waiting out the seven lean years that are not expected to pay for themselves. We shall view, in turn, the results of the Research Corporation, government laboratories, and universities.

University technology transfer offices have, in recent years, internalized a task performed for some years by an organization founded for that purpose, The Research Corporation, now Research Corporation Technologies (RCT). During the pre-war era, even MIT had this intermediary organization, independent of the university, market its intellectual property, not wanting the university to be too closely identified in the public mind with pecuniary interests. In the 1960s, MIT took full control of its patent management activities when its interests diverged from RCT in a dispute with IBM over core memory. RCT wished to fight in court for the maximum amount; MIT had other interests to consider. Since IBM was an important philanthropic donor and sometime joint developer of Institute technologies it was more imortant to maintain good relations with the company than to extract the maximum royalty. (Etzkowitz 1994b).

RCT is the longest-established technology transfer organization serving academic institutions, having been founded in 1917 by Frederick Cottrell, a professor of physical chemistry at the University of California, who had invented the electrostatic precipitator technology to solve emission problems from copper smelters in the San Francisco Bay Area. For several decades, RCT, with a few exceptions such as the Wisconsin Alumni Foundation, had the academic technology transfer field to itself, visiting campuses to identify inventions and distributing its earnings in the form of small research grants to faculty members.

TABLE 10.2
RCT Royalty Receipts and Disbursements

	Total	*Retained*	*Distributed*
1987	13,478	9,295	4,183
1990	32,273	21,259	11,014
1993	57,664	36,085	21,579

RCT operates by taking title to inventions and marketing them at its own expense, in return for a significant share in the proceeds, typically in the 40–50 percent range, and distributing the balance to the originating institution. One of its most successful transactions in recent years has been the licensing of Michigan State's platinum chemotherapy compounds to Bristol-Myers Squibb. As part of the 1986 tax reform act, RCT transferred its invention identification and development activities to a taxable nonprofit corporation set up by the original foundation, which remained as a grant giving agency.[2] RCT's results since the 1987 reorganization are shown in Table 10.2.

Federal Laboratories

The role of national laboratories in technology transfer has increased greatly, with the end of the Cold War, as some government laboratories have entirely lost their previous mission. In order to stay in existence, they are eagerly taking up the tasks of technology transfer and providing research services to industry as one of their main missions. Until recently, it was assumed that most of the money that the federal government gave to national laboratories and universities for research, with the exception of basic research, health, and agriculture, was tied to military purposes. Now that these purposes have lessened or even disappeared, uses for those funds for new purposes must be found or we can expect the research universities and the national laboratories to shrink greatly, reflecting the extent that their research activities were tied to defense-related projects that are no longer needed. Should technology transfer be successfully implanted as the primary, rather than as merely a subsidiary, mission of a significant number of national laboratories, the United States would gain the virtual equivalent of the German Fraunhaufer system of industrial support laboratories.

The GOA study "Technology Transfer: Federal Agencies' Patent Licensing Activities" (GAO/RECD-91-80 (April 1991), prepared for the House and Senate Judiciary Committees and the House Committee on Science, Space and Technology, gave a ten-year summary for 1981–1990 (see Table 10.3).[3]

TABLE 10.3
Federal Laboratory Royalty Income ($000's)

1981	346
1986	1,642
1990	9,389
1993	18,000

TABLE 10.4
Adjusted Total PSR Technology Transfer Royalty Income

Year	$ millions
1980	7.3
1986	38.1
1990	136.5
1993	344.4

TABLE 10.5
Academic Institutions with Largest Royalty Income and Licensees Thereof

Institution	Royalty Income	Major Licences	Licensees
City of Hope	18	Insulin, hGH	Genentech
Stanford	14	Cohen-Boyer	Biotech, Pharm
U. California	12	Patch,Cohen-Boyer	Pharm, Biotech
Wisconsin	12	Warfarin, Vit. D	Pharm
New York Blood Center	8	Viral decont.	Various
Columbia	7	Co-transformation	Amgen
Michigan State	7	cis-platin	Bristol-Myers
MIT	4	Miscellaneous	Small
Sloan-Kettering	4	G-CSF	Amgen
U. Florida	3	Gatorade (trademark)	Coca-Cola

The figures shown in Table 10.4 estimate total royalty receipts from Public Sector Research (PSR) consisting of U.S. academic institutions and government laboratories. The 1993 earnings of $344 million represent a small (8.6 percent), but increasingly significant amount, in comparison to the $4 billion of federal expenditures for basic research at U.S. universities per annum (Office of Technology Assessment 1991, 188).[4] As Table 10.5 suggests, most of the funds earned by universities, thus far, derive from a fairly narrow research stream of biotechnology-related pharmaceuticals. Some critics take

TABLE 10.6
Estimated Economic Impact of PSR Technology
($ million)

	Product Sales	Employment
1980	365	2,920
1986	1,905	15,240
1990	6,825	54,600
1993	17,220	137,760

this to mean that technology transfer is largely confined to a single sector of the university and will remain a minor factor in academia. Proponents argue the contrary, that this same table represents only a beginning and that significant software patents and multimedia companies will appear, not only from computer science and engineering but even from the arts and humanities departments of the university.

Economic Impact

These data on royalty income can be used to provide a very crude estimate of the economic impact of PSR technology transfer activity. Based upon the average royalty rate paid to the universities and government laboratories of $344.4 million in royalties at a two percent average royalty, the total sales of the licensed products can be estimated to be $17.2 billion.[5] Product sales can also be used to estimate the employment generated by technology transfer to consist of 137, 800 jobs created.[6] The economic impact of technology transfer from universities and government laboratories has evolved since the passage of Bayh-Dole and Stevenson-Wydler to a point where it can be considered to be playing a recognizable and increasingly significant role in aiding the growth of the U.S. economy (see Table 10.6).

The drafters of the Bayh-Dole Act realized their legislative intent to attain public benefit from university technology transfer through contribution to tax revenues. The economic activity arising from tech transfer shows a return to federal and state governments of approximately $3.9 billion in 1993. It is also worth noting that these estimates are undoubtedly low, for two reasons:

1. Once patents expire, royalties cease, but the products remain in the market. For instance, in the mid-1960s, MIT had licensed two very important technologies—synthetic penicillin and computer core memory. Both patents have now expired, but were the foundation of major markets.

2. This methodology doesn't capture the induced investment effect, when technologies are in development and are employing people but not yet generating revenues. Thus, the above figures are conservative estimates of the economic impact of indirect industrial policy.

Conclusion: Inching Toward Industrial Policy

In the United States, government intervention in the civilian economy did not take place directly, as it did in France. Nevertheless, emerging companies funded by the Department of Defense (DOD) Advanced Research Projects Agency (ARPA) such as SUN Microsystems and Silicon Graphics, created a new category of computer "workstations" with significant spillover to the civilian economy. These companies, achieving $10 billion of sales within a decade, did not sprout from Stanford University unaided, (the SUN acronym stands for Stanford University System); the DOD acted as venture capitalist to the workstation industry in the 1980s even as it had served the same function in the 1960s for the mini-computer and military electronics industries on Route 128. These defense-related exceptions apart, government intervention in commercialization of civilian technology had been largely discredited in the energy crisis of the 1970s when government-funded company efforts to commercialize shale oil did not achieve results quickly.

Such examples gave rise to a rhetoric touting the inability of government to "pick winners" and appeared to justify the confinement of government to the role of funding basic research during the Reagan/Bush administrations on the accepted grounds of the inability of the market to undertake such a task. Full wisdom was imputed to the market to select technologies despite the prescient efforts of DARPA. Another significant exception to prevailing ideology, arising from industry pressure, was the DOD funding of the SEMATECH cooperative research scheme to revive the technology of the semiconductor industry, then believed to be in severe danger of loss to competition from Japan. Despite taking ideological exception, the Reagan administration committed the necessary funds at the behest of the Semi-Conductor Industry Association in the mid-1980s. Less than a decade later, the industry declared both the utility of the effort in regaining competitive superiority and the lack of need for further government funds to maintain the cooperative pre-competitive research scheme. Current opposition in Congress to renewing the funding of the Advanced Technology Program (ATP), part-funding the development of generic technologies, mostly by large companies, is another expression of such ideological opposition to industrial policy.

Despite such opposition, the United States has taken range of initiatives at the federal and state levels, during the postwar era, to facilitate knowledge-based economic development. Taken together, they comprise an incipient industrial policy. In this chapter we have focused on one aspect of these initiatives: the effects of the adjustment of patent policy at the federal level. Changes in patent policy have induced a reordering of relationships among the knowledge sector, the economy, and the state. The Carter administration was unable to establish an explicit industrial policy during the late 1970s in the face of laissez-faire objections. Instead, universities were encouraged to act as a surrogate for government through incentives offered to induce schools to become technology transfer agents and commercialize research.

The Bayh-Dole Act altered the regulatory infrastructure that determined how the results of research which would have been funded anyway could be utilized. No funds were appropriated for its implementation or administration. By changing the rules of the game, placing responsibility for technology transfer in the university where it was being conducted rather than with government, the funder, potentially useful research was moved closer to users. In the context of federal research budgets that were not growing at a fast enough rate to meet academic researchers' needs, universities were given the opportunity to earn monies from the royalties and equity that they could generate from federally sponsored research on their campuses.

The Morill Act of 1862 donated federal land to support the development of higher education for the improvement of agricultural and industrial practice. The laws of 1980 turned over intangible property of scientific and technological knowledge to the universities with similar intentions. A few universities were already oriented toward technology transfer; others soon turned in this direction. The legislation led universities to experiment with a variety of arrangements to develop fruitful relations with industry such as research parks, incubator facilities, and offices for the transfer of technology and, by stimulating the universities to undertake these initiatives, encouraged interested academics to include commercial activities in their roles.

The purpose of the federal legislation was to speed up the transfer of scientific technological knowledge from university to private industrial firms. It was to be left to the academic institutions to make their own arrangements for the commercial disposition of the results of governmentally supported research. Many universities acquired and took control of patent rights and established offices to promote their commercial exploitation. These changes in academic practice and organization were quickly accepted by most academic scientists and engineers; others were skeptical as to whether the university was taking on a function that would be detrimental to the traditional academic culture of disseminating knowledge through publication. Since active participation on the part of the faculty was voluntary, the level of controversy was relatively low.

Technology transfer is one of several ways that the United States conducts an industrial policy without officially having one (Etzkowitz 1994a). The primary licensees of academic technology patents are small companies that are generally located close to universities. These companies are more receptive to new ideas and have mechanisms available to attract and compensate academic scientists who are interested in seeing their ideas utilized. As Vannevar Bush put it, "The purpose of issuing a patent is not to reward the inventor, but to enable the investment of venture capital, without which many inventions would die on the vine. The patent also enables small companies to carve out a corner for themselves in a large field, and to grow and prosper in the midst of large, powerful competitors" (Bush 1970, 84). The crucial role of the federal government in funding basic research that is carried out in universities, and in fashioning the patent policies that have encouraged the economically productive usage of this research by small firms, is the single most important way that government supports high technology innovation in the United States.

Arising over the past century, the institutional mechanisms for handling academic patent rights have been generalized from a few universities such as MIT, where they originated, to the academic system as a whole (Etzkowitz and Webster 1994). These practices represent a potentially fundamental modification of the traditional view of universities as institutions supported by governmental, ecclesiastical, and lay patronage. The new arrangements open the possibility that universities will become, at least in part, financially self-supporting institutions, entities obtaining revenues through licensing agreements and other financial arrangements for the industrial use of new knowledge discovered at the universities. At present, this possibility is little more than that but it certainly represents a novel idea in the history of universities—at least on the scale in which it is envisaged.

Notes

Chapter 3

Paper presented at the Advanced Research Workshop on University-Industry Relations, Acquafredda, Italy, Sept 1–6, 1991. Portions of this paper appeared in "The changing locus of control over faculty research: From self-regulation to dispersed influence," in John C. Smart, ed., *Higher Education: Handbook of Theory and Research*, vol.VII (New York: Agathon, 1991).

Karen Seashore Louis is Associate Dean of the College of Education and Human Development and Professor of Educational Policy and Administration. Melissa S. Anderson is Associate Professor of Higher Education.

1. In addition to the specific trends outlined below, one can take a broader view of the changing structure of academic research as it relates to the control of faculty work. Weingart (1982), for example, points to three major threats to autonomy. First, there is an increasing disjuncture between the knowledge that is being produced by science and the values of society at large. Thus, controversy over biotechnological efforts to develop new or altered life forms reaches beyond the specific research project to question the basis for posing the question. Second, science may be losing its internal consensus: there are debates about what constitute appropriate behavior and practices, and dissenters are turning to the public for support. Finally, there are definite changes taking place in the social order, pointing largely to the increasing complexity of government, and the increasing predominance of government as the chief or indirect client of many fields of science.

2. Data from the mid-1980s suggest that, among the 200 leading research universities, only twenty-five receive more than ten percent of their research funds from industry (Fink 1985). As of 1983, less than four percent of total research and development expenditures by industry went to universities; moreover, ten companies accounted for one-third of all industrial support for universities, and two accounted for twenty percent (Culliton 1983). Blumenthal et al. (1986a) note that the average grant to a university made by non-Fortune 500 firms engaged in biotechnology was only $19,000 and that neither small nor large firms anticipated increasing their investment in universities in the coming years.

3. Moderate consulting does not appear to interfere with scholarly productivity, but is associated with a reduced commitment to teaching (Boyer and Lewis 1985).

4. Wofsy (1986) notes some of the special aspects about the rapid development and potential exploitation of biotechnological results. The suddenness with which the new university-environment ties were sought and established was matched by a sharp contrast between faculty members' earlier focus on academic concerns and their later orientation to market aspects of research. The social and political climate of research changed as government funding and oversight were supplemented or replaced by private sector involvement, leading to changes in social priorities and public policy issues. Finally, biotechnology represents a case of strong governmental support for fundamental academic work, predicated on a commitment to improvements in public health, which has resulted in substantial financial return to researchers and private corporations.

5. ". . . the environment is conceptualized in terms of understandings and expectations of appropriate organizational form and behavior that are shared by members of society. . . . Such normative understandings constitute the institutional environment of organizations" (Tolbert 1985, 1).

Chapter 5

This research was carried out as part of a project entitled "Public-private research linkage in advanced technologies"; it was funded by the Economic and Social Research Council (ESRC award number: Y 306 25 3001) and conducted under the Science Policy Support Group program *Public Science and Commercial Enterprise.* Our thanks to colleagues in both Sussex and Edinburgh who have commented at various stages on our work, also to Andrew Webster of Anglia Polytechnic University.

1. The findings and implications of this study have been reported at greater length in Faulkner, Senker, and Velho 1995, Faulkner and Senker 1994, Senker and Faulkner 1995, and Faulkner and Senker 1995. For a fuller account of the methodology, see Faulkner 1995.

2. For simplicity, we use the terms "academia" and "academic" to encompass government as well as university research and researchers. However, it should be remembered that government laboratories can be important contributors to industrial innovation—as, for example, in the case of the U.S. parallel computing firms in our study.

3. We use the term RD&D in preference to R&D to highlight the importance of design activities in innovation.

4. De Solla Price uses the term instrumentalities "to carry a general connotation of a laboratory method for doing something to nature or to the data in hand" (1984).

5. One survey-based study by CEST (Barden and Good 1989) considered the pattern of information flows into industrial research laboratories, but failed to analyze these information flows in the context of the *overall* inputs to new product development.

6. Unlike Gibbons and Johnston, we did not attempt to quantify the science and technology inputs in terms of equally weighted units of information.

7. These charts were suggested in part by Gibbons and Johnston (1974) and in part by an earlier study of industry-academic research linkage in biotechnology by Faulkner (1986), and subsequently refined in the pilot of this study. Our categories for knowledge type and impact are substantially different from those used by Gibbons and Johnston; we largely share their approach to source and channel.

8. We refer to our interviewees generically in this paper as "researchers."

9. This was also noted in a recent study of networking in biotechnology (Kreiner and Schultz 1993).

10. These data were derived from lengthy discussion in which interviewees were asked to detail the specific types of knowledge they utilize, under each broad heading.

11. The impact of knowledge inputs from academia in these two categories combined accounts for 64 percent of all responses in biotechnology, 54 percent in ceramics, and 44 percent in parallel computing.

12. Sixty-six percent of responses in ceramics, compared with 24 percent and 7 percent respectively in biotechnology and parallel computing, identified academia as contributing to these activities.

Chapter 6

1. See, among others, Segal (1982), Dorfman (1983), Rogers and Larsen (1984), Saxenian (1985), Segal Quince (1985), Miller and Coté (1987), Rosengrant and Lampe (1992), Garnsey et al. (1994), and Saxenian (1994).

2. One should add that the concept of technopolis owed much to that of "science city" as it was developed in the '60s and '70s in the Soviet Union (Novosibirsk) and Japan (Tsukuba).

3. For example, Bari region in the Southern Italy, Côte d'Azur in France, Twente region in the Netherlands, and so forth.

4. This is an old theory that goes back to the writings on creativity and invention by Poincaré, Ogburn, and Hadamard. Recently it was forcefully argued by David and Foray (1995).

5. This is related to the importance of the tacit dimention of technological knowledge. The more important the tacit knowledge is and the less it is shared between the communicating parties, the greater the necessity of direct face-to-face interactions.

Chapter 7

1. The International Study Group on Academy-Industry Relations had an Eastern European Network carrying out an empirical study in the region in 1993–1994. The project, "Innovation Potential Embodied in Changing Academy-Industry Relations," was supported by the Central European University, Research Support Scheme. It was carried out by a network of researchers and organized by Z. Andrási and K. Balázs (Hungary), A. Jasinski (Poland), M. Lenardic and S. Radosevic (Croatia), W. Meske (Germany), K. Müller (Czech Republic), S. Sandu and C. Vlaicu (Romania), K. Simeonova (Bulgaria). (Thus the empirical study was carried out in the Central and Eastern European countries excluding any from the former Soviet Union.) This activity also was part of the TERAIN (Trans European Research: Academy—Industry Network) managed by Andrew Webster and supported by the EC. See for results: EASST Special Issue, *Social Studies of Science* (guest editors: Balázs, Faulkner, Schimank), Volume 25, Number 4, and "Building New Bases for Innovation," edited by A. Webster, Anglia Polytechnic University, 1996.

Chapter 8

1. Noteworthy, R&D entities, as well as shares of joint-stock companies established in the privatization process cannot be sold at money auctions.

Chapter 10

1. The most direct and readily measurable consequences of the Bayh-Dole Act have been the royalties that have been earned by academic institutions that have licensed the inventions to which they have elected title. Taking the passage of the Bayh-Dole Act as a starting point, the National Science Board of the National Science Foundation, "University-Industry Research Relations" provides a comprehensive analysis of all aspects of university-industry relations as they entered the "Bayh-Dole" era. The authors report that they surveyed the top thirty-six recipients of federal funding. Twenty-five responded and reported royalty income as follows: 1981, $7.3 million; 1982, $9.2 million. The next year for which good quality data exist is 1986. In that year, the General Accounting Office carried out a study, "R&D Funding: Foreign Sponsorship of U.S. University Research." (GAO/RCED-88–89BR.) The royalty data is buried in the questionnaire in the appendix, on page 33, and isn't actually discussed

in the body of the text. Although the schools were not identified, 112 institutions reported royalty income of: 1986, $30.3 million.

Four studies were conducted in 1988. The first was a comprehensive survey carried out by Marjorie Forster of the University of Maryland at Baltimore and reported at the May 1990 AUTM Conference on technology transfer performance assessment. Seventy institutions, sixty-three U.S. and seven Canadian, reported to this survey that they had received royalty income of $60.4 million. Of the U.S. institutions, twenty-five allowed their royalty income to be individually reported, while the rest asked that it not be individually disclosed. One Canadian institution allowed its royalty income to be reported. Of the remaining thirty-eight U.S. institutions, seventeen reported that they had no licenses generating royalties and twenty-one reported royalty income on a confidential basis.

The second survey was carried out by John Preston, Director of Technology Transfer at MIT. He queried seven of the largest recipients of royalties and importantly included data for several universities that were not included in Forster's study. Total royalty income for the seven was $38.3 million. The third study was by Terri Wiley of the Indiana Corporation for Science and Technology, as part of a study of technology transfer practices. Individual figures are very similar to those in the 1988 AUTM survey, but one or two additional institutions were included. The fourth study was carried out by the law firm Pravel, Gambrel, Hewitt and Kettleberger. They surveyed thirty-eight institutions and found total royalty income of $18.9 million.

Assuming that every institution surveyed by Marjorie Foster reported its royalty income, then the other studies allow a further thirteen institutions to be added, giving: 1988, $70.1 million.

Two studies are available for 1989, 1990. The first is the second AUTM survey, carried out by Marjorie Forster and Steve Atkinson of Harvard Medical School and reported to the San Francisco 1992 Annual Meeting. This survey included data for twenty-two universities and hospitals for 1989, 1990, and 1991. For 1990, it included data for seven non-AUTM members who chose to respond to a questionnaire. The 1990 data included the $50 million lump sum payment from Amgen to Memorial Sloan Kettering. For the consensus figure, this was not included. The second source was another GAO study "University Research—Controlling Inappropriate Access to Federally Funded Research Results" (GAO/RCED-92–104), carried out at the request of Senator Ted Weiss's Subcommittee on Human Resources and Intergovernmental Relations of the Committee on Government Operations. This report included data for thirty-one institutions. The study combined the figures for the two years into a single total, $113.1 million. For the purposes of this analysis, they were dissaggregated by assuming that 45 percent of the total pertained to 1989 and 55 percent to 1990. This is in line with the estimated growth rate of 20–30 percent in royalties throughout the 1980s. Importantly, some of the institutions with high royalty incomes, such as Michigan State and Wisconsin, who had not reported to AUTM, had to report to GAO. An interesting part of this study is the differentiation between licenses and royalties derived from NSF and NIH funded technology and from all other funding sources. $82.1 million out of the $113.1 million was derived from NSF and NIH funded technology.

The result is a rather unsatisfactory figure for 1989, covering only fifty-three institutions and barely exceeding the 1988 figure, which covered sixty-six institutions. For 1990, the data are rather better and cover sixty-three institutions: 1989, $89.2 million; 1990, $125.4 million. For 1991, 1992, and 1993, comprehensive surveys are available from AUTM.

2. Separate figures for RCT were not included in these earlier studies. (RCT has reported to the 1991–1993 AUTM surveys.) While the distributed portion of the royalty proceeds will show up in the reported royalty income of the originating institutions, the retained portion will not. This portion should therefore be added to the individually reported figures. With the 1991 and on AUTM surveys, the opposite problem pertains—the distributed portion is double-counted and must be subtracted from the total.

3. The largest single federal royalty earner is the AIDS test kit, accounting for almost half the total. It is also worth noting that the 1991 and 1992 AUTM data only includes NIH, resulting in probably a $1 million under count.

4. Several adjustments need to be made in the data. First, the income from the Cohen-Boyer patent is paid to Stanford, which subtracts a fifteen percent management fee and pays half of the remainder (42.5 percent of the payments) to the University of California. The UC component is therefore double reported and must be removed.

Second, one of the early, major royalty generators, City of Hope Hospital in Los Angeles, did not report to any of the surveys before the AUTM survey. City of Hope had carried out the genetic engineering of both insulin and human growth hormone for Genentech before Genentech had its own laboratories. We have obtained these data by personal communication and added them to the data.

5. The consensus of a workshop at the 1993 Annual Meeting of AUTM, which included representatives of many of the academic institutions with large royalty incomes, was that two percent was a good figure. Looking at some of the specific contributors to the total, the Cohen-Boyer patent is non-exclusively licensed for rates in the 1–1.5 percent range (and only applies to U.S. sales); the Columbia co-transformation patent is a production patent that is also non-exclusively licensed; the royalty rate on the Memorial Sloan-Kettering G-CSF patent was bought down to three percent and only applies to sales over $350 million per year; so this rate certainly appears reasonable.

6. The average sales per employee of the S&P 500 in 1992 was $169,000 per employee. The consensus of a workshop at the 1993 Annual Meeting of AUTM was that the small high tech companies that are the primary licensees of academic technology have sales per employee of $125,000. 137,800 jobs workers would be required to generate $17.2 billion in product sales at $125,000 in sales per employee. In the future, this figure could be more precisely defined by using database summaries of actual company data by industry.

References

Introduction

Blumenthal, D. et al. 1986. University-industry research relations in biotechnology. *Science* 232: 1361–1366.

Branscomb, L. 1993. *Empowering technology*. Cambridge: MIT Press.

Bulthuis, K. 1996. New arrangements for the science base of our industry: How the industry of Europe is managing its knowledge resources. Amsterdam: The Triple Helix Conference (3 January).

Chancellor, Duchy of Lancaster. 1993. Realising our potential: A strategy for science, engineering and technology (HMSO).

Etzkowitz, H. 1994. Knowledge as property: The Massachusetts Institute of Technology and the debate over academic patent policy. *Minerva* (Winter) 32: 383–421.

Etzkowitz, H. 1996. Conflict of interest and commitment in academic science in the United States. *Minerva* (Autumn) 34: 259–277.

Etzkowitz, H., and L. Leydesdorff, eds. 1997. *Universities in the global knowledge economy: A triple helix of academic-industry-goverment relations*. London: Cassell.

Faulkner, W., and J. Senker. 1995. *Knowledge frontiers: Public sector research and industrial innovation in biotechnology, engineering ceramics, and parallel computing*. Oxford: Oxford University Press.

Feller, I. 1986. Universities as engines of economic development: They think they can. *Research Policy* 19: 335–348.

Jencks, Christopher, and David Riesman. 1968. *The academic revolution*. New York: Doubleday.

Ogbimi, F. E. 1990. Preparing for commercialisation of scientific research results in Nigeria. *Science and Public Policy* (December) 17: 370–380.

Packer, K., and A. Webster. 1996. Patenting culture in science. *Science Technology and Human Values* 21: 427–453.

Weber, Max. [1922] 1946. Science as a vocation. In Hans Gerth and C. Wright Mills, eds. *From Max Weber.* New York: Oxford University Press.

Wall Street Journal. 1996. Columbia University Denies Fired Economist's Charges (Friday, August 23).

Chapter 1

ASTEC. 1989. *Public policies for exploitable areas of science: A comparison of the UK, Japan, The Netherlands and Sweden.* Canberra: Australian Science and Technology Council.

Bell, D. 1974. *The coming of post-industrial society.* New York: The Free Press.

Cotgrove, S., and S. Box. 1970. *Science, Industry and Society.* London: Allen and Unwin.

CNRS. 1989. *Les CNRS et les enterprises la valorisation. Le Courner du CNRS* 74 (November).

EIRMA. 1987. (European Industrial Research Managers Association) Working Group Report, No. 37.

Etzkowitz, H. 1990. The capitalization of knowledge. *Theory and Society* 19: 107–121.

Etzkowitz, H. 1992. Individual investigators and their research groups. *Minerva* (Spring) 30: 28–50.

Etzkowitz, H. 1996. The triple helix: Academic-industry-government relations; implications for the New York regional innovation environment. In Susan Raymond, ed. *The technology link to economic development.* Annals of the New York Academy of Science, Vol. 787.

Genuth, J. 1987. Groping towards science policy in the United States in the 1930s. *Minerva* 25: 238–268.

Gore, Albert. 1996. The technology challenge: What is the role of science in American society. American Association for the Advancement of Science Annual Meeting. February 12. Baltimore, Md.

Greenberg, D. 1967. *The politics of pure science.* New York: New American Library.

Gustin, B. 1975. The emergence of the German chemical profession. Ph.D. Dissertation, Department of Sociology, University of Chiago.

Handler, P. 1980. When science becomes a public venture, to whom is the scientist accountable? *Chronicle of Higher Education* (March 3): 64.

Kemelgor, C. 1989. Organizational styles in molecular biology research groups. BA Thesis, SUNY Purchase.

Loveridge, R., and M. Pitt, eds. 1990. *The strategic management of technological innovation.* Chichester: Wiley.

Merton, R. K. 1938. *Science, Technology and Society in 17th Century England.* OSIRIS 3: 60–75.

Mustar, P. 1997. Triple Helix Special Issue. *Science and Public Policy* 24: 37–44.

OECD. 1984. *Industry and university, new forms of cooperation and communication.* Paris: OECD.

OECD. 1990. University enterprise relations in OPECD member countries, DSTI/SPR/89.37 (1st Rev). Paris: OECD.

OTA. 1984. Technology, innovation and regional economic development. Washington, D.C.: Office of Technology Assessment.

Packer, K., and A. Webster. 1996. Patenting Culture in Science, *Science, Technology and Human Values* 21: 427–453.

Peters, L. 1987. Academic Crossroads. RPI Center for Science and Technology Policy. New York: Rensselaer Polytechnic Institute.

Peters, L., and H. Fusfeld. 1982. *University-industry research relationships.* Washington, D.C.: National Science Foundation.

Rappert, B., and A. Webster. 1997. Regimes of Ordering. *Technology Analysis and Strategic Management* 9: 115–129.

Remington, J. 1988. Beyond big science in America: The binding of inquiry. *Social Studies of Science* 18: 45–72.

Smilor, R. W. 1990. University spin-out costs. *Journal of Business Venturing* 15: 63–76.

Stankiewicz, R. 1986. *Academics and entrepreneurs.* London: Pinter.

Webster, A. 1990. Institutional stability. *Science and Public Policy* 17: 381–86.

Wise, G. 1985. *Willis Whitney: General Electric and the origins of United States industrial research.* New York: Columbia University Press.

Chapter 2

Balazs, K. 1995. Special Issue. *Social Studies of Science* 25(4): 655–684.

Benson, J. K. 1978. Interorganizational network as a political economy. In L. Karpik, ed. *Organization and Environment.* New York: Sage.

Borys, B., and D. B. Jemison. 1989. Hybrid arrangements as strategic alliances: Theoretical issues in organisational combinations. *Academy of Management Review* 14(2): 234–249.

Constable, J., and A. Webster. 1990. Strategic research alliances and hybrid coalitions. *Industry and Higher Education* (December).

Cricelli, L. et al. 1996. A system of science and technology parks for the Rome area. COST A3 Workshop. February 1–2. Milan.

Faulkner, W., and J. Senker. 1995. *Knowledge frontiers.* Oxford: Oxford University Press.

Feller, I. 1991. Issues for the HE sector: Lessons from the US experience with collaboration. Symposium on the True Price of Collaborative Research. January 22. Royal Society, London.

Garnsey, E., and S. Wright. 1990. Technical innovation and organisational opportunity. *International Journal of Technology Management* 5(3): 267–291.

Hicks, D. et al. 1995. The changing shape of British science. STEEP Special Report, no. 3. SPRU, University of Sussex.

Hoch, P. 1990. New UK interdisciplinary research centres: Reorganisation for new generic technology. *Technology Analysis and Strategic Management* 2(1): 35–47.

Hull, F. 1988. Inventions from R&D: Organisational designs for efficient research performance. *Sociology* 22(3): 393–416.

In Vivo. 1989. Upjohn's global discovery programme. (December): 3–6.

Jencks, C., and D. Reisman. 1968. *The academic revolution.* New York: Doubleday.

Kameoka, A. 1996. A corporate technology stock model and its application. International Conference on Technology Management. June 24–26. Istanbul.

Krimsky, S. et al. 1991. Academic-corporate ties in biotechnology: A quantitative study. *Science, Technology and Human Values* 16(3): 275–287.

Lawton-Smith, H. 1993. Public and private interfaces in technology. Society for Research in Higher Education, Annual Conference. December. London.

Malerba, F. et al. 1991. The nascent globalisation of universities and public and quasi-public research organisations. Brussels: FAST/Monitor Programme, CEC.

Massey, D. et al. 1992. *High tech fantasies.* London: Routledge.

Organisation for Economic Cooperation and Development (OECD). 1989. *The changing role of government research laboratories.* Paris.

Packer, K. 1995. The role of patenting in academic-industry links in the UK: Fool's gold? *Industry and Higher Education* 9(3): 154–159.

Park, R. L. 1996. What's new? The American Physical Society. August 30. Washington, D.C.

Powell, W. W. 1987. Hybrid organisational arrangements. *California Management Review* 30(1): 67–87.

Rip, A. 1996. On tacit and codified knowledge in engineering communities. Paper presented to the Information Diffusion and Economics Seminar, All Souls College, Oxford. June 22.

Samuelson, P. 1987. Innovation and competition: Conflicts over intellectual property in new technologies. *Science, Technology and Human Values* 11(1): 6–21.

Stankiewicz, R. 1986. *Academics and entrepreneurs: Developing university-industry relations.* London: Frances Pinter.

Vollmer, H. 1962. *A preliminary investigation and analysis of the role of scientists in research organisations.* Menlo Park: Stanford Research Institute.

Webster, A. 1988. Changing structural relationship between public sector science and commercial enterprise. SPSG Concept Paper No. 4. London.

Webster, A., and K. Packer, eds. 1996. *Innovation and the intellectual property system.* Doredrecht: Kluwer.

Webster, A., and B. Rappert. 1996. The commercial exploitation of knowledge: Towards an institutional convergence of firms and the science base? *Strategic Management Journal*: Special issue on Knowledge and the firm. (Forthcoming.)

Chapter 3

Anderson, M. S., and K. S. Louis. 1994. The graduate student experience and subscription to the norms of science. *Research in Higher Education* 35(3): 273–299.

Ashford, N. A. 1983. A framework for examining the effects of industrial funding on academic freedom and the integrity of the university. *Science, Technology, and Human Values* 8: 16–23.

Barber, A. A. 1985. University-industry research cooperation. *Society of Research Administrators Journal* 17: 19–29.

Ben-Yehuda, N. 1986. Deviance in science. *The British Journal of Criminology* 26: 1–27.

Bird, B. J., and D. N. Allen. 1989. Faculty entrepreneurship in research university environments. *Journal of Higher Education* 60: 583–596.

Blevins, D. E., and S. R. Ewer. 1988. University research and development activities: Intrusion into areas untended?: a review of recent developments and ethical issues raised. *Journal of Business Ethics* 7: 645–656.

Blumenthal, D., M. Gluck, K. Louis, and D. Wise. 1986a. Industrial support of the university research in biotechnology. *Science* 23: 242–246.

Blumenthal, D., M. Gluck, K. Louis, M. Stoto, and D. Wise. 1986b. University-industry research relationships in biotechnology: implications for the university. *Science* 23: 1361–1366.

Blumenthal, D., M. Gluck, S. Epstein, K. Louis, and M. Stoto. 1987. *University-industry relationships in biotechnology: Implications for federal policy* . Cambridge, Mass.: Kennedy School of Government, Harvard University.

Bok, D. C. 1981. Business and the academy. *Harvard Magazine* (May–June), 23–24.

Bok, S. 1982. Secrecy and openness in science: ethical considerations. *Science, Technology, and Human Values* 7: 32–41.

Boyer, C., and D. Lewis. 1985. *And on the seventh day: Faculty consulting and supplemental income*. Washington, D.C.: Association for the Study of Higher Education.

Braxton, J.M. 1989. Institutional variability in faculty conformity to the norms of science: a force of integration or fragmentation in the academic profession? *Research in Higher Education* 30: 419–433.

Bremer, H. W. 1985. Commentary on Rosenzweig. *Science, Technology, and Human Values* 10: 49–54.

Brooks, H. 1988. The research university: doing good, and doing it better. *Issues in Science and Technology* (Winter): 49–55.

Brown, T. L. 1985. University-industry relations: is there a conflict? *Society of Research Administrators Journal* 17: 7–17.

Buchbinder, H., and J. Newson. 1985. Corporate-university linkages and the scientific-technical revolution. *Interchange* 16: 37–53.

Burke, A. 1985. University policies on conflict of interest and delay of publication: report of the Clearinghouse on University-Industry Relations Association of American Universities, February 1985. *Journal of College and University Law* 12: 175–189.

Buttel, F. H., and J. Belsky. 1987. Biotechnology, plant breeding, and intellectual property: social and ethical dimensions. *Science, Technology, and Human Values*, 12: 31–49.

Caldart, C. C. (1983). Industry investment in university research. *Science, Technology, and Human Values* 8: 24–32.

Caplan, Arthur. 1993. Ethical prophylaxis: research design, conduct and dissemination. *University of Minnesota Research Review* 22(8): 3, 10–12.

Chalk, R. 1985. Overview: AAAS Project on secrecy and openness in science and technology. *Science, Technology, and Human Values* 10: 28–35.

Chubin, D. E. 1985. Open science and closed science: tradeoffs in a democracy. *Science, Technology, and Human Values* 10: 73–81.

Coberly, C. A. 1985. Conflicts in university-industry interactions. *Engineering Education* 75: 320–323.

Cohen, J. 1981. Publication rate as a function of laboratory size in three research institutions. *Scientometrics* 3: 467–487.

Culliton, B. J. 1983. Academe and industry debate partnership. *Science* 219: 150–151.

Dialogue: "Disclosure of conflicts of interest." 1985. *Science, Technology, and Human Values* 10: 36–40.

Etzkowitz, H. 1984. Entrepreneurial scientists and entrepreneurial universities in American academic science. *Minerva* 21: 198–233.

Fink, I. 1985. The role of land and facilities in fostering linkages between universities and high technology industries. *Planning for Higher Education* 13: 1–12.

Fowler, D. R. 1982–83. University-industry research relationships: the research agreement. *Journal of College and University Law* 9: 515–532.

Giamatti, A. B. 1982. The university, industry, and' cooperative research. *Science* 218: 1278–1280.

Gluck, M., D. Blumenthal, and M. Stoto. 1987. University-industry relationships in the life sciences: implications for students and post-doctoral fellows. *Research Policy* 16: 327–336.

Goldman, A. H. 1987. Ethical issues in proprietary restrictions on research results. *Science, Technology, and Human Values* 12: 22–30.

Grobstein, C. 1985. Biotechnology and open university science. *Science, Technology, and Human Values* 10: 55–63.

Hackett, E. J. 1988. Funding and academic research in the life sciences: results of an exploratory study. *Science and Technology Studies* 5: 134–147.

Hackett, E. J. 1990. Science as a vocation in the 1990s. *Journal of Higher Education* 61: 241–279.

Hearn, J. C. 1988. Strategy and resources: Economic issues in strategic planning and management in higher education. In Smart, J. S., ed. *Higher education: Handbook of theory and research*, Vol. 4. New York: Agathon Press.

Lepkowski, W. 1984. University/industry research ties still viewed with concern. *Chemical and Engineering News* 62: 7–11.

Liebert, R. 1977. Research-grant getting and productivity among scholars: recent national patterns of competition and favor. *Journal of Higher Education* 48: 164–192.

List, C. J. 1985. Scientific fraud: social deviance or the failure of virtue? *Science, Technology, and Human Values* 10: 27–36.

Louis, K., M. Anderson, and J. Swazey. 1988. The university's role in regulating graduate education and research. Paper presented at the Annual Meeting of the Association for the Study of Higher Education, St. Louis, November.

Louis, K., D. Blumenthal, M. E. Gluck, and M. A. Stoto. 1989. Entrepreneurs in academe: an exploration of behaviors among life scientists. *Administrative Science Quarterly* 34: 110–131.

Marsh, H., and K. Dillon. 1980. Academic productivity and faculty supplemental income. *Journal of Higher Education* 51: 546–555.

Merton, R. 1942. The normative structure of science. Reprinted in *The sociology of science: Theoretical and empirical investigations* (1973). Chicago: University of Chicago Press.

Merton, R. 1968. The Matthew Effect in science. *Science* 159: 56–65.

Meyer, J. W., and B. Rowan. 1977. Institutionalized organizations: Formalized structure as myth and ceremony. *American Journal of Sociology* 83: 340–363.

Mitroff, I. I. 1974. Norms and counter-norms in a select groups of the Apollo moon scientists: a case study of the ambivalence of scientists. *American Sociological Review* 39: 579–595.

Mulkay, M. 1976. Norms and ideology in science. *Social Science Information* 15: 637–656.

Mulkay, M. 1979. *Science and the sociology of knowledge.* London: George Allen and Unwin.

Mulkay, M. 1980. Interpretation and the use of rules: The case of the norms of science. *Transactions of the New York Academy of Sciences*, series 2, 39: 111–125.

Nora, A., and M. A. Olivas. 1988. Faculty attitudes toward industrial research on campus. *Research in Higher Education* 29: 125–147.

Olswang, S. G., and B. A. Lee. 1984. *Faculty freedoms and institutional accountability: Interactions and conflicts.* ASHE-ERIC Higher Education Research Report, no.5. Washington, D.C.: Association for the Study of Higher Education.

Pfeffer, J., and W. Moore. 1980. Power in university budgeting: a replication and extension. *Administrative Science Quarterly* 25: 398–418.

Pfeffer, J., and G. Salancik. 1974. Organizational decision making as a political process: the case of a university budget. *Administrative Science Quarterly* 19: 135–151.

Pfeffer, J., and G. R. Salancik. 1978. *The external control of organizations: A resource dependence perspective.* New York: Harper and Row.

Riordan, C. A., and N. A. Marlin. 1987. Some good news about some bad practices. *American Psychologist* 42: 104–106.

Rosenzweig, R. M. 1985. Research as intellectual property: influences within the university. *Science, Technology, and Human Values* 10: 41–48.

Ruscio, K. 1984. Prometheus entangled: academic science in the administrative state. *Public Administration Review* 44: 353–359.

Samuelson, P. 1987. Innovation and competition: conflicts over intellectual property rights in new technologies. *Science, Technology, and Human Values* 12: 6–21.

Schmandt, J. 1984. Regulation and science. *Science, Technology, and Human Values* 9: 23–38.

Schultz, T. 1980. The productivity of research: the politics and economics of research. *Minerva,* 18: 644–651.

Scott, W. R. 1987. The adolescence of institutional theory. *Administrative Science Quarterly* 32: 493–511.

Sechrest, L. 1987. Approaches to ensuring the quality of data on performance: some lessons for science? In Jackson, D., and Rushton, J. P, eds. *Scientific excellence: Origins and assessment.* Beverley Hills: Sage.

Shenhav, Y. A. 1986. Dependency and compliance in academic research infrastructures. *Sociological Perspectives* 29: 29–51.

Smith, K. A. 1984. Industry-university research programs. *Physics Today* 37: 24–29.

Steneck, N. H. 1984. Commentary: the university and research ethics. *Science, Technology, and Human Values* 9: 6–15.

Tolbert, P. S. 1985. Institutional environments and resource dependence: sources of administrative structure in institutions of higher education. *Administrative Science Quarterly* 30: 1–13.

Varrin, R. D., and D. S. Kukich. 1985. Guidelines for industry-sponsored research at universities. *Science* 227: 385–388.

Weese, J. A. 1985. How NSF encourages industry-university partnerships. *Engineering Education* 75: 646–649.

Weick, K. 1976. Educational organizations as loosely coupled systems. *Administrative Science Quarterly* 21: 1–19.

Weingart, P. 1982. The social assessment of science, or the de-institutionalization of the scientific profession. *Science, Technology, and Human Values* 7: 53–55.

Wheeler, David L. 1989. Academy panel recommends a new review process for outdoor tests of genetically altered organisms. *Chronicle of Higher Education* (September 27), A4, A10.

Wofsy, L. 1986. Biotechnology and the university. *Journal of Higher Education* 57: 477–492.

Chapter 4

Anderson, C. 1993. Scripps backs down on controversial Sandoz deal. *Science* 260 (25 June): 1872–1873.

Archibugi, D. 1992 Patenting as an indicator of technological innovation: a review. *Science and Public Policy* 19 (6 December): 357–368.

Borys, B., and D. B. Jemison. 1989. Hybrid arrangements as strategic alliances: theoretical issues in organisational combinations. *Academy of Management Review* 14, 2: 234–249.

Company Reporting Ltd. 1993. *The 1995 UK R&D Scoreboard.* Edinburgh.

Constable, J., and A. Webster. 1991. Strategic research alliances and hybrid coalitions. *Industry and Higher Education*: 225–230.

Cukor, P. 1992. How GTE Laboratories evaluates its university collaborations. *Research Technology Management* (March–April): 31–37.

Drews, J. 1993. The changing research roles of industry and academia. *Scrip Magazine* (June): 38–41.

Faulkner, W. 1992. Conceptualising knowledge used in innovation. Paper presented at Edinburgh PICT Workshop *Exploring Expertise.* 20–22 November.

Gambardella, A. 1992. Competitive advantages from in-house scientific research: The US pharmaceutical industry in the 1980s. *Research Policy* 21: 391–407.

Gershon, D. 1993. Amgen to spend $80 million to create Canadian institute. *Nature* 361 (18 March): 194.

Longman, R. 1989. Upjohn's global discovery program. *In Vivo: The Business and Medicine Report* (December): 3–6.

Mansfield, E. 1991. Academic research and industrial innovation. *Research Policy* 20: 1–12.

Marsh, P. 1990. Pharmaceuticals: in tough times, bigger is better. *Financial Times* (8 January).

NIH (National Institutes of Health). 1992. Congressional report on conflict of interest. Washington, D.C.

Orsenigo, L. 1989. *The emergence of biotechnology*. London: Pinter.

OTA (Office of Technology Assessment). 1993. *Pharmaceutical R&D: Costs, risks and rewards*. Washington, D.C. Report submitted to the Subcommittee on Health and the Environment, House of Representatives, U.S. Congress, March 4.

Rosenberg, N. 1990. Why do firms do basic research? *Research Policy* 19: 165–174.

Rappert, B., and A. Webster. 1996. University spin-off firms, SMEs and the science base: preliminary report. SATSU Working Paper. Cambridge. June.

Roessner, J. David, and A. S. Bean. 1991. How industry interacts with Federal laboratories. *Research Technology Management* 4: 22–25.

Sapienza, A. 1989. R&D collaboration as a global competitive tactic—Biotechnology and the ethical pharmaceutical industry. *R&D Management* 19: 285–295.

Schimank, U. 1988. The contribution of university research to the technological innovation of the German economy. *Research Policy* 17: 329–340.

Schrage, M. 1992. Single-company deals are no way for universities to promote research. *The Washington Post* (March 13).

Spurgeon, D. 1992. Merck promises large grant to university if Canada extends patent protection. *Nature* 359 (1 October): 351.

Thomas, D. 1992. Imperial college's research: the business dimension. Mimeo, London, 25.

Wade, N. 1984. *Betrayers of the truth*. London: Penguin.

Webster, A. 1994. University-corporate ties and the construction of research agendas. *Sociology* 28, 1: 123–142.

Webster, A., and K. Packer. 1996. Patenting in public sector research: Tensions between theory and practice. In J. Kirkland, ed. *Barriers to international technology transfer*. Dordrecht: Kluwer.

Webster, A., and V. Swain. 1991. The pharmaceutical industry: Towards a new innovation environment. *Technology Analysis and Strategic Management* 3, 2: 127–141.

Weil, V. 1991. Conflicts of interest. Mimeo. Paper for Academic-Industry Relations NATO Advanced Research Workshop, Acquafredda, Italy. September.

Chapter 5

Barden, P., and B. Good. 1989. *Information flows into industrial research.* London: CEST.

Barnes, B., and D. Edge. 1982. The interaction of science and technology. In B. Barnes and D. Edge, eds. *Science in context: Readings in the sociology of science.* Milton Keynes: Open University Press, pp. 147–154.

CVCP (Committee of Vice Chancellors and Principals of the Universities of the United Kingdom). 1981. *Universities and industry.* London: CVCP.

Edge, D. 1992. Mosaic array cameras in infrared astronomy. In R.Bud and S. Cozzens, eds. *Invisible connections: Instruments, institutions and science.* Bellingham, Wash.: SPIE Optical Engineering Press.

Faulkner, W. 1986. *Linkage between industrial and academic research: The case of biotechnological research in the pharmaceutical industry.* Ph.D. Thesis, Science Policy Research Unit, University of Sussex, Brighton.

Faulkner, W. 1994. Conceptualising knowledge used in innovation: A second look and the science-technology distinction and industrial innovation. *Science, Technology, and Human Values* 19(4): 425–458.

Faulkner, W. 1995. Getting behind industry-public sector research linkage: A novel research design. *Science and Public Policy* 22(5): 282–294.

Faulkner, W., and J. Senker. 1994. Making sense of diversity: Public-private sector research linkage in three technologies. *Research Policy* 23: 673–695.

Faulkner, W., and J. Senker. 1995. Policy and management issues in company links with academic and government laboratories: A cross-technology study. *Journal of High Technology Management Research* 6(1): 95–112.

Faulkner, W., J. Senker, and L. Velho. 1995. *Knowledge frontiers: Industrial innovation and public sector research in biotechnology, engineering ceramics and parallel computing.* Oxford: Clarendon Press.

Feller, I. 1990. Universities as engines of R&D-based economic growth—they think they can. *Research Policy* 19: 335–348.

Fleck, J., and M. Tierney. 1991. The management of expertise. *Edinburgh PICT Working Paper no 29*. Edinburgh: Research Centre for Social Science, University of Edinburgh.

Fowler, D. 1984. University-industry research relationships. *Research Management* (January–February): 35–41.

Gambardella, A. 1992. Competitive advantages from in-house scientific research: The US pharmaceutical industry in the 1980s. *Research Policy* 21: 391–407.

Gibbons, M., and R. Johnston. 1974. The roles of science in technological innovation, *Research Policy* 3: 220–242.

Kreiner, K., and M. Schultz. 1993. Crossing the institutional divide: Networking in biotechnology. *Organizational Studies* 14(2): 189–209.

Lieberman, M. B. 1978. A literature citation study of science-technology coupling in electronics. *Proceedings of the IEEE* 6: 5–13.

MacKenzie, I., and R. Rhys Jones. 1985. *Universities and industry: New opportunities from collaboration with UK universities and polytechnics*. London: The Economist Intelligence Unit.

Martin, B. R., and J. Irvine. 1981. Spin-off from basic science: The case of radio astronomy. *Physics in Technology* 12: 204–212.

Metcalfe, J. S., and M. Gibbons. 1988. Technology, variety and organisation: a systematic perspective on the competitive process. In R.S. Rosenbloom, ed. *Research on technological innovation, management and policy* 4: 153–193. JAI Press Ltd.

Narin, F., and E. Noma. 1985. Is technology becoming science? *Scientometrics* 7: 369–381.

National Science Board. 1983. *University-industry research relationships: Selected studies*. Report to the National Science Foundation. Washington, D.C.: Government Printing Office.

Nelson, R. 1982. The role of knowledge in R and D efficiency. *Quarterly Journal of Economics* 97(3): 453–470.

Oakey, R., R. Rothwell, and S. Cooper. 1988. *Innovation in small high technology firms*. London: Pinter.

Pavitt, K. 1984. Sectoral patterns of technical change: Towards a taxonomy and a theory. *Research Policy* 13: 343–374.

Pavitt, K. 1991. What makes basic research economically useful? *Research Policy* 20: 109–119.

Pelaez, E. 1990. From symbolic to numerical computing: the story of thinking machines. *Edinburgh PICT Working Paper, No 23*. Edinburgh: Research Centre for Social Sciences, University of Edinburgh.

Rosenberg, N. 1990. Why companies do basic research (with their own money)? *Research Policy* 19: 165–174.

Rothwell, R. 1973. The communication problems of small firms. *R&D Management* 3: 151–153.

Rothwell, R. 1977. The characteristics of successful innovators and technically progressive firms. *R&D Management* 7: 191–206.

Segal Quince Wickstead. 1988. *Universities, enterprise and local economic development: An exploration of links*. Report for the Manpower Services Commission, HMSO, London.

Senker, J. 1991. Evaluation of the funding of strategic science: Some lessons from British experience. *Research Policy* 20: 29–43.

Senker, J. 1993. The contribution of tacit knowledge to innovation. *AI and Society* 7: 208–224.

Senker, J., and W. Faulkner. 1995. Networks, tacit knowledge and innovation. In R. Coombs, P. Saviotti, and V. Walsh, eds. *Technological Collaboration: Causes and Consequences*. Cheltenham: Edward Elgar.

Solla Price, D. J. de. 1984. The science/technology relationship, the craft of experimental science, and policy for the improvement of high technology innovation. *Research Policy* 13: 3–20.

Vincenti, W. 1990. *What engineers know and how they know it: Analytical studies from aeronautical history*. Baltimore: John Hopkins University Press.

Webster, A., and J. Constable. 1990. Strategic research alliances and "hybrid coalitions." *Industry and Higher Education* 4: 225–230.

Winter, S. 1987. Knowledge and competence as strategic assets. In D. Teece, ed. *The competitive challenge: Strategies for industrial innovation and renewal*. Cambridge, Mass.: Ballinger, pp. 159–183.

Chapter 6

David, P., and D. Foray. 1995. Accessing and expanding the science and technology base. *STI Review*, OECD: 13–68.

Dorfman, N. 1983. Route 128: The development of a regional high technology economy. *Research Policy* 12: 299–316.

Garnsey, E., S. Galloway, and S. Mathisen. 1994. Flexibility and specialisation in question; Birth, growth and death rates of Cambridge new technology firms 1988–1992. *Entrepreneurship & Regional Development* 6: 81–107.

Gibb, J., ed. 1985. *Science parks and innovation centers: Their economic and social impact*. Amsterdam: Elsevier.

Jonsson, A., A. Klingström, and B. Westerstrandh. 1991. *Så föds företag ur forskning. Exempel från Uppsala*. [The growth of academic spinoff companies. Examples from Uppsala]. Uppsala: Kontakt sekretariatet.

Macdonald, S. 1987. British science parks: Reflections on the politics of high technology. *R&D Management* 17, 1: 25–37.

Massey, D., P. Quintas, and D. Wield. 1992. *High tech fantasies*. London: Routledge.

Miller, R., and M. Coté. 1987. *Growing the next Silicon Valley*. Lexington, Mass.: Lexington Books.

Monck, C., R. Porter, D. Storey, and D. Winarczyk. 1988. *Science parks and the growth of high technology firms*. London: Croom Helm.

OTA. 1984. *Technology, innovation and regional development—encouraging high technology development*. Washington, D.C.: Office of Technology Assessment.

Quintas, P., D. Wield, and D. Massey. 1993. Academic industry links and innovation: Questioning the science park model. *Technovation* 12, 3: 161–175.

Rogers, E., and J. Larsen. 1984. *Silicon Valley fever*. New York: Basic Books.

Rosegrant, S., and D. Lampe. 1992. *Route 128*. New York: Basic Books.

Saxenian, A. 1985. The genesis of Silicon Valley. In P. Hall and A. Markusen. *Silicon landscapes*. Boston: Allen & Unwin.

Saxenian, A. 1994. *Regional advantage: Culture and competition in Silicon Valley and Route 128*. Cambridge, Mass.: Harvard University Press.

Segal, N. 1982. *Universities, small firms and science parks in the United Kingdom*. Stockholm: Six Countries Programme Workshop.

Segal Quince. 1985. *The Cambridge phenomenon: The growth of high technology industry in a university town*. Cambridge: Segal Quince Wicksteed.

SPRU. 1996. *The relationship between publically funded and basic research and economic performance. A SPRU review*. Report prepared for The Lords Commissions of HM Treasury. Brighton: SPRU, Falmer.

Stankiewicz, R. 1986. *Academics and entrepreneurs: Developing university-industry relations*. London: Frances Pinter.

Stankiewicz, R. 1992. Technology as an autonomous socio-cognitive system. In H. Grupp, ed. *Dynamics of science-based innovation*. Berlin: Springer-Verlag.

Stankiewicz, R. 1994. Spin-off companies from universities. *Science and Public Policy* 21, 2: 99–107.

Stankiewicz, R. 1996. The development of beta blockers at Astra-Hässle and the technological system of the Swedish pharmaceutical industry. Forthcoming in B. Carlsson, ed. *Technological Systems and Economic Performance*. Vol 2. Kluwer Publishers; to appear in 1996.

Van Dierdonck, R., K. Debackere, and M. Rappa. 1991. An assessment of science parks: Towards a better understanding of their role in the diffusion of technological knowledge. *R&D Management* 21, 2: 109–123.

Whittaker, E., and D. Bower. 1994. A shift to external alliances for product development in the pharmaceutical industry. *R&D Management* 24, 3: 249–260.

Chapter 7

Balázs, K., and G. A. Plonski. 1994. Academic-industry relations in middle-income countries: Eastern Europe and Ibero-America. *Science and Public Policy* 21(2): 109–116.

Balázs, K. 1993. Lessons from an economy with limited market functions: R&D in Hungary in the 1980s. *Research Policy* 22: 537–552.

Balázs, K. 1994. Transition crisis in Hungary's R&D sector. *EconomicSystems* 18(3): 281–306.

Balázs, K. 1995. Innovation potential embodied in research organisations in Central and Eastern Europe. EASST Special Issue, *Social Studies of Science* 25: 655–684.

Balázs, K. 1996. Is there any future for the Academy of Sciences? In David Dyker, ed. *Technology of Transition*. Budapest: CEU Press, forthcoming.

Balázs, K., W. Faulkner, and U. Shimank. 1995. Transformation of the research systems of post-communist Central and Eastern Europe: An introduction. EASST Special Issue, *Social Studies of Science*: 613–632.

Balzer, D. 1989. Soviet science at the edge of reform. Boulder: San Francisco, and London: Westview Press.

Dierdonck, R. V., and K. Debackere. 1991. An assessment of science parks: Towards a better understanding of their role in the diffusion of technological knowledge. *R&D Management* 21, 2: 102–123.

Etzkowitz, H., and C. Kemelgor. 1993. Institutionalized collaboration: The transition from academic departments to centers. State University of New York at Purchase. Mimeo.

Faulkner, W., and J. Senker. 1995. *Knowledge frontiers. Public sector research and industrial innovation in biotechnology, engineering, ceramics and parallel computing.* Oxford: Clarendon Press.

Fortescue, S. 1990. Science policy in the Soviet Union. New York: Routledge.

Gaponeneko, N. 1995. Transformation of the research system in a transition society: The case of Russia. *Social Studies of Science* 25: 685–704.

Gibb, A. 1993. Small business development in Central and Eastern Europe—Opportunity for Rethink? *Journal of Business Venturing* 8: 461–486.

Gokhberg, L. 1994. Basic research in Russia: Human resources and funding. *Economic Systems* 18(2) (June 1994): 159–179.

Hoffman, O. 1992. Some question about the science and technology policy during the transition period in Romania. Mimeo.

Jasinski, A. 1996. Academy-industry relations and the transition in Poland. In A. Webster, ed. *Building bases for innovation. The transformation of the R&D system in post-socialist countries.* Cambridge: Anglia Polytechnic University.

Jasinski, A. H. 1991. Recent changes in the Polish R&D system. *Science and Public Policy* 18(4): 245–249.

Jawitt, A. 1991. Science Parks, Academic Research and Economic Regeneration. In Hilpert, ed. *Regional innovation and decentralisation. High tech industry and government policy.* London: Routledge, pp. 113–133.

Joseph, R. A. 1994. New ways to make technology parks more relevant. *Prometheus* 12(1) (June 1994): 80–92.

Josephson, P. R. 1994. Russian scientific institutions: Internationalisation, democracy and dispersion. *Minerva* 32(1): 1–20.

Kontorovich, V. 1994. The future of the Soviet science. Research Policy 23: 113–121. North Holland.

Kornai, J. 1980. *Economics of shortage.* Amsterdam: North Holland.

Laki, M. 1992. A vallalati magatartas valtozasa es a gazdasagi valsag [Changing behavior of firms and the economic crisis]. *Kozgazdasagi Szemle* XXXIX: 565–579.

Lavados Montes, I. 1994. Visión histórica de las relaciones en América Latina. In *Gestión y Desarrollo Tecnológicos: Rol de la Universidad Latinoamericana.* Santiago: CINDA.

Lenardic, M. 1996. Science and technology policy and academy-industry links in Croatia: Structural problems and their resolution. In A. Webster, ed. *Building bases for Innovation. The transformation of the R&D system in post-socialist countries.* Cambridge: Anglia Polytechnic University.

Lubrano, L. 1993. The hidden structure of Soviet science. *Science, Technology and Human Values* 18(2): 147–175.

Maier, C. S. 1991. Why Communism Collapsed in 1989? Program on Central and Eastern Europe Working Papers Series: 7. Harvard University.

Massey, D., P. Quintas, and D. Wield. 1992. Academy-industry links and innovation: Questioning the science park model. *Technovation* 12(2): 161–175.

Meske, W. 1996. Academic-industry relations and eastern German innovation. In A. Webster, ed. *Building bases for innovation. The transformation of the R&D system in post-socialist countries.* Cambridge: Anglia Polytechnic University.

Meske, W. 1993. The restructuring of the Eastern German research system—a provisional appraisal. *Science and Public Policy* 20(5): 298–312.

Müller, M. 1996. Academy-industry relations and economic reform in the Czech republic. In A. Webster, ed. *Building bases for innovation. The transformation of the R&D System in post-socialist countries.* Cambridge: Anglia Polytechnic University.

Olofson, C., and A. Wahlbin. 1993. Firms started by university researchers in Sweden—roots, roles, relations and growth patterns. *Frontiers of Entrepreneurship Research.* Wellesley, Mass.: Babson College.

Pavitt, K., and P. Hanson. 1987. The comparative economics of research development and innovation in Eastern and West: A survey. Churr, Switzerland: Harwood Academia Publisher.

Pavitt, K. 1995. Transforming centrally planned systems of science and technology—The problem of obsolete competencies. In D. Dyker, ed. *Technology of Transition.* Prague: Central European University Press.

Piskunov, D., and B. Saltikov. 1992. Transforming the basic structures and operating mechanisms of Soviet Science. *Science and Public Policy* 19(2): 111–119.

Plonski, G. A. 1992. University-industry trends in Brazil. In T. M. Khali and B. A. Bayraktar. *Management of Technology III: The Key to Global Competitiveness.* Norcross: IIE Press, pp. 1387–1396.

Plonski, G. A., ed. 1993. Cooperacion empresa-universidad en Iberoamerica. Programa CYTED, Brazil.

Plonski, G. A., ed. 1995. Cooperación empresa-universidad en Iberoamérica: Avances recientes. Programa CYTED, Brazil.

Radosevic, S. 1996. Restructuring of R&D institutes in post-socialist economies: Emerging patterns and issues. In A. Webster, ed. *Building bases for innovation. The transformation of the R&D system in post-socialist countries.* Cambridge: Anglia Polytechnic University.

Ray, G. 1991. Innovation and productivity in Eastern Europe: An international comparison. National Institute Economic Review, No. 183: 75–84.

Review of National Science and Technology Policy: Czech and Slovak Federal Republic. 1992. Paris: OECD.

Review of National Science and Technology Policy: Hungary. 1992. OECD.

Rothwell, R., and M. Dogson. 1992. European technology policy evolution: Convergence towards SMEs and regional technology transfer. *Technovation* 12(4): 223–238.

Sábato, J., and N. Botana. 1968. La ciencia y tecnología en el desarrollo futuro de América Latina. *Revista de Integración* (Nov.): 15–36.

Sandu, S. 1996. Innovation potential and research-industry relations in Romania. In A. Webster, ed. *Building bases for innovation: The transformation of the R&D system in post-socialist countries.* Cambridge: Anglia Polytechnic University.

Schenberg, S., and S. Alange. 1991. The role of new enterprises in the transforming economies in Russia and Estonia. EIASM 5th Workshop on Research in Entrepreneurship. Vaxjo.

Schimank, U. 1995. Transformation of the research systems in Central and Eastern Europe: A coincidence of opportunities and trouble. *Social Studies of Science* 25: 633–653.

Senker, J. 1994. Small and medium size firms' access to the science base. *Revue International P.M.E.* 7(3–4): 121–146.

Simeonova, K. 1993. Conflicts in Bulgarian scientific system in the transition to market economy. *Science Studies* 6(1): 196–208.

Simeonova, K. 1995. Radical and defensive strategies in the democratisation of the Bulgarian academy of sciences. *Social Studies of Science* 25: 755–776.

Simeonova, K. 1996. Academy-industry relations and the transition within Bulgaria. In A. Webster, ed. *Building bases for innovation. The transformation of the R&D system in post-socialist countries.* Cambridge: Anglia Polytechnic University.

Stal, E. 1994. A contratação empresarial da pesquiisa universitária. In R. Sbragia. *Gestão da inovação tecnológica.* São Paulo: USP, pp. 391–415.

Stankiewicz, R. 1994. Spin off companies from universities. *Science and Public Policy* 21(2) (April 1994): 79–87.

Stankiewicz, R. 1996. Science parks and innovation centres. Mimeo. University of Lund, Sweden.

Stankiewicz, R. 1986. *Academics and enterprises: Developing university industry relations*. London: Pinter.

Tither, D. 1990. A case study of technology transfer and funding mechanisms in an industrially supported multi-centered university research initiative. *Technovation* 10(1): 39–46.

Török, A. 1992. International patterns versus the Hungarian structure of market protection in industry. Budapest: Research Institute of Industrial Economics.

Tyson, L. d'A., T. Petrin, and H. Rogers. 1994. Promoting entrepreneurship in Eastern Europe. *Small Business Economics* 6: 165–184.

Velho, S. M. 1993. Relações universidade-empresa em três estudos de caso: Produção de ciência ou interesse de mercado? Ph.D. Dissertation, University of Brasilia.

Vessuri, H. 1995. Introduction to the special issue on "The Latin American University and R&D." *Industry and Higher Education* 9(6): 365.

Webster, A. 1993. Bridging institutions: The role of contract research organizations in technology transfer. *Science and Public Policy.*

Webster, A., ed. 1996. *Building bases for innovation. The transformation of the R&D system in post-socialist countries.* Cambridge: Anglia Polytechnic University.

Weiss, C. Jr. (1993). The re-emergence of Eastern European science and technology. *Technology in Society* 15: 3–23.

World Development Report, The World Bank. 1992. Washington.

Chapter 8

Afanas'ev, V. 1991. Nauka i rynok. *Pravda* (18 April), p. 3.

Anisin, N. 1990. Bar'er pered naukoi. *Pravda* (9 April), p. 1.

Anon. 1989. Rezul'taty i zarplata. *Ekonomicheskaya Gazeta* 36: 9.

Berry, M. J., ed. 1988. *Science and Technology in the USSR.* Harlow: Longman.

Berry, M. J. 1991. Perestroika and the changing nature of East-West scientific contacts. *Technology in Society* 13: 160.

Bobylev, Y. 1990. Sbrosim tsepi gigantizma. *Inzhenernaya Gazeta* (December 19).

CSRS. 1992. *Science in the USSR: Analysis and statistics.* Moscow: Data Book.

CSRS. 1996. *Russian science and technology at a glance: 1995.* Moscow: Data Book.

Dickma, S. 1991. Soviet science: A struggle for survival. *Science* (December 20).

Holusha, J. 1990. Trade in brainpower: An East-to-West trend. *International Herald Tribune* (21 February).

Ivakhnov, A. 1987. Nauka na khozraschete. *Izvestiya* (21 September).

Lavrov, I. 1990. Cherez terni nauki. *Pravitel'stvennyi vestnik* 12: 7.

Lynnik, N. V. 1990. Novye organizatsionnye struktury, orientirovannye na uskorenie ispol'zovaniya naucho-tekhnicheskikh dostizhenii. *Voprosy Izobretatel'stva* 5: 16.

Makarov, I. M. 1991. Razvitie Akademii nauk SSSR v sovremennnykh usloviyakh. *Vestnik Akademiinauk SSSR* 6: 31–40.

Mindeli, L. E., and L. K. Pipiia. 1995. Small and middle-sized innovation enterprise: Conditions of development and international cooperation. Moscow.

Nesvetailov, G. A. 1990. Bol'naya nauka v bol'nym obshchestve. *Sotsiologicheskie Issledovaniya* 11: 54.

Nevzorov, A., and Z. Trofimenko. 1991. Deyatel'nost' sovmestnykh predpriyatii v 1990 g. *Vestnik Statistiki* 6: 10.

Nikolin, V. K. et al. 1990. Akademicheskie instituty v novykh usloviyakh khozyaistvovaniya. *Vestnik Akademii Nauk* 10: 120–128.

Oambovtsev, V. L. 1995. Spontaneous privatization in R&D organizations. *Voprosy Prognozirovania* 4: 74–81.

Panin, V. 1991. Mozhet li uchenyi byt'negotsiantom? *Inzhenernaya Gazeta* 2: 1.

Perminov, S. B., and A. I. Petrov. 1990. Malye nauchno-tekhnicheskie firmy. *Znanie: Praktika sotsialisticheskogo khozyaistvovaniya* 3: 43.

Shukshunov, V. 1990. Vykhod est'—nauchnyi park. *Izvestiya* (August 31).

Webster, A., ed. 1996. *Building new bases for innovation: The transformation of the R&D system in post-socialist states.* Cambridge: APU Press.

Chapter 9

Anderson, R. D. 1992. The Scottish tradition. In J. C. Carter and D. J. Withrington, eds. *Scottish universities: Distinctiveness and diversity.* Edinburgh: John Donald Publishers Ltd.

Carter, J. C., and D. J. Withrington. 1992. Introduction. In *Scottish universities: Distinctiveness and diversity.* Edinburgh: John Donald Publishers Ltd.

Cheese, J. J. 1991. *Attitudes to innovation in Germany and Britain: A comparison.* London: Centre for Exploitation of Science and Technology.

Cheese, J. J. 1993. Sourcing technology: Industry and higher education in Germany and the UK. *Industry and Higher Education.*

Anon. 1993. *Financial Times.* Wednesday, April 14, p. 14.

von Hippel, E. 1986. *Lead users: A source of novel product concepts.* Management Science 32(7).

Leaver, A. 1992. *A survey of the new biotechnology firm sector in Scotland.* MSc Thesis, University of Strathclyde.

McNicoll, I. 1993. *The impact of Strathclyde University on the economy of Scotland.* University of Strathclyde.

National Research Council. 1991. *The competitive edge—research priorities for U.S. manufacturing.* Washington, D.C.: National Academy Press.

Niwa, F. 1992. *Rediscovering the core of national science and technology: Ourselves as others see us.* London: jointly sponsored by SPSG (Science Policy Support Group) and the Parliamentary Office of Science and Technology. Mimeo.

OECD. 1991. *Science and technology policy, review and outlook 1991.* Paris: OECD.

Porter, M. E. 1991. *The competitive advantage of nations.* London: Macmillan.

Scottish Enterprise. 1991. *Annual report.* Edinburgh: HMSO.

Scottish Enterprise. 1992. *Innovation for competitiveness: A framework for Scotland.* Edinburgh: HMSO.

Sheen, M. R., and M. E. Jack. 1992. *A technology audit: A profile of one UK university's collaboration with industry.* London: Technology Transfer and Implementation Conference.

Sheen, M. R. 1993. Technology diffusion: Mechanisms for linking supply and demand in the UK and Denmark. *Industry & Higher Education,* pp. 86–92.

Turok, I. 1993. Loose connections? Foreign investment and local linkages, in Silicon Glen. *University of Strathclyde Paper on Planning, no. 23.* Strathclyde: University of Strathclyde.

Watkins, T. A. 1991. A technology communications model of R&D consortia as public policy. *Research Policy* 20: 87-107.

Wooten, C. 1992. Funding the gap from science to prototype. *Exploiting the science base—the American experience.* London: Department of Trade and Industry.

Chapter 10

Etzkowitz, Henry. 1990. The second academic revolution. In Susan Cozzens and Peter Healey, eds. *The research system in transition.* Amsterdam: Kluwer.

Etzkowitz, Henry. 1993. Enterprises from science: The origins of science-based regional economic development. *Minerva* 31(3): 326–360.

Etzkowitz, Henry. 1994. Beyond the frontier: The convergence of military and civilian R&D in the U.S. *Science Studies* 7(2): 5–22.

Etzkowitz, Henry. 1994a. Technology centers and industrial policy: The emergence of the interventionist state in the USA. *Science and Public Policy* 21(2): 79–87.

Etzkowitz, Henry. 1994b. Knowledge as property: The Massachussetts Institute of Technology and the debate over academic patent policy. *Minerva* 32(4): 383–421.

Etzkowitz, Henry. 1995. The turn to universities and SME's: The emergence of the "triple helix" in Scandinavia. *Technology Access Report* 8(11) (November): 10–11.

Etzkowitz, Henry, and Andrew Webster. 1994. Science as intellectual property. In *Handbook of science and technology studies.* Beverly Hills: Sage, pp. 480–505.

Faulkner, Wendy, and Jacqueline Senker. 1995. *Knowledge frontiers: Public sector research and industrial innovation in biotechnology, engineering ceramics, and parallel computing.* Oxford: Oxford University Press.

Feller, Irwin. 1990. Universities as engines of R&D based economic growth—They think they can. *Research Policy* 19: 335–348.

Guston, David, and Kenneth Kenniston. 1994. *The fragile contract.* Cambridge: MIT Press.

Hofstadter, Richard, and Wilson Smith. 1962. *American higher education: A documentary history,* Volume Two. Chicago: University of Chicago Press.

Jencks, Christopher, and David Riesman. 1968. *The academic revolution.* New York: Doubleday.

Kloppenberg, Jack. 1988. *First the seed: The political economy of plant biotechnology; 1492–2000.* Cambridge: Cambridge University Press.

Kohler, Robert. 1979. Warren Weaver and the Rockefeller Foundation program in molecular biology: A case study in the management of science. In Nathan Reingold, ed. *The sciences in the American context: New perspectives.* Washington, D.C.: The Smithsonian Institution.

Latker, Norman. 1977. Patent counsel, Dept. of Health, Education and Welfare, House subcommittee on Science, Research and Technology, May 26. 95th Congress, 1st session, p. 8.

Latker, Norman. 1996. Former Chief Patent Counsel to the National Institutes of Health and to the Department of Health, Education and Welfare. Personal Communication to Ashley Stevens National Science Board. 1982. *University-Industry Research Relations*. Washington, D.C.: U.S. Government Printing Office.

Office of Technology Assessment. 1991. *Federally funded research: Decisions for a decade*. Washington, D.C.: U.S. Government Printing Office.

Office of Technology Assessment. 1993. *Pharmaceutical R&D: Costs, risks and rewards*. Washington, D.C.: U.S. Government Printing Office.

Owen, Larry. 1994. The counterproductive management of science in the Second World War: Vannevar Bush and the Office of Scientific Research and Development. *Business History Review 68* (Winter): 515–576.

Pursell, Carroll. 1979. Science agencies in World War II: The OSRD and its challengers. In Nathan Reingold, ed. *The sciences in the American context: New perspectives*. Washington, D.C.: The Smithsonian Institution.

Contributors

Melissa S. Anderson is Associate Professor of Higher Education at the University of Minnesota. Her current research interests include graduate education, ethics in research, academic-industry relations, and faculty demography.

Katalin Balázs is Research Fellow, Policy Research in Engineering, Science and Technology (UK) and a member of the Institute of Economics, Hungary. She has researched on science policy and firm dynamics in post-socialist central Europe and undertaken related comparative research funded by the Central European University.

Mike Berry is Lecturer, Centre for Russian and East European Studies, University of Birmingham. His research interests include science and technology in the former Soviet Union and developments in Russian language after the collapse of the USSR. He is editor and main author—*Science and Technology in the USSR, Longman Guide to World Science and Technology*, vol. 6, Harlow, Longman, 1988.

Henry Etzkowitz is Associate Professor of Sociology and Director of the Science Policy Institute, Purchase College, State University of New York. His latest books include *The Triple Helix: MIT and the Rise of Entrepreneurial Science*, London: Gordon and Breach; and *Athena Unbound: Women, Social Capital and Science* (with Carol Kemelgor), Cambridge University Press, in press.

Wendy Faulkner is Senior Lecturer at the Science Studies Unit, Department of Sociology, University of Edinburgh, Scotland. She has undertaken research in science policy, academic-industry linkage and knowledge flows, and gender and technology. She is currently working on the construction and dynamics of masculinity in engineering environments.

Peter Healey is managing director of the Science Policy Support Group (SPSG), London. SPSG organizes programs of research on science and technology policy issues, which are funded by a range of sources and performed

269

by UK and European networks of scholars. Current programs include strategic priority setting in Science and Technology, defense technology management, and the public understanding of science.

Karen Seashore Louis is Professor of Education Policy and Administration, and Associate Dean for Academic Affairs at the University of Minnesota. Her recent publications include articles on ethical issues in higher education, the changing institutional context for science and science education, and university-industry relations.

Lioudmila Pipiia is a principal researcher at the Centre for Science Research and Statistics in Moscow, Russia. She is a Candidate in Economics and she works in the field of R&D funding, priority setting, and the interrelations between science, technology, and innovation policy.

Guilherme Ary Plonski is Professor in the Engineering and Management Schools and Executive Coordinator for University Cooperation at the University of Sao Paulo, Brazil. He is also International Coordinator of the Ibero-American Network of Industry-University Cooperation Management (CYTED) and a member of the Board of Governors of the Technion—Israel Institute of Technology.

Margaret Sheen is Director of the Emerging Technologies Research and Assessment Centre, University of Strathclyde, Scotland. She has a background in natural sciences and has worked in technology transfer as a practitioner and researcher for a number of years.

Jacqueline Senker is Senior Research Fellow at the Science Policy Research Unit (SPRU) at Sussex University, UK. She has a background in urban and regional planning and has published extensively on academic-industry links, national systems of innovation and firm strategies in biotechnology.

Rikard Stankiewicz is Professor of Technology Dynamics at the Research Policy Institute, University of Lund, Sweden. Between 1997 and 1998 he was also Research Professor at Copenhagen Business School, Denmark. His current research interests are evolutionary models of technological change generally, and studies of R&D processes in the pharmaceuticals/biotechnology and software engineering sectors.

Ashley Stevens is Director of the Community Technology Fund at Boston University. He was formerly Director of the Office of Technology Transfer at the Dana-Farber Cancer Institute of the Harvard Medical School. His research interests include university-industry strategic alliances and the impact of academic technology, and the Bayh-Dole Act on economic development.

Lea Velho is Associate Professor in the Department of Science and Technology Policy, State University of Campinas, Brazil. She has a PhD from the Science Policy Research Unit, Sussex University, UK, and has published extensively on different aspects of science policy, from science indicators and research evaluation to decision making processes and dynamics of science.

Andrew Webster is Professor in the Sociology of Science and Technology at Anglia University, Cambridge, UK, and Director of SATSU (Science and Technology Studies Unit). He has published extensively in the area of academic-industry relations and is currently working on various projects related to the sociology of science policy. His forthcoming book (as co-author) is *Valuing Technology: Organisations, Culture and Change* (Routledge: London).

Author Index

274   AUTHOR INDEX

Subject Index

academia
    commercialization of, 36–38, 44, 59,
        61, 128
    norms within, 74 et passim
    revolution in, 1, 4, 21–46
academic-industrial relations, 5, 22, 25,
    50
    benefits of, 120–24
    collaboration, 50–59, 61–62, 66,
        145–46
    developments in, 56–59
    disadvantages of, 79–83
    evolution of, 43–45, 67
    in Eastern Europe, 151–61
    in Ibero-America, 161–67
    in Russia, 169–85
    in Scotland, 187–213
advanced engineering ceramics,
    111–32
Association of University Technology
    Managers (AUTM), 225–26, 232

Bayh-Dole Act, 215, 222–25
British Technology Group, 11
biotechnology, 79, 82, 111–32, 159
bridging institutions, 159–60

conflict of interest, 12–16, 49, 52,
    63–65
cooperatives (UUSR), 173–74
corporations, 59–61
CRADA, 13, 228–29
CYTED, 166

entrepreneurial university 16–17, 40
entrepreneurship, 48, 77 et passim, 139,
    171
European Union, 23, 163, 208

FINEP, 164–65
Foresight Exercise, 211
Frounhofer Gesellschaft, 40, 159,
    194

generic technologies, 196
government, 8, 35–36, 163–64, 182,
    215–38
    laboratories, 227–29, 233–35

hybrid coalitions, 100–102
    incubators, 31, 41, 136, 153, 160
    intellectual property, 11, 15–16, 21,
        42, 59, 83, 129, 178, 198, 206,
        220–22

Interdisciplinary Research Centers,
    57–58, 207
innovation, 7–9, 35, 54, 112, 130,
    195–96
    in transitional economies, 151, 181
innovation centers, 153–47
international co-operation, 166

Knowledge, 2, 8
    capitalization of, 2, 9, 10–16, 24, 39,
        41, 46
    flows of, 5–7, 111, 113, 114, 128

277

SUNY series
FRONTIERS IN EDUCATION
Philip G. Altbach, editor

List of Titles